Beyond the Doll Tests

Beyond the Doll Tests

Affirming and Uplifting Black Students' Well-Being

CHERYL HOLCOMB-McCOY

HARVARD EDUCATION PRESS
CAMBRIDGE, MASSACHUSETTS

Paperback ISBN 9798895570661

The Library of Congress Cataloging-in-Publication Data is on file.

Published by Harvard Education Press,
an imprint of the Harvard Education Publishing Group

Harvard Education Press
8 Story Street
Cambridge, MA 02138

Cover design by Dave Kessler Design
Cover description: On a yellow background, there is a colorful, artistic image of a young Black girl with a joyful expression. The girl is depicted as if she is running, and she is hugging a doll which is also Black. The cover shows the book's title and subtitle at the top and the author's name at the bottom.

The typefaces in this book are Adobe Garamond Pro and Myriad Pro.

To my beloved family—Alvin, Niles, Nia, and Niko—
You are my purpose, my peace, and my power.
In moments when my spirit wanes, your love fuels me forward.
Thank you for filling my life with joy, laughter, and unwavering support.

To my father, Frederick Holcomb—
For over sixty remarkable years, you have fathered me with quiet strength and unshakable faith.
Whenever I face uncertainty, I ask myself, "What would Dad do?"
Your devotion to God, family, and community continues to guide me.
You were the rock beside Mom, Colethia R. Holcomb, the heart of our family.
I love you deeply, Daddy.

And to you, the reader, thank you for choosing this book.
Your decision to engage with these words is an act not just of reading but of resistance, love, and purpose.

To every educator, advocate, and healer who cares for and loves Black children, may these pages fuel your passion for justice in education and remind you that you are not alone.

Contents

Foreword

JOHNNETTA BETSCH COLE, PhD

It is an honor and a joy for me to write this foreword for *Beyond the Doll Tests: Affirming and Uplifting Black Students' Well-Being.* I am deeply moved that President Cheryl Holcomb-McCoy—my colleague, my sister, my friend—has found in my words and legacy a spark for her own work. As I witness how she does the work that she is called to do, Cheryl Holcomb-McCoy continues to inspire me to do what I can to affirm and uplift Black students.

There is so much in my lived experience that speaks to all that is addressed in this book. I was born in 1936 in Jacksonville, Florida, and came of age in the deeply segregated South. I learned early what it meant to be deemed "less than." But I was also the product of a family and community that poured love, expectation, and pride into me. I am the child of pushy Black parents who believed—fiercely and unapologetically—in the power of education to transform not just a single life but the life of a people.

My first school experience was in a segregated school. But how fortunate I was that Ms. Bunny Vance, my first-grade teacher, not only affirmed me, she uplifted me as she looked me square in the eyes and said, "Johnnetta, never mumble your name. And remember, in this class, we are preparing leaders." That moment has stayed with me. So too have the words of my mother, who would often tell me that segregation was an evil system invented by some white people, but I could be whatever I worked hard to be.

Those affirmations became my foundation. Education should not be about just acquiring information but also better understanding one's self, one's people, one's community, one's nation, and one's world. And yes, it should be about accepting one's responsibility to help to create a more just and equitable world.

South African President Nelson Mandela said, *"Education is the most powerful weapon which you can use to change the world."* My generation used that weapon to crack open the doors of opportunity, and we did so not just for ourselves but for those who would follow. And yet, as I reflect on this moment in history, I am prepared to say: There has never been a more urgent time to assure Black people that children are seen, uplifted, and fiercely supported.

Over seventy years ago, Kenneth and Mamie Clark conducted the famous "Doll Tests," in which Black children showed a preference for White dolls, naming them as "good" or "nice"—a painful revelation of how racism infiltrates even the youngest minds. Their findings helped shape *Brown v. Board of Education* and exposed the psychological toll of segregation. Although legal segregation has ended, the work of affirming Black children's full humanity remains unfinished.

Today, our children may sit beside white classmates, but they still carry invisible burdens: the sting of low expectations, the pain of implicit bias, and the exhaustion of constantly proving their worth in systems not built with them in mind. Racism may no longer wear the same signs, but it still speaks—in exclusion, in silence, and in the narrowing of curriculum and banning of books.

This is a time when every educator must be called upon to not only demand bold curricula—but to teach with a boldness rooted in love. As the great educator Marva Collins once said, *"I'm a teacher. A teacher is someone who leads. There is no magic here. I do not walk on water. I do not part the sea. I just love children."* That kind of love is not sentimental—it is radical. It demands preparation, intentionality, and courage.

Sister President and CEO of the American Association of Colleges for Teacher Education Cheryl Holcomb-McCoy has the courage to write this mighty important book. *Beyond the Doll Tests* is not content with pointing out harm—it insists we imagine healing. It draws from Black psychology, self-efficacy theory, and strength-based, trauma-informed practice. It centers the voices of those who know our children best and challenges educators to not simply include but to affirm Black children. It provides a roadmap for what it means to meet Black students with high expectations and genuine care.

This book reminds us that teachers do not do this work alone. According to an African saying, *"It takes a village to raise a child."* That village includes not only teachers and principals but social workers, school counselors, policymakers, parents, aunties, uncles, elders, religious leaders, and government officials on all levels.

James Baldwin reminded us, *"A child cannot be taught by anyone who despises him, and a child cannot afford to be fooled."* What our children need is not lectures but advocates; not pity, but affirmation of their presence; and above all, love tied to action.

As a lifelong educator, I've worn many hats—professor, college president, and museum director. But in every role, one truth has remained: our children are our most sacred responsibility—to nourish them, protect their joy, fuel their brilliance, and uplift their identity—and certainly, through our children, to secure the future of our people.

If we ever needed this book, we certainly need it now—when truth itself is under attack, and teachers are told not just what to teach but what they must not say. We are in a time of moral urgency. But I believe that, together, we will press forward. For as Maya Angelou said, *"And still, we rise."*

President Cheryl Holcomb-McCoy has long understood that the work of education should never be in opposition to the ongoing struggle for equality and justice for all. I am proud to stand alongside her as she boldly declares that Black students deserve to be nurtured, not merely taught, to be inspired, and not merely instructed.

Let those who read this book be moved to reflection, stirred to action, and reminded that Black children are not a problem to be solved but a promise to be fulfilled. Let us proceed with hearts open and minds focused toward a future where all Black children can soar to the height of their possibilities.

Preface

Over seventy-five years ago, psychologists Mamie and Kenneth Clark (fig. P.1) asked a simple but profound question: *What happens to Black children when the world teaches them they are inferior?* Their famous "Doll Tests" study, in which children as young as three years of age preferred white dolls over Black ones, offered a disturbing answer (fig. P.2). The internalization of racism begins early, and it leaves lasting scars.

The Clarks' research was significant evidence in the landmark 1954 *Brown v. Board of Education* decision, which ended legal racial segregation in public schools. But although the laws may have changed, the emotional consequences of racism on Black youth have endured. Despite progress, the United States is still a nation where Black students experience harsher discipline and under-supported schools and are systemically devalued in classrooms across the country.

I know its relevance personally. In 1972, eighteen years after *Brown*, schools in my hometown of Hampton, Virginia, were finally integrated through busing. I was in the third grade. Until then, I had attended all-Black schools filled with nurturing Black educators who believed in my potential. Their classrooms were places where I felt seen. But when I stepped into that newly integrated school, the environment shifted. Blackness meant something different there, something less valued.

It was in that moment of cultural disorientation that a white teacher, my third-grade teacher, unknowingly changed the trajectory of my life. One day, she looked at me and said, "You would make an excellent teacher." Her affirmation may have seemed casual, but it was profound. I held onto those words. They worked. They planted a seed of belief, and over time, they bloomed.

This book is about that kind of affirmation, not just from teachers who share a student's background, but from any educator willing to truly see Black students in their full humanity. It's about how simple moments of recognition, when

FIGURE P.1 Kenneth and Mamie Clark in their living room in Hastings-on-Hudson, New York, 1958.

Source: Charlotte Brooks, *LOOK* Magazine Photograph Collection at the Library of Congress.

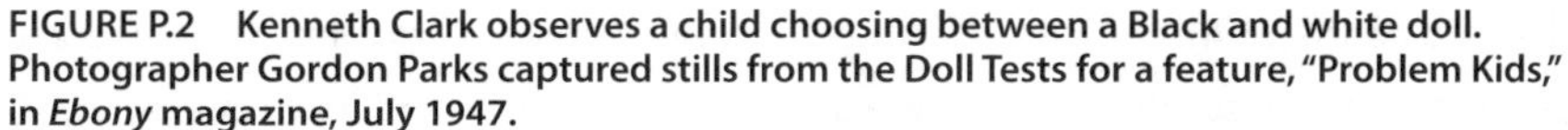

FIGURE P.2 Kenneth Clark observes a child choosing between a Black and white doll. Photographer Gordon Parks captured stills from the Doll Tests for a feature, "Problem Kids," in *Ebony* magazine, July 1947.

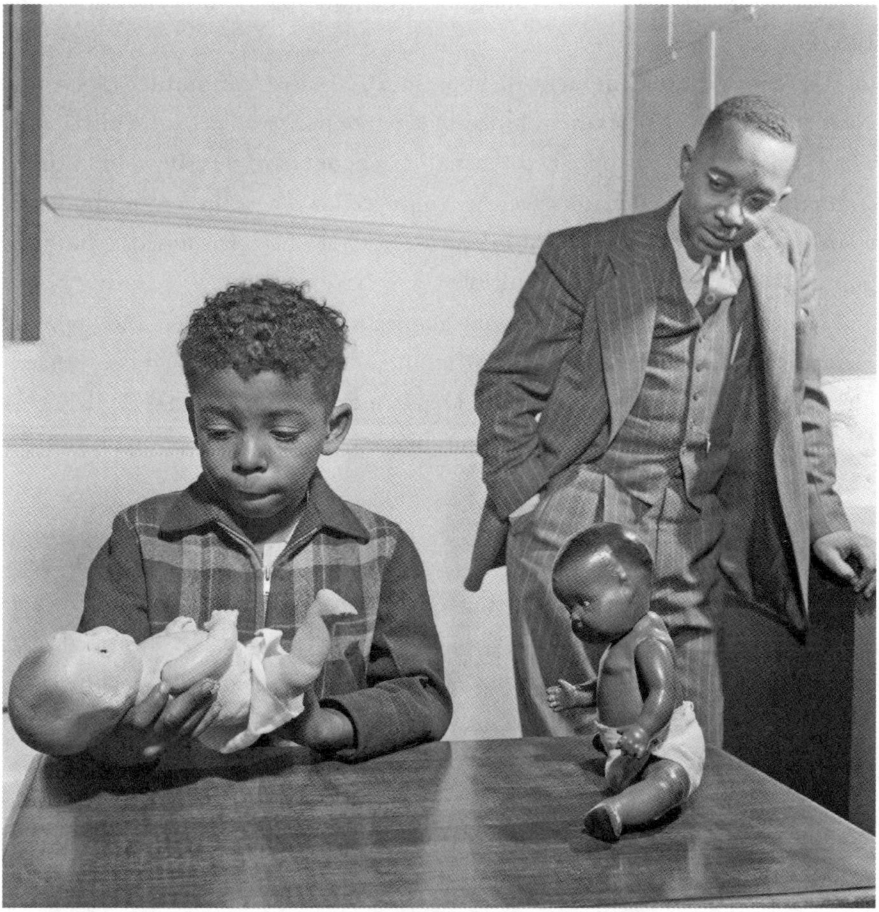

Source: Gordon Parks, *Untitled*, Harlem, New York, 1947. Courtesy of and copyright The Gordon Parks Foundation.

grounded in high expectations and care, can disrupt the legacy of harm. And it's about how, too often, our schools fail to offer those moments at all.

I wrote this book because the question—*How does racism shape the emotional well-being of Black children?*—remains relevant today. Sadly, Black students are navigating school systems that too often deny their history, ignore their trauma, and fail to affirm their brilliance. This is not just about implicit bias or underfunded schools. It's also about the growing national movement to end discussions about the cruelty and pervasiveness of racism and to erase Black history altogether. In many ways, the push to return to "separate and unequal" education systems is more evident now than at any time since the 1960s.

There was a brief moment of hope in 2020 after the murder of George Floyd, an unarmed Black man killed by a white police officer in Minneapolis, when racial equity was openly discussed in school board meetings, in business communities, and educators were encouraged to teach the truth about the country's history of racism. But in recent years, we have witnessed a dramatic political shift. Legislators in multiple states have passed laws banning books and restricting classroom discussions about race/racism, gender, and systemic inequality. And the Trump administration has hindered civil rights by lessening many protections (e.g., the US Department of Education's Civil Rights Division) designed to guarantee that Black citizens have opportunities for success.

These are not neutral acts.

This book addresses these acts and urges educators, school leaders, counselors, and policymakers to prioritize the foundation of education: recognizing and affirming the full humanity of every child. As the Clarks' research illustrated years ago, Black children continue to confront the psychological effects of ongoing anti-Black sentiments, beliefs, and practices in schools, regardless of setting—urban, suburban, or rural. These psychological effects of self-hatred and inferiority stifle dreams and development.

This book is organized into three overarching sections: (1) Roots of Oppression in Black Communities, (2) Interventions That Uplift Black Students' Well-Being, and (3) Changing Systems of Oppression. Across nine chapters, I weave historical context, theoretical frameworks, and practical insights to explore how systemic anti-Black racism has shaped the educational and psychological experiences of Black students. Each chapter begins with key histories and theories and then examines how those forces play out in contemporary educational settings. To bridge theory with practice, each chapter includes two case studies: one in which actions and outcomes are fully explained and a second that is left unresolved, prompting readers to engage in critical dialogue and collaborative problem-solving with their colleagues. These cases are designed to spark meaningful conversations and foster professional reflection. I also provide reflection questions and a curated reference list for deeper exploration.

Central to the book is my belief that supporting the well-being of Black youth in schools requires a four-pronged approach: (1) creating student-centered, self-efficacious, antiracist learning environments, (2) implementing trauma-informed practices, (3) utilizing strength-based helping strategies, and (4) ensuring access to well-trained, culturally responsive and self-proclaimed antiracist educators and mental health professionals.

At its core, this book argues that Black students and their families deserve to be heard, honored, and respected in their school communities. And for that to happen, educators must understand the enduring impact of anti-Black racism on the Black psyche and be committed to transformation, not just in policy, but in practice and purpose.

Beyond the Doll Tests offers practical strategies grounded in research and draws on my experience from over thirty years as a teacher, school counselor, educator trainer, and dean. More important, it provides a vision in which Black students are not seen as "problems to fix" but as young people full of potential, resilience, and brilliance, a vision in which their emotional well-being is not an afterthought but the foundation for academic success. The truth is: Black children are still carrying the weight of generations of discrimination through racist policies, poverty, over-policing, and exclusion from opportunity. And too often, schools amplify that trauma instead of helping to heal it. We must change that.

Will this book be banned for highlighting Black children and addressing racism? I don't know. But I'm sure some people will not be pleased that it focuses on Black children. In today's climate, where books that candidly discuss race, identity, and justice are being removed from libraries, *Beyond the Doll Tests* boldly reveals the truth about the root cause of the underachievement of Black children. It's not because other racial groups are "superior." Rather, it's due to the lack of attention to the relationships we cultivate with Black students and the insufficient effort to uplift them as valued individuals. For me, writing this book is about restoring the stolen dignity, joy, and belief that Black children deserve every chance to thrive and live productively. Just as the Clarks once helped the nation recognize the problems of racial segregation, *Beyond the Doll Tests* aims to continue the discussion that the Clarks initiated over fifty years ago. Now, we must envision and restructure schools where all students are welcomed by and learn from educators who understand the history of anti-Black racism in this country, as well as the power of undoing racism through affirmation and altering harmful policies and practices.

PART 1

Roots of Oppression in Black Communities

If you know whence you came, there is really no limit to where you can go.

—James Baldwin, author and activist

CHAPTER 1

Racism, Trauma, and Education

In a high school gym, an eighteen-year-old Black girl tells her physical education teacher, "I don't feel good," as she sits on the bleachers, with her head hanging low and her eyes puffy. Instead of checking on her, the PE teacher assumes that she is being defiant and calls the school resource officer (SRO). The SRO, visibly irritated, climbs the bleachers and forcibly pulls the young girl to the gym floor by her hair. The girl fights back and yells, "Stop!" Students record the event with their phones; the recording goes viral and captures national attention. The national attention causes some concern among the school staff and the school system, but no disciplinary action is taken against the SRO. The student is left with physical as well as psychological scars.

This story reflects a pattern of how Black youth are disproportionately harmed and denied dignity in school settings.[1] These moments are not about just discipline. They involve treating Black students with little to no humanity and traumatizing (or retraumatizing) them.

Now, consider a second version.

The same student says she's feeling sick. This time, the physical education teacher sits beside her on the bleachers and asks in a caring way, "What's wrong? You don't look well." The student looks at the teacher and says her head and stomach hurt. The teacher calls the nurse and asks another student to walk with her to the school clinic. Later, the teacher learns that the student's mother is dying of cancer. The counselor is contacted, and a care plan is developed for the student.

This case reflects the essence of this book. *What impact do these harmful experiences have on the well-being of Black students, and how can we address these issues?* In one scenario, a student is criminalized; in the other, she is humanized and cared for. These stories are not unique or isolated. They are embedded in a long history of anti-Black racism and punitive treatment of Black students in school settings.[2]

RACISM IN US EDUCATION

The story of education in the United States cannot be separated from the enduring legacy of anti-Black racism, which continues to shape the lives and learning conditions of Black youth. This book's title, *Beyond the Doll Tests*, denotes the important research and extensive work of psychologists Mamie and Kenneth Clark in the 1940s. Their series of experiments, now known as the "Doll Tests," revealed the profound effects of long-term systemic racism on the psychological and mental well-being of Black children. In these studies, young children were asked to choose between white and Black dolls. Most children, regardless of race, consistently preferred the white dolls, attributing positive characteristics such as beauty, intelligence, and goodness to them, while assigning negative traits to the Black dolls.[3] The findings exposed how young Black children internalize racist messages in a segregated society, shaping how they see themselves and their worth. The Clarks' research provided key social science evidence in the landmark 1954 *Brown v. Board of Education* decision, which ruled that segregation in public schools was inherently unequal and psychologically damaging.[4] Though legal segregation was dismantled, the Doll Tests continue to resonate today, reminding us that the educational system remains a site where the psychological consequences of racial bias are deeply embedded and too often left unchallenged by policies and practices.

To begin the journey of correcting racism in schools, educators must confront and grapple with the long history of racism in the United States. Central to this history is the institution of chattel slavery, a uniquely brutal system in which African people were treated as property. They were bought, sold, inherited, and exploited to build the economic foundation of the United States and other countries across the globe[5] (see Appendix A for a map of the African Slave Trade). Unlike other forms of servitude, chattel slavery in the United States was considered permanent, inheritable, and justified by white racial ideology or white supremacy. It served not only to dehumanize enslaved Africans but also to establish a racial hierarchy that supported and fueled the growth of American capitalism. Wealth accumulated through unpaid Black labor financed industries, built universities, and secured public institutions, including early school systems that excluded Black children.

Although slavery ended after the Civil War, anti-Black racism was extended by a century of legalized segregation, state-sanctioned discrimination, and the continued devaluation of Black intellectual capacity. These forces embedded false narratives about Black inferiority into the very fabric of US education. Today's racial disparities in school discipline, academic tracking, funding, and opportunity are not accidental. They are the predictable outcomes of a system built on racial exclusion. In recent years, terms such as *wokeism* have been weaponized to undermine educational efforts that address systemic racism. Originally a Black vernacular term meaning awareness of racial injustice, *woke* has been co-opted and distorted to frame accurate racial history and racial equity as cultural threats.[6] This "anti-woke" backlash has accelerated the removal of inclusive curricula, the banning of books that discuss race, and policies that censor educators. These efforts prevent students from learning important and horrific history that has impacted millions of US citizens. Rather, these efforts maintain the status quo by erasing the truths necessary for justice. To create an education system rooted in equity and equality, we must acknowledge how chattel slavery shaped our institutions, and we must continue to resist the ideologies that preserve inequality today.

No group of immigrants entered the United States involuntarily for solely chattel slavery purposes other than Africans.[7] This unique history has impacted the education of Black youth ever since. During slavery, Black children were systematically denied the right to learn. The education of enslaved people was viewed as a threat to a system of white supremacy and a danger to the economic system of the time. Laws made it illegal to teach enslaved individuals to read or write, and those who dared to defy these laws faced punishment. Denying education was central to the process of dehumanization and control. Many white slaveholders feared that educating enslaved people would foster an environment of increased resistance and potentially lead to the end of slavery. Consequently, laws, customs, and violent punishments were employed to control, restrict, and criminalize Black education.

However, there was resistance to the laws and customs related to the education of enslaved people. Religious groups, particularly the Quakers and other missionaries, taught enslaved people to read so that they could read the Bible. However, as enslaved rebellions became more frequent, even more rigid laws and punishments resulted. By the early nineteenth century, many states passed explicit anti-literacy laws. For example, in 1740, South Carolina passed one of the earliest laws (e.g., South Carolina Negro Act) making it illegal to teach enslaved people to write.[8] Despite these restrictions, many enslaved people pursued education in secret and at great personal risk. Frederick Douglass described how he initially learned the alphabet from his owner's wife in Baltimore and then taught himself to read in secret. Douglass famously wrote in *Narrative of the Life of Frederick Douglass* (1845), "Once you learn to read, you will be forever free."[9]

Even after slavery ended, US laws were created to deny Black children the same education as their white peers. Black children were subjected to underfunded all-Black schools, and many lacked access to education altogether. The doctrine of "separate but equal" governed education from 1896 (*Plessy v. Ferguson*) until 1954.[10] *Plessy v. Ferguson*, a significant US Supreme Court case, upheld racial segregation in schools and other areas of US society. The Louisiana case involved Homer Plessy, a man of mixed race, who intentionally violated the state's Separate Car Act by sitting in a "whites-only" railroad car. Plessy was arrested and challenged the law, arguing that it violated the Equal Protection Clause of the Fourteenth Amendment. However, in a 7–1 decision, the US Supreme Court ruled against Plessy. The majority opinion, written by Justice Henry Billings Brown, asserted that segregation was constitutional if the facilities provided to both races were allegedly equal. The Court reasoned that the Fourteenth Amendment was not meant to eliminate racial injustice or enforce social equality.[11] The *Plessy* decision legitimized nearly six decades of legalized educational segregation, until it was overturned by *Brown v. Board of Education* in 1954.[12] Although the *Brown* decision legally dismantled school segregation, it did not eradicate the racist ideologies or institutional practices that sustained unequal systems.

In US education, it can be argued that every advance for Black student progress encounters a wave of resistance or "backlash" that persists to this day. From the demotion of Black educators after schools were integrated to the excessive policing of Black students, the US education system continues to pathologize, surveil, and silence Black children and educators.[13] This is particularly concerning because of the resurgence of this resistance in 2025 through anti-DEI (diversity, equity, and inclusion) policies, book bans, and curricular censorship. The Trump administration intensified these efforts by leveraging executive actions and federal influence to restrict civil rights enforcement, dismantle teacher preparation programs that emphasize the education of diverse student populations, and block funding for institutions focused on equity-driven education.[14] These actions are part of a broader anti-Black policy agenda that undermines not only what is taught but also who gets to teach and who is welcome in public education spaces.[15] The attempts to erase Black history, limit teacher autonomy, and prohibit open discussions about America's racial history are not new, but they represent just the latest chapter in a long-standing backlash against Black children's right to learn and self-determination.[16]

Derrick Bell, one of the founders of critical race theory (CRT), warned that racism is ingrained in the DNA of the United States. Anti-Black racism, he argued, is embedded in the national psyche because of the long history of enslavement and second-class treatment of Black Americans. Although there has been undeniable progress and extraordinary resilience within Black communities, that progress remains fragile. Every gain in civil rights and educational equity has triggered swift and often strategic efforts to reverse it, a pattern seen from Reconstruction to the backlash against *Brown v. Board of Education*, and again today with the dismantling of diversity, equity, and inclusion (DEI) efforts and civil rights protections.[17]

At the center of this backlash is the persistent myth of meritocracy. The academic difficulties faced by Black students are frequently interpreted as a deficiency in knowledge, effort, or ability, instead of being acknowledged as unequal access to resources and opportunities.[18] In contrast, white students typically gain advantages from a history of generational wealth, attendance at well-funded schools, and institutional bias, aspects that often are unrecognized as unmerited benefits. This misguided notion of meritocracy, which attributes success entirely to personal effort, obscures systemic obstacles and perpetuates racial hierarchies in schools.[19]

The current wave of anti-Black rhetoric and policies affects the civil rights of Black students, the accuracy of history curricula, financial aid support for Black college students, and any initiatives focused on racial equity and equality in education. These efforts have created a chilling effect on PK–12 schools and higher education institutions that have made significant strides in implementing inclusive practices. In an environment where even naming racism is deemed controversial, students are denied the opportunity to engage in truthful education and self-affirmation. As Bell (1992) reminds us, the permanence of racism requires that we challenge the structures that sustain racist practices.[20]

Although many books address the issues facing Black students, this book is different. It focuses on what can be made right. Written as a guide for educators, school leaders, policymakers, and advocates, this book encourages moving beyond passive awareness toward intentional, sustained action. Research, historical analysis, and modern case studies highlight both challenges and possibilities, demonstrating how we can create educational systems that affirm Black life, nurture Black brilliance, and celebrate Black joy. To repair what was broken, we must first understand how it was shattered. That work begins here.

FROM "SEPARATE BUT EQUAL" TO RESISTANCE

As mentioned previously, for almost sixty years, the doctrine of "separate but equal" legally approved racial segregation in US public schools. Established in the 1896 Supreme Court decision *Plessy v. Ferguson*, the "separate but equal" doctrine permitted states to maintain racially segregated schools if *they claimed* to offer equal resources, services, and materials. Separate was never equal. For decades, Black students suffered from severely underfunded schools, which were housed in crumbling buildings filled with outdated textbooks and materials. In the 1940s, Black schools in Mississippi, for example, were funded at only about one-third the rate of white schools.[21] Yet, Black educators continued to teach and offer support to Black students with little to no support. Black teachers stood as pillars of strength, hope, and excellence and brought an unparalleled understanding of their students' lived experiences. Black educators created schools that nurtured Black students' academic development while instilling in them a sense of pride and possibility.

Earlier findings note the hugely significant *Brown v. Board of Education* US Supreme Court case challenged the injustice of segregated schools and the violation of the Fourteenth Amendment. Led by Black civil rights lawyer Thurgood Marshall, the case overturned the *Plessy v. Ferguson* legal finding of separate but equal schools. However, the *Brown* decision was met with noncompliance and massive resistance. Instead of ushering in an era of racial reconciliation and reckoning, the Brown decision ignited a fierce backlash from white Americans.

White politicians, school boards, and community members worked to delay or outright defy school desegregation. For instance, in Virginia, Senator Harry F. Byrd led a massive resistance to integrated schools. A striking example occurred in Prince Edward County, Virginia, where officials chose to shut down all public schools between 1959 and 1964 instead of integrating. For five years, Black children were denied formal education, while white families established and ran private "academies" funded by public money.[22] This intentional act of snubbing the US Supreme Court decision demonstrated the extreme measures white authorities were willing to take to maintain white supremacist structures and hierarchies, even sacrificing children's futures in the process.

Another example of resistance to the integration of schools occurred in Little Rock, Arkansas. In 1957, nine Black students, later recognized as the Little Rock Nine, faced hostile white mobs and National Guard troops while attempting to enter Central High School in Little Rock (fig. 1.1). President Eisenhower was

FIGURE 1.1 A 1959 rally at Arkansas state capitol protesting the racial integration of Little Rock Central High School. Protesters carry US flags and signs reading "Race Mixing is Communism" and "Stop the Race Mixing March of the Anti-Christ." Protests continued two years after the "Little Rock Nine" crisis.

Source: John T. Bledsoe, *U.S. News & World Report Collection*, Library of Congress Prints and Photographs Division, August 20, 1959. Accessed via Wikimedia Commons: https://commons.wikimedia.org/wiki/File:Little_Rock_integration_protest.jpg.

forced to send federal troops to ensure their safe entry. The images of these young students surrounded by soldiers and hostile crowds became a symbol of the nation's deep divide on racial justice.

The aftermath of *Brown* and white resistance resulted in a psychological conundrum for Black students and families. Although they were pleased to have the promise of equal schooling, racial integration and the resistance to it were tough. Many Black students who integrated white schools faced daily hostility, isolation, and racial trauma. They were often harassed or ignored by white peers and teachers. Meanwhile, Black communities lost local control of schools that had once been cultural anchors and sources of racial pride. Ironically, school desegregation disrupted Black students' educational stability and eroded community-based schooling. Consequently, the failure to implement integration with equity and care created new forms of inequality that we are still living with today. Many urban and rural districts are more racially and economically segregated now than they were in the 1970s, a trend exacerbated by housing policy, district zoning, and school choice laws.[23] Sadly, the vision of *Brown* has yet to be realized.

THE DISPLACEMENT OF BLACK EDUCATORS AFTER *BROWN V. BOARD*: A LASTING INJURY TO EDUCATION

After the *Brown* case, the widespread demotion, dismissal, and marginalization of Black educators were pervasive. Tens of thousands of Black principals, teachers, and administrators, who had long been part of segregated Black schools, were reassigned or otherwise forced out of their positions. Between 1954 and 1970, around 38,000 Black educators lost their jobs.[24] Instead of being integrated into the newly racially integrated schools, Black teachers were devalued and lost their positions of authority. In contrast, white administrators and teachers mostly kept or secured their roles of authority. This systemic displacement not only resulted in job losses but also represented an erasure of professional dignity and educational leadership in Black communities.

In all-Black schools of the past, Black educators served as role models, mentors, and community leaders. They understood their students' lived experiences and delivered culturally affirming curricula and teaching methods, even in the face of inequality. The racial integration of schools resulted in fewer Black teachers and leaders for students who shared their racial and cultural backgrounds, which are elements that have a significant influence on academic engagement, performance, and long-term achievements.[25] Interestingly, the dissolving of Black teacher and leader authority resulted in a series of US Senate Select Committee hearings in 1971 about the status of Black school leaders in integrated schools. The hearings did not result in any action toward reinstating Black educators.[26]

Desegregation introduced a dilemma for Black communities. Although most Black parents wanted their children to learn alongside white students, they were required to endure schools with educators and administrators who maintained deficit-oriented or explicitly racist perceptions of their children's abilities. This transition led to long-lasting patterns of racial bias in disciplinary actions, special education referrals, and academic tracking that continue today in a multitude of formats. The absence of Black educators not only harmed Black students but also weakened the overall American education system by reducing its pool of culturally competent professionals. Black educators crafted adaptable teaching strategies to support students during the Jim Crow era, creating enriching educational experiences despite inadequate funding. The exclusion of these experiences signified a loss of pedagogical diversity and voided numerous knowledge systems rooted in resilience and cultural validation. Moreover, the misconception that desegregation served as a clear victory for educational equity underestimated the fact that education was still vastly unequal. Consequently, education reform emphasized inclusion without justice and access without agency.

The ongoing impact of this erasure is still evident today. Black teachers are significantly underrepresented in the workforce, accounting for only about 6 percent of all teachers, with charter schools hiring the highest number of Black teachers (10 percent).[27] Research indicates that all students, particularly Black students, benefit from having diverse teachers.[28] The mistrust and alienation felt by many Black families toward schools also stems from systemic neglect in providing Black educational leadership and presence in schools. We are at a crossroads in education, where districts must determine the best pathway forward for recruiting and retaining Black educators. If not, the shortage of Black educators exacerbates a system where equity often remains symbolic rather than structural.

SYSTEMIC RACISM IN US SCHOOLS TODAY

As discussed earlier, systemic racism in education has historically positioned Black students as inferior. This is reflected in both policies and practices, in which Black youth face disproportionately higher rates of suspension and expulsion compared to their white counterparts for similar actions and are less likely to experience advanced coursework and gifted and talented opportunities.[29] These disparities do not result from higher rates of misbehavior or inferior intelligence but stem from entrenched racial biases in how educators and institutions perceive and respond to Blackness.

Systemic racism in education is also evidenced by the long-lasting inequities in Black students' academic outcomes. Black students' average test scores in reading and math are significantly lower than those of other students. And, after the COVID-19 pandemic, they have experienced high rates of health consequences and loss resulting from COVID-19, in addition to mental health issues. As such, Black students are facing rising suicide risks and heightened feelings of disconnection.

To grasp the implications of racism in education, it is crucial to differentiate between individual racism and systemic racism as they relate to Black students. *Individual racism* refers to the discrimination or oppression of Black students. Examples of individual racism in schools include assuming a Black student is less capable and offering her easier assignments, limiting her academic development or a school counselor discouraging a Black student from applying to competitive colleges assuming he will not "fit in." In contrast, *systemic racism* transcends personal biases and represents the institutionalization of racist beliefs and assumptions within various systems. For instance, systemic racism is evidenced by less funding for majority Black schools, the underrepresentation of Black students in gifted and talented programs, and the erasure of Black history in a school system's curriculum. Systemic racism not only mirrors but also magnifies individual racism by leveraging institutional power. Systemic racism can be so pervasive in policies, classroom practices, and educator beliefs that it maintains unequal resources and treatment of Black students. These long-standing inequities result in Black students' lack of opportunity to learn and achieve academic success. Ultimately, systemic racism complicates and often stops the path to opportunity for Black students.

Research consistently indicates that racist attitudes and biases affect educators' perceptions and responses to Black students.[30] In short, educators with biased views about Black people are more likely to view Black students as aggressive, defiant, or threatening.[31] Most importantly, anti-Black racism can cause an educator to perceive Black students as less intelligent and capable. These altered perceptions lead to inferior and disparate opportunities for Black students' success. For young Black girls, educators may tend to "adultify" them, leading to viewing them as older, more mature, and less innocent compared to white girls. This perception denies Black girls the protection typically given to children, leading to increased surveillance and harsher disciplinary measures in schools.[32] Consequently, Black girls often lack the social-emotional support that others receive, which reinforces exclusionary practices and emotional trauma.[33] This process of adultification reflects broader societal dynamics in which Black children are not viewed through a lens of care or compassion; rather, they are perceived as adults to be controlled. Many educators, including Black educators, respond with punishment instead of offering healing. Thus, schools often are spaces where Black students are pushed out or excluded. These schooling practices mirror societal patterns of criminalizing Black people, which deny them their right to learn and become fully productive and thriving adults.

To interrupt systemic and individual racist systems, educators must commit to antiracist and healing-centered classroom approaches that affirm and respect the humanity, agency, and cultural wealth of Black students. Comprehensive antiracist professional development for educators, culturally responsive pedagogy, and restorative justice practices result in school communities that uplift all students, not just Black students.[34] When white students see racism in action, their perception of justice and its implications for Black identity significantly impact their social identity and moral development. Research indicates that unchecked racial injustice in school settings can lead to moral disengagement, where all students become numb to inequality and learn to justify or overlook harm done to their peers.[35] Pettigrew and Tropp's research indicates that when racially unjust systems are normalized in school environments, rather than challenged, cross-group empathy decreases; and desensitization among majority group students increases.[36] In the absence of critical discourse about the harm of racism, witnessing unchecked racism in schools can lead to the normalization of racist actions and reinforce institutional racism.

Another consequence of institutional racism in schools is the emergence of what is termed "white silence." This practice involves avoiding conversations about race to maintain comfort or social cohesion.[37] In environments where anti-Black racism remains unchallenged, students—including Black students—internalize the belief that silence is acceptable or even expected. Such silence perpetuates racial injustice by shielding individuals from the responsibility of allyship and weakening their capacity for empathy, civic engagement, and the establishment of cross-racial solidarity.[38] Conversely, as discussed earlier, when educators take proactive measures to confront racial bias and instruct students about the history of racism, they foster critical consciousness. This awareness of social inequalities cultivates a sense of duty to challenge these injustices.[39] Curricular and pedagogical strategies that reflect a commitment to inclusion and antiracist beliefs, where every child is regarded as equal, can enhance the overall school climate. This not only benefits all students but also encourages white students to become more thoughtful, empathetic, and active contributors to equitable communities.

It is essential to recognize that majority-Black schools are not immune to anti-Black racism. Research indicates that even within all-Black contexts, educators may propagate anti-Black messages inherited from the broader society.[40] These detrimental messages can manifest as colorism, where lighter skin tones are prioritized, or the devaluation of Black cultural knowledge in favor of mainstream "white" norms. Love and Ladson-Billings highlight that curricula in all-Black schools can still emphasize white or Eurocentric narratives. Ultimately, when students lack exposure to representations of Black excellence and history within their learning, it reinforces Black inferiority, even in the absence of white peers.[41]

THE HISTORICAL CONTEXT OF TRAUMA IN BLACK COMMUNITIES

The trauma of enslavement did not end in 1865. Nearly a century of Jim Crow laws, racial segregation, and racialized terror, including lynchings, sexual violence, and disenfranchisement, followed. These systems were designed to uphold white supremacy and suppress Black freedom and advancement.[42] Numerous examples of racialized trauma occurred across the United States, impacting every aspect of Black life. Table 1 provides information about those laws and events, particularly regarding how many Black people were affected. One of the most egregious examples of racialized violence and trauma took place in Tulsa, Oklahoma, in 1921, when a white mob, fueled by a false accusation, attacked the prosperous Black neighborhood of Greenwood, often referred to as "Black Wall Street." More than three hundred Black individuals lost their lives, eight hundred sustained injuries, and thousands were forced to flee. Homes, businesses, schools, and churches were destroyed in one of the most tragic and deliberate attacks on Black prosperity in

US history.[43] This massacre targeted not only individuals but also the collective self-determination and economic independence of a thriving Black community.

The traumatic impact of such events on individuals and communities has never been fully addressed or remedied. Instead, these wounds have been transmitted across generations, influencing the psychological, emotional, and educational journeys of Black children and families.[44] The repercussions of this legacy of racial violence persist both as historical memory and as lived experience. And today, many Black youth's experiences in schools are shaped by these racialized beliefs and generations of harm.

It's important to acknowledge that the racial violence during the Jim Crow era (1877–1965) was especially abhorrent. The lynching of Black youth, often for alleged minor infractions or perceived breaches of racial etiquette, served as a brutal tool of white supremacy intended to instill fear and uphold racial dominance. Between 1877 and 1950, more than 4,400 Black individuals were lynched, many of whom were young boys and teens falsely accused of minor or fabricated offenses.[45] One of the most infamous cases was the 1955 lynching of fourteen-year-old Emmett Till in Mississippi, after he was accused of whistling at a white woman. His brutal murder and the decision of his mother, Mamie Till-Mobley, to hold an open-casket funeral exposed the horrors of racial violence and became a catalyst for the civil rights movement. These lynchings were frequently treated as public spectacles, infused with religious overtones and justified by white communities as necessary for moral order, revealing a deep-rooted belief in their divine and civic entitlement to control Black lives.[46] The legal system provided no protection for Black Americans. Lynchers were seldom prosecuted and almost never convicted. For Black youth, the consequences of pervasive lynching left them vulnerable, traumatized, and acutely aware that their lives were perpetually at risk and unvalued.

The impact of racialized trauma over hundreds of years continues to affect individuals today. Table 1.1 shows the legacy of anti-Black policies and trauma on Black youth. Although Black children may not face lynching by members of the Ku Klux Klan, they still experience a significant amount of racialized trauma. This trauma includes the ongoing emotional and psychological damage caused by both systemic and individual racism. The national attention on the brutal deaths of unarmed Black individuals such as Trayvon Martin, George Floyd, Ahmaud Arbery, Yusef Hawkins, and Breonna Taylor spotlights the everyday racialized violence

TABLE 1.1 Legacy of anti-Black policies and collective trauma

Each link directs you to the primary Equal Justice Initiative (EJI) report, article, or interactive site where the underlying data and narrative are presented.

	EJI Resource	*Data and Narrative*
Slavery and the Middle Passage	*Slavery in America: The Montgomery Slave Trade* https://eji.org/reports/slavery-in-america/	Documents the forced transport of 10–12 million Africans, mortality on the Middle Passage, and the domestic slave trade's scale inside the United States.
Black codes and convict leasing	"Convict Leasing" history brief (EJI Racial-Injustice Calendar entry) https://eji.org/news/history-racial-injustice-convict-leasing/#:~:text=After%20the%20Civil%20War%2C%20slavery,and%20often%20deadly%20work%20conditions.	Explains how post-Emancipation criminalization and leasing systems re-enslaved hundreds of thousands well into the twentieth century.
Lynchings and mob violence	*Lynching in America: Confronting the Legacy of Racial Terror* (3rd ed., 2017) https://eji.org/reports/lynching-in-america/	Provides the definitive count of 4,400+ documented racial-terror lynchings (1877–1950) and their community-wide impact.
Destruction of Black communities (e.g., Tulsa, Rosewood)	"Lynching in America: Outside the South" interactive and Tulsa massacre narratives https://lynchinginamerica.eji.org/explore	Details large-scale racial attacks—including the 1921 Tulsa and 1923 Rosewood massacres—that erased wealth and displaced thousands.
Jim Crow Laws and segregated apartheid	*Segregation in America: Separate and Unequal in the 1950s* (2018 report and companion site) https://eji.org/reports/segregation-in-america/	Traces legalized segregation, voter suppression, and the denial of civil rights affecting virtually the entire Black population of the South.
Police violence and mass incarceration	EJI "Mass Incarceration" issue hub and related news archive https://eji.org/criminal-justice-reform/	Connects historical criminal-control regimes to modern policing disparities and the disproportionate imprisonment of millions of Black Americans.
Contemporary anti-Black violence and policy backlash	"The History of Violent Opposition to Black Political Participation" https://eji.org/news/the-history-of-violent-opposition-to-black-political-participation/	Examines ongoing legislative rollbacks (e.g., voting-rights curbs) and racially motivated violence as current manifestations of the same legacy of racial terror.

experienced by Black people. This trauma is further intensified by additional challenges, such as inferior schooling, poverty, housing instability, and community violence, to which Black children are more frequently subjected compared to their white peers.[47] However, when Black students exhibit signs of trauma, such as anxiety, withdrawal, hypervigilance, or emotional outbursts, they are often misinterpreted as being disruptive, defiant, or disengaged. Instead of receiving the necessary mental health support, they face disproportionate punishment, suspension, or criminalization, resembling the traumatic processes of earlier times.

The modern extension of historical systems designed to police Black behavior, deny Black children their innocence, and erase Black brilliance is real. However, educators can disrupt this cycle by fostering school environments that acknowledge trauma, affirm Black identity, and promote healing instead of harm. This begins with acknowledging history, rather than avoiding it. Culturally responsive teaching and restorative practices are essential, along with consistently recognizing Black children as resilient, creative individuals brimming with potential. To uplift Black students, we must first confront the truth regarding racialized violence and recognize the incredible strength Black communities have demonstrated despite enduring these challenges.

THE ROLE OF EDUCATORS IN ENDING RACIALIZED TRAUMA

Educators from all racial backgrounds enter the profession with a genuine desire to support students. However, without a clear understanding of the historical and emotional experiences of Black students, teachers can unknowingly perpetuate the very inequities they aim to dismantle. Many educator preparation programs, for instance, focus on pedagogy, including culturally responsive educational strategies. But ways to address racialized trauma are often least understood by new and experienced teachers.[48]

Frequently, educators are unaware of how to discuss or broach issues of race or racism with Black students. For most educators, they learn about the consequences of racialized trauma through the lens of Black underachievement. Statistics, such as test scores, graduation rates, attendance trends, and suspension rates, are often used in schools without considering the generational impacts of racialized policies such as redlining, disinvestment in schools, Black history exclusion from curricula, and the cultural disconnect between predominantly white educators and students of color.[49] This negative framing strengthens implicit bias and causes educators to view Black students as issues to address rather than as children deserving support.

As a result of this absence in educator training, educators frequently misinterpret trauma-based behaviors (e.g., emotional withdrawal, emotional outbursts) as signs of defiance, disrespect, or lack of motivation. These behaviors are often symptoms of racialized trauma, grief, psychological distress, or identity-related crisis. When teachers respond with punitive measures rather than inquiry or support, they reinforce cycles of harm that alienate Black students from their own learning environments. Schoolwide policies (e.g., discipline codes with zero tolerance, school policing) also illustrate a larger trend of systemic exclusion. Moreover, the daily microaggressions (e.g., being overcorrected, underaffirmed, ignored) attest that many Black students are tied to a long legacy of educational exclusion and anti-Black surveillance. Collectively, these acts harm. Although not always intentional, they are deeply consequential.

The responsibility of educators and preparation programs is paramount. Educator preparation programs must shift from neutrality to explicit antiracist pedagogy, equipping teachers and all educators to understand not only child development but also trauma-informed care and critical consciousness.[50] Educators need training to pose more profound questions about Black student behavior and how to support Black students' success. The main questions include: Am I retraumatizing Black students? What beliefs and biases am I introducing into the classroom? How can I guarantee that every student feels seen, heard, and valued? Until we address the effects of trauma in Black communities—all communities—even well -meaning educators may unknowingly contribute to the retraumatization of the very students they mean to serve.

TRAUMA AND BLACK IDENTITY: WHO IS CONSIDERED BLACK?

Historically, Black students are not just learning academics in school; they are also learning what it means to be Black in a society that has historically devalued and excluded them. The trauma of systemic racism deeply impacts racial identity formation, as well as the multiple intersecting identities that many Black students carry, such as gender, religion, sexual orientation, and ability. Although this chapter focuses primarily on racial identity, it is essential for educators to recognize that Black students are often navigating a complex web of identities that shape their school experiences and sense of self. The messages Black students receive about "Blackness," their worth, their culture, and their place in the world are all significant factors in their development. In many ways, schools are spaces where students' identities, particularly racial identity, are constantly negotiated and explored. This negotiation can be confusing, especially when Black students are exposed to conflicting narratives about the meaning of "Blackness." In school, they may be told by teachers that they can be whatever they want to be, but in their neighborhoods, they are often followed by police because they are perceived as potential threats. The internal conflict that emerges can manifest as self-doubt, anger, or even rejection of one's own Black identity. For students navigating these tensions, racialized trauma is about not only external harm but also the psychological dissonance that comes from living in a society that simultaneously urges you to embrace and erase your Blackness. Psychologist William Cross's Nigrescence Theory outlines the stages of Black racial identity development, providing educators with insights into a student's possible position in their identity formation.[51] Cross's stages include:

- Pre-encounter: a disconnection from or devaluing of Black identity: *"I don't really see myself as different from anyone else. I just try to fit in and not cause problems. I don't think race has much to do with how people treat you."*
- Encounter: an awakening to the realities of racism: *"I thought if I just worked hard and stayed out of trouble, I'd be treated fairly. But now I see that being Black changes how people see me, no matter what I do."*
- Immersion/Emersion: deep exploration of Black identity and culture: *"I'm learning everything I can about Black history and culture. I only want to be around people who understand what it means to be Black. I've wasted too much time trying to fit into white spaces."*
- Internalization: a secure and integrated sense of Black self: *"I know who I am, and I'm proud to be Black. I don't need to distance myself from anyone, but I also won't let anyone define me or diminish my worth."*

These stages are not fixed, and students may move through them fluidly, depending on their experiences. Black racial identity can develop differently in all-Black or predominantly Black school settings compared to racially diverse or predominantly white institutions. Racial identity often develops in response to encounters with systemic racism or what he calls a "disorienting encounter," an experience that forces an individual to confront the reality of racism and re-evaluate their identity in relation to it. In predominantly white schools, these encounters are frequent and often unavoidable through microaggressions, isolation, biased discipline, or curriculum erasure. Such experiences can accelerate the progression of racial identity development by forcing Black students to grapple with their racialized existence in opposition to dominant white norms.[52]

In contrast, students in all-Black schools may experience more *racial affirmation*, peer validation, and representation. As a result, the early stages of racial identity development may not involve the same kind of reactive dissonance often triggered by exposure to whiteness. This does not mean identity is less developed. However, it means it may emerge through *affirmation* **or** forming a collective and internalized understanding of Black identity from the outset.[53] However, even in all-Black schools, students are not immune to structural racism. They are still navigating a society dominated by white norms in media, politics, and public life. Thus, their racial identity development is still shaped by broader social forces. Scholars such as Beverly Daniel Tatum argue that racial identity continues to evolve over time, particularly as students transition into racially integrated spaces such as college or the workplace.[54]

Consider Maya, a ninth-grade Black student who says during a history class discussion: *"Slavery wasn't that bad, why do we keep talking about it? It just makes me feel bad like I'm a slave."* Her Black classmates react with shock and anger, and Maya becomes the target of ridicule. *"You aren't Black, Maya,"* the students keep saying to her in class and later stating as a reason to exclude her from "Black student groups." An educator in this case might focus on correcting Maya or silencing her, *but an identity-conscious, strength-based educator* would understand that Maya is still forming her relationship to Blackness. Thus, Maya doesn't need condemnation; instead, she needs an opening for further exploration. In fact, all the students in this class would benefit from exploring their racial identities. Teasing others about their identities is not appropriate. However, given Maya's experience, the affirming educator in this case will provide her with a safe space, free from teasing, to ask questions, explore her heritage, and reframe her understanding of Blackness. When educators understand identity development, they can meet students where they are and provide them with the space to learn and explore more about their identities.

Colorism is another dynamic related to exploring one's understanding of their Blackness or Black identity. Colorism is the preferential treatment of Black people with lighter skin tones over those with darker complexions. It is a persistent and painful issue within Black communities that is often overlooked in schools. Although racism functions through power structures that elevate whiteness and marginalize Blackness, colorism operates as an intraracial hierarchy, privileging proximity to white physical features (such as lighter skin, straighter hair, or narrower facial features) and devaluing darker skin and African features.[55] Though rooted in white supremacy, colorism is sustained within Black communities through intergenerational messaging, media representation, and even classroom dynamics. In educational spaces that serve primarily Black students, colorism can shape peer relationships, teacher perceptions, discipline rates, and students' racial identity development.

Colorism is deeply tied to racial identity, especially for Black students navigating questions of self-worth, belonging, and acceptance. It can distort or complicate stages of Black racial identity, as students receive mixed messages about what it means to be "Black enough" or desirable within their own community. Lighter-skinned Black students may experience privilege and inclusion, but they may also wrestle with questions about authenticity and belonging. Darker-skinned Black students may encounter exclusion, ridicule, and lowered expectations, which can result in internalized racism, social anxiety, and disengagement.[56] Colorism may play out in school policies through white norms such as dress codes, hair policies, and informal social cues. Research by Dumas and Nelson indicated that Black students are frequently disciplined or ridiculed for hairstyles such as braids or Afros, implying their appearance is "unprofessional" or disruptive.[57] White beauty standards still dominate in US schools, and Black girls in particular must navigate a society where they are often perceived as the opposite of beauty while still developing a positive self-perception and strong cultural pride.

These dynamics are further compounded by the fact that many teachers, both Black and non-Black, are not trained to recognize or interrupt colorism. Research has found that educators may unconsciously favor lighter-skinned students.[58] The psychological and emotional impact of colorism is real. For children and teens, being teased for their skin tone, hair texture, or other physical features can lead to long-term trauma, especially when educators do not address these experiences. This trauma may manifest as:

- low self-esteem or body dysmorphia
- internalized anti-Blackness
- depression or anxiety
- social withdrawal or identity confusion

Educators must also be vigilant about internalized racism among Black students that is due to colorism. In a worst-case scenario, Black students may establish hierarchies within peer groups based on skin tone or challenge each other's Black identities based on color or appearance. These divisions are often reinforced by broader societal messages, including portrayals of lighter skin as more beautiful or aligned with beauty in the media.[59] When left unaddressed, however, colorism undermines the very goals of inclusivity and unity in schools, creating further division and hurt within a community already burdened by systemic racism. For educators and school leaders committed to affirming Black students, understanding and disrupting colorism must be integral to their work.

MICROAGGRESSIONS: *"YOU DON'T BELONG"*

Today, particularly in an anti-DEI culture, Black students frequently confront daily microaggressions that deliver a clear and damaging message: "You don't belong here." These experiences can result in trauma-related symptoms, such as anxiety, emotional numbness, distrust, self-doubt, and disengagement, which are often misinterpreted as defiance or disinterest by educators. Microaggressions are subtle, often unintentional slights or insults that convey hostile, derogatory, or dismissive messages toward minoritized groups.[60] In school settings, examples include: "You're so articulate" (which implies surprise at a Black student's intelligence) or "Can I touch your hair?" (reducing cultural identity to mere curiosity). Additional examples include consistently being overlooked in classroom discussions or facing disciplinary actions for behaviors tolerated in white peers. Over time, these microaggressions can detrimentally impact Black students' mental health, identity development, and academic motivation.

To truly support Black students, educators must understand that these students are navigating the psychological burden caused by systems that were never designed to affirm them. Supporting Black students involves nurturing their racial identity development and facilitating their healing. For educators, disrupting microaggressions against Black students is crucial for their success. For instance, Jameel is a Black tenth grader at a mixed-race high school, where a majority of the teachers identify as white. In every class, his teachers mispronounce his name, calling him "Jaleel" or "Jaime," or some other incorrect name, but never "Jameel." Finally, a Black teacher interrupted another teacher's mispronunciation, stating, "*His name is Jameel. Mispronouncing his name is hurtful. Please pronounce his name right.*" Jameel thanked the teacher.

LINGERING IMPACT OF RACIALIZED TRAUMA ON BLACK STUDENT DEVELOPMENT

To understand the challenges many Black students face in educational spaces today, we must first understand the lingering pain of racialized trauma and violence on Black students' development. Racialized violence is not limited to physical acts of brutality; it encompasses a wide spectrum of psychological and emotional harm, which has been carried out through schools for hundreds of years. The history of violence associated with the desegregation of schools has been maintained by the current racial segregation of schools and the sustained attacks on Black students' safety, dignity, and humanity.

Black students' academic and social development progresses through a series of critical stages, each profoundly influenced by the realities of racism within and beyond schools. Although growth across physical, cognitive, emotional, and social domains is a natural process for all children, Black students experience a developmental journey uniquely disrupted and complicated by individual and systemic racism and exclusionary schooling practices. Black scholars, such as James Comer, Beverly Tatum, Signithia Fordham, John Ogbu, and others, have highlighted how educational structures and the racism embedded within them interact with Black students' development. For instance, early childhood is a critical stage for identity development, emotional regulation, and social learning. However, for Black children, this foundational period is often disrupted by early experiences with bias and exclusion in educational settings. Research by Gilliam et al. revealed that Black preschoolers, particularly boys, are nearly four times more likely to be suspended or expelled than their white peers, even when controlling for similar behaviors.[61] These disciplinary disparities are not reflections of student conduct, but rather adult perceptions shaped by implicit racial bias. Such early punitive measures have profound developmental consequences. They contribute to a diminished sense of belonging, erode self-esteem, and interrupt the natural development of emotional and behavioral regulation. Black children begin internalizing harmful messages about their worth and potential at a young age, which can result in disengagement from school and heightened vulnerability to future discipline. These patterns help establish the foundations of the school-to-prison pipeline, where exclusionary discipline becomes a precursor to long-term academic and social marginalization.

Decades ago, Comer's School Development Program emphasized that Black students' emotional and social development is foundational to academic success, arguing that educators must nurture, rather than punish, the natural exuberance and exploration of young Black children.[62] As students progress into middle childhood, typically in grades 3 through 5, they begin to compare themselves to others and become more aware of fairness and societal norms. During this period, Black students often face the damaging effects of lowered teacher expectations and harmful race-based tracking decisions. Fordham and Ogbu argued that Black students and their parents must navigate the painful reality of Black identity formation, choosing between pursuing academic excellence and maintaining cultural solidarity in a racialized educational environment.[63]

The transition to early adolescence (grades 6–8) brings new challenges as racial identity development accelerates. According to Tatum, adolescence is a critical time for racial consciousness, during which Black students begin to understand racism as a structural and systemic force rather than isolated incidents.[64] At the same time, school discipline disparities widen at this time. The cumulative effects of biased and racist discipline policies, exclusion from advanced coursework, and invisibility within the curriculum significantly impact and erode the motivation and academic development of Black students over time.

During high school, all students face important decisions about their futures. Black students often face additional pressures from teachers and school counselors who emphasize the need to accelerate their preparation for college and careers—for example, by insisting that they participate in college access programs designed to "catch them up" on academics and improve college-going metrics such as standardized test scores. If these students and their caregivers had been given more information earlier about the processes and expectations of college preparation, they would likely have been better positioned to succeed without additional stress. Nevertheless, such supports and guidance are too often not prioritized for Black students. Also, academic tracking often locks students out of advanced placement (AP) and college preparatory courses, not because of a lack of ability but because of racialized gatekeeping practices.[65] Comer's work remains especially relevant during these high school years. He emphasizes the importance of developmental pathways: physical, cognitive, psycho-emotional, social-interactive, moral-ethical, and linguistic. He argues that the academic success of Black students depends on support of the whole child, particularly amid structural barriers.

Throughout these stages, it becomes evident that racism does not merely affect Black students' outcomes; it actively distorts the very process of development. Emotional security, intellectual curiosity, social belonging, and self-concept are all compromised when schools fail to affirm Black students' full humanity. As Comer insisted, educational success for Black youth requires systems that prioritize relationships, culture, and community.

Racialized violence affects Black students' development when it is transmitted across generations through a process known as *intergenerational trauma*. Families who have survived historical or contemporary racial violence often pass on adaptive survival mechanisms, such as racial socialization, resilience narratives, and community vigilance; however, they also pass on unresolved grief, fear, and caution. These emotional legacies shape parenting/caregiving practices, perceptions of safety, and relationships with institutions, including schools.[66] This trauma is compounded when school systems fail to validate these realities or, worse, reinforce them through harsh discipline, lowered expectations, or cultural erasure. When educators deny the presence of racism or adopt color-blind approaches, they risk deepening the disconnect between Black students' lived experiences and the narratives upheld in school. This dissonance creates additional emotional labor for students and undermines their ability to thrive. Schools that serve Black children well are those that acknowledge racial harm, celebrate Black resilience, and provide space for critical conversations, creative expression, and leadership.

HISTORY OF THRIVING: BLACK STUDENTS' PROTECTIVE FACTORS

Although the history of Black education in the United States is a story of struggle, it is also a rich story of resilience and success. From the inception of secret schools during enslavement to the establishment of historically Black colleges and universities (HBCUs) and Freedom Schools, Black communities have consistently found ways to nurture their youth. This legacy persists today through protective factors, or sources of strength that enable Black students to succeed despite the struggles they encounter.

Research indicates there are factors that protect Black students from the negative impacts of trauma and inequitable systems.[67] These "protective factors" counteract risks and foster resilience. Protective factors exist at multiple levels: within the individual, the family, the community, and broader systems like education. For Black children, whose trauma often stems from systemic racism, it is important for educators to build upon and include these protective factors in their daily work. Research shows the presence of supportive, identity-affirming educators is one of the most influential school-based protective factors for Black children facing racial stress.[68] When educators intentionally create spaces that recognize and affirm Black identity, they not only support academic achievement but also help students heal, grow, and thrive. Below is a list of key protective factors for Black students:

- positive racial identity and cultural pride
- affirming, trusting relationships with caring adults
- racial socialization that teaches coping, resistance, and cultural affirmation
- safe and inclusive classrooms that actively challenge racism and bias
- opportunities for leadership, creativity, and self-expression
- mindfulness, emotional regulation, and future orientation
- culturally relevant mental health supports and enrichment opportunities

For educators, affirming Black students means recognizing the protective power of racial identity, validating their lived experiences, and acting as co-constructors of healing spaces. Educators cannot be bystanders to this process. Studies show that Black youth with strong racial identity formation and solid social support report higher levels of psychological well-being, better academic performance, and greater resilience in the face of discrimination.[69]

Overall, educators have the power to transform classrooms into healing spaces by strengthening the protective factors that research shows are vital for Black students' development. In classrooms where protective factors are intentionally woven into daily practice, the atmosphere shifts to spaces where students feel valued.

CASE STUDY: BREAKING THE PATTERN—A PRINCIPAL'S STAND AGAINST ANTI-BLACK RACISM

Hawthorne Middle School, located in a racially diverse suburban district, had long been known for its high test scores and structured discipline approach. However, beneath the surface of academic success was a troubling pattern: Black students, particularly boys, were being suspended at nearly four times the rate of their white peers. Parents and teachers raised concerns, but the former principal dismissed the disparities as unfortunate but necessary for maintaining order in the school.

That changed when Pat O'Leary took on the role of principal.

Two weeks into the school year, a sixth-grade student named Marcus, an energetic and expressive Black boy, was referred to the principal's office for "disrupting class." The incident report from the teacher stated that Marcus had "challenged her authority" by asking why he couldn't finish his drawing during quiet time. The teacher claimed he had an "attitude."

Ms. O'Leary reviewed the incident report and followed up with important questions for the teacher. Did he use inappropriate language? Did he disrupt class? Did he complete his assignments? She noted that Marcus had not used inappropriate language, had not disrupted other students, and had completed all his assignments on time. Moreover, she discovered that a similar incident involving a white student had been resolved with a quiet conversation and no referral.

Ms. O'Leary knew that she needed to model how to solve this problem in a way that was nurturing rather than punitive. Marcus would soon become another statistic in the school's disciplinary data. So, Ms. O'Leary took several deliberate steps:

- She called Marcus and his mother into her office, not to reprimand, but to listen. She apologized to them. "You didn't deserve to be sent out of class for asking a question," she told Marcus. "That wasn't fair, and I'm going to make it right."
- Instead of publicly criticizing the teacher, Ms. O'Leary scheduled a private coaching session. She used the incident as a learning opportunity, introducing the teacher to the concept of implicit bias and

adultification. She recommended readings and offered access to a cultural humility workshop.

- Within weeks, Ms. O'Leary launched a discipline audit, examining who was being referred, for what reasons, and by whom. She disaggregated data by race and gender and shared the findings with the staff during a professional development day.
- The school replaced zero-tolerance policies with restorative circles. Students who felt harmed by disciplinary action were given space to speak. Marcus, with his mother's support, chose to share his experience during a community circle. The impact was powerful: several teachers acknowledged the need to shift their lens.

By the end of the year, suspensions of Black students had dropped by 60 percent. Student engagement increased, particularly among boys who had previously been labeled "challenging." Marcus, once on the verge of being written off, had become an outspoken leader in student government.

Staff surveys revealed a significant shift in school culture: more than 80 percent of teachers reported increased awareness of their own biases and greater confidence in using restorative approaches.

Case Study Reflection Questions

1. What forms of anti-Black racism (individual vs. systemic) are evident in this case? How does this case reflect US historical themes of anti-Black racism in education?
2. What specific steps did the school leader take to shift culture and practice?
3. How did Ms. O'Leary center both accountability and healing? What systems did she change?
4. How could this case inform your own practice or your school's policies?

CASE STUDY: SCHOOL REOPENING AMID GRIEF AND INEQUITIES

In the spring of 2020, at the height of the COVID-19 pandemic, a predominantly Black elementary school in a historically under-resourced neighborhood was pressured to reopen. The decision was largely driven by demands from the school board and working parents, many of whom were essential workers in roles such as public transit, health care, sanitation, and food service. These families faced a devastating dilemma: risk exposure to the virus by sending their children back to school, or lose income and job security to care for them at home.

Tragically, the surrounding community had already experienced disproportionately high COVID-19 death rates. The pandemic's toll exacerbated a long-standing legacy of grief, loss, and systemic neglect. Students returned to classrooms carrying the emotional weight of family deaths, economic instability, and profound uncertainty—yet the school had no on-site counselors or mental health professionals to support them.

Teachers quickly began to report rising levels of student anxiety, depression, and disengagement. Chronic absenteeism and behavioral challenges surged. But these challenges were not new. Even before COVID-19, this school had struggled with low student achievement and motivation. The community itself had long suffered from structural racism: food deserts, inadequate health infrastructure (including mental health services), and persistent underinvestment in public education. Geographically isolated, this neighborhood was often ignored in policy decisions until reopening schools became a matter of economic necessity.

As reopening unfolded, the decision reignited difficult questions about whose lives and needs are prioritized and what it means to educate children amid collective trauma without appropriate support.

Case Study Discussion Questions

1. What were the primary forces driving the decision to reopen this school during the pandemic? How do these forces reflect historical patterns of devaluing Black life and labor?
2. In what ways does the lack of mental health professionals and resources compound racialized trauma in this context?
3. How do structural inequities—such as food insecurity, poor health-care access, and school underfunding—relate to the historical oppression and racism that Black communities have experienced?

4. What might a racially just and trauma-informed reopening plan have looked like for this school?
5. How should schools address systemic racism during crises like the pandemic? How should educators communicate with wider audiences?
6. Reflecting on your own role (as an educator, policymaker, or leader), how would you advocate for the needs of this school and community moving forward?

CONCLUSION

Racism causes harm and leaves an indelible wound that seeps into the everyday experiences of Black students in American schools. From punitive discipline policies to erasure in the curriculum and casual microaggressions, schools often become sites of racial trauma that reside in the bodies, minds, and spirits of Black children. Although we hear from legislative leaders that they care about the success of all students, they continue to ignore how the legacy of racial violence and trauma has shaped how Black children view themselves, how they engage with learning, and how safe they feel in spaces meant to support their growth. Looking ahead, educators must resist the notion that school choice and meritocracy alone will rectify the racial inequalities in education. We must confront and address the brutal history of racial trauma through systemic change and boldly affirm and uplift Black students' well-being.

This chapter has examined the impact of racism and racial trauma on Black youth today. Healing begins with recognition and continues through action. Educators and school leaders must create environments that not only acknowledge racial trauma but also actively work against it. This includes affirming racial identity and building relationships rooted in dignity and care.

CHAPTER 2

Black Psychology: A Framework for Affirmation

Mainstream psychological theories, largely based on Eurocentric norms and paradigms, often fail to capture the cultural, historical, and collective experiences of Black people.[1] This gap between theoretical frameworks and real educational practices poses a major hurdle in educating Black students. To fully appreciate and affirm Black students, educators must embrace an educational framework grounded in Black psychology. Founded during the Black Power and civil rights movements, Black psychology emerged as a direct challenge to the deficit-based models of traditional psychology and educational practices in general. Black psychology recognizes the cultural brilliance of Black youth. It positions core cultural values such as communalism, spirituality, and self-determination as fundamental to Black students' well-being and identity.[2] When applied in educational contexts, Black psychology shifts the focus from "fixing" students to transforming the systems and structures that harm them. Rather than pathologizing behavior, it encourages educators to ask: What strengths has this child developed in response to their environment? What cultural knowledge and historical memory must be understood and applied? Amid today's ongoing attacks on issues of equity and justice in education, understanding Black psychology enables educators to become agents of healing and affirmation. This chapter focuses on the background and foundational aspects of Black psychology in schools and how it serves as the basis for transforming classrooms into environments where Black students are not merely surviving systems of harm but are thriving in settings designed with their full humanity in mind.

RECLAIMING THE PSYCHE: WHAT IS BLACK PSYCHOLOGY?

The field of Black psychology formally emerged in the 1970s during a time of political resistance. Joseph White, a pioneering voice in psychology, published his seminal article "Toward a Black Psychology" in 1970.[3] The article laid the foundation for an entirely new way of conceptualizing the unique mental health needs of Black Americans. He called for a psychology that centered the lived experiences, cultural identity, and historical trauma of Black people. White claimed it is inappropriate and harmful to use traditional theories developed by white psychologists to explain Black people.

Black psychology challenges the pathology-focused lens of mainstream psychology by offering a strength-based approach grounded in cultural integrity and resilience. It acknowledges that racial trauma from centuries of enslavement, segregation, and systemic racism has shaped the development and "psyche" of Black people. At the same time, it emphasizes collective memory, spirituality, and a deep-rooted sense of self as tools of resistance and healing. Black psychology, or African-centered psychology, calls on educators and mental health providers to understand wellness not as individual achievement but as a balance between self, community, and spirit.

Evolving Schools of Black Psychology

Maulana Karenga identified three ideological branches within Black psychology: traditional, reform, and radical. Traditional thinkers, such as Kenneth Clark, critiqued racism in psychology but remained grounded in its universalist assumptions.[4] Clark's "Doll Tests," conducted with his wife, Mamie Phipps Clark, demonstrated the internalized self-hate among Black children exposed to racial segregation. Though the work was instrumental in *Brown v. Board of Education*, it was framed largely through the lens of traditional psychological tenets.

The reform school, exemplified by Joseph White, James Jackson, and Margaret Beale Spencer, acknowledged the distinctiveness of Black psychology while also finding utility in select mainstream theories. Their work sought to expand traditional frameworks by integrating cultural context.[5] On the other hand, the radical school marked a clear break from traditional theories. Scholars such as Asa

Hilliard, Wade Nobles, Na'im Akbar, and Linda James Myers rejected Eurocentric psychological constructs altogether, proposing instead an African-centered worldview. This orientation placed collective identity, spiritual connectedness, and historical memory at the center of Black people's psychological health.

Narratives from Ancestors: Contributions of Psychologists That Shaped Black Psychology and Education

Mainstream education and psychology frequently overlook the transformative contributions scholars have made to enhance the mental health and well-being of Black communities. This neglect stems not from a lack of information or research but from the omission of culturally rooted perspectives within prevailing frameworks. The field of Black psychology, in particular, has developed as a significant counternarrative, emphasizing the lived experiences, cultural strengths, and communal values of Black individuals in both psychological theory and educational practice.

In addition to the research of Mamie and Kenneth Clark, this section introduces key thought leaders whose groundbreaking contributions have redefined what it means to support Black youth. These scholars challenged deficit models and exposed the harmful effects of systemic racism while offering culturally responsive and healing-centered approaches. Their work has paved the way for more affirming, identity-conscious practices. Despite their influence, many of their insights remain underutilized in today's schools and educator preparation programs. These brief introductions seek to honor the legacy of Black mental health researchers and remind readers that the tools to uplift Black students have long existed. They simply need to be embraced.

Inez Beverly Prosser, often recognized as the first Black woman to earn a PhD in psychology, studied the impact of segregated and integrated schools on Black students. She concluded that segregated schools, despite their lack of resources, often nurtured Black children's confidence more effectively than integrated settings, where students encountered daily racism.

William Cross, a white psychologist, offered the Nigrescence Model, a groundbreaking theory of Black identity development. His theoretical stages—arc from pre-encounter to internalization—mapped the emotional and psychological shifts that occur as Black students move toward racial self-awareness and pride. This model continues to shape educational and counseling practices.

Beverly Tatum deepened our understanding of racial identity development, particularly among adolescents navigating predominantly white spaces. In her influential book, *Why Are All the Black Kids Sitting Together in the Cafeteria?*, Tatum argues that identity formation is not only normal but necessary for Black youth living in a racially stratified society.

Robert Williams disrupted conventional intelligence testing by creating the Black Intelligence Test of Cultural Homogeneity (BITCH-100), which is designed to reflect Black language and cultural references. His work exposed the racial biases inherent in standardized testing and helped legitimize African American Vernacular English (AAVE), a dialect he called "Ebonics."

Wade Boykin's "Triple Quandary" theory describes the conflicting cultural contexts Black children must navigate in mainstream society, Black culture, and minority status. As a Howard University professor, Boykin's research underscored the importance of culturally responsive pedagogy and affirmed the need to view academic success through a cultural lens.

Asa Hilliard, an educational psychologist and African historian, fiercely advocated for African-centered curricula in public schools. He emphasized Black children are not broken; they are brilliant. What they lack is not ability but affirmation. Hilliard insisted that every child must be treated as a genius until proven otherwise.

Margaret Beale Spencer is a distinguished developmental psychologist whose work has been instrumental in revealing how race, ethnicity, and culture shape identity development in children, especially among Black youth. Building on the legacy of Black psychology, she introduced the Phenomenological Variant of Ecological Systems Theory (PVEST), emphasizing how Black students derive meaning from their experiences within racially stratified social environments. Her research illustrates Black children are not merely passive victims of bias; rather, they actively interpret their surroundings, continually negotiating their identity and self-worth.

CENTERING BLACK PSYCHOLOGY IN SCHOOLS AND CLASSROOMS

If not intentionally corrected, school curricula can reinforce white superiority and Black inferiority. Over time, anti-Black narratives have been normalized, leading both white and Black students to internalize their presumed place in society. More than three decades ago, Janice Hale emphasized that Black children need an educational system that affirms their strengths, intelligence, and cultural identity.[6] Similarly, Bettina Love has highlighted the systemic violence schools enact against Black students, referring to these harmful practices as spiritual, emotional, and intellectual assaults.[7]

At its core, Black psychology calls for an educational model grounded in love, cultural integrity, and a commitment to the thriving of Black children, which includes the following:

1. Integrating Black and African History into the PK–12 Curriculum

In *The Mis-Education of the Negro*, Carter G. Woodson, a pioneering Black historian and educator, argued that miseducation instills compliance and a sense of internalized inferiority among Black people. He wrote, "When you control a man's thinking you do not have to worry about his actions . . . He will go without being told. In fact, if there is no back door, he will cut one for his special benefit."[8] Woodson's critique remains a cornerstone of Black educational thought, highlighting how systemic indoctrination discourages critical consciousness and reinforces racial subordination.

Miseducation today takes many forms, including the banning of Black authors' and historians' contributions from the curriculum, presenting the enslavement of Black Africans in sanitized terms ("Slaves learned critical work skills"), or failing to teach literacy and critical thinking equitably. These practices distort Black students' history and identity and diminish potential. Classrooms that affirm Black psychology must present a comprehensive and truthful account of Black history, including both struggle and excellence. This requires more than token celebrations in February. Instead, it calls for a year-round commitment to historical accuracy and cultural relevance.

2. Celebrating Social Identities

Black psychology affirms identity as central to human development. Schools must create space for students to express their full identities, including those shaped by race, ethnicity, gender, spirituality, and language. In a world that teaches Black youth to doubt their worth, loving and embracing one's identity is radical. Curriculum and pedagogy must challenge dominant narratives that label schools serving Black and Brown students as "bad," and instead affirm the cultural practices, brilliance, and resilience present in those communities.

3. Using a Strength-Based Approach to Relationship Building

Rather than focusing on deficits, Black psychology promotes a strength-based philosophy in which educators recognize and nurture each child's potential. Building relationships grounded in respect, affirmation, and high expectations fosters resilience and empowerment. Practices such as restorative justice reflect this philosophy by centering healing, accountability, and community.

4. Truth-Telling as a Pathway to Healing

bell hooks reminds us that healing begins with truth. By naming racial pain and inviting students to share their stories, educators can cultivate classrooms rooted in empathy and collective healing.[9] Storytelling serves as both a tool for truth-telling and a catalyst for transformation. Models such as Community Healing and Resistance Through Storytelling (C-HeARTS) emphasize justice, cultural memory, and collective consciousness as key components of psychological healing. The C-HeARTS model positions these elements as essential for the psychological healing of racially marginalized communities. Rather than pathologizing trauma, this model honors the intergenerational stories and wisdom of Black communities, fostering resilience and resistance through culturally grounded practices and collective narrative work.[10]

5. Recruiting and Retaining Black Educators and Counselors

Although efforts to recruit Black teachers, counselors, principals, and other educators are vital for representation, retaining these professionals necessitates intentional actions, including affirming Black educators' identities, addressing racial dynamics in schools, and centering their voices in decision-making about students. As Achinstein and Proctor note, many Black educators are pushed out because of systemic racism within the profession. Recruitment without retention is performative; true inclusion requires structural change.[11]

6. Affirming Black Psychology in Practice

Psychologists and mental health providers who subscribe to Black psychology principles encourage educators to view Black children as geniuses and to love them unconditionally. Black psychology, in practice, means embedding affirming images, histories, and pedagogies in every aspect of school life, from classroom materials to discipline policies to counseling theories. It means rejecting narrow definitions of achievement and honoring the excellence inherent in Black communities. To center Black psychology in schools is to imagine education not as a site of harm but as a space of liberation. When we educate with love, history, and justice in mind, we honor the full humanity of every Black child and begin the work of collective healing.

Black psychology offers not only a critique of the past but a vision for the future—one rooted in cultural pride, holistic wellness, and educational justice. As Dr. Asa Hilliard once said, "There is no mystery on how to teach them [Black children]. The first thing you do is treat them like human beings and the second thing you do is love them."[12] To center Black psychology in schools is to affirm that every Black child is worthy of care, brilliance, and belonging. It is to reimagine what education can be—not just informative, but transformative.

The activity "Tell Your Story: Naming and Understanding Racialized Experiences" is a classroom activity that affirms students' identities by creating space for them to voice their lived realities, acknowledge the impact of race on their experiences, and connect their personal narratives to broader systemic patterns. By encouraging students to reflect on and share how race has shaped their educational, social, or emotional journeys, the activity affirms their perspectives and challenges the invisibility and dismissal they often experience in predominantly white or color-evasive school environments. Naming racialized experiences is a powerful act of self-definition and resistance, helping students develop a positive racial identity and critical consciousness. This process fosters a sense of belonging, agency, and pride, all of which are essential to affirming Black identity in educational spaces.

Activity: "Tell Your Story: Naming and Understanding Racialized Experiences"

Objective: To create a safe and reflective space for participants to explore personal experiences with racial bias, microaggressions, and racialized trauma, and to build empathy and awareness in learning communities.

Target Audience: Middle school, high school, college students, educators, and education stakeholders

Time: 45–60 minutes

Materials Needed:

- printed handouts of the experience checklist (see below)
- journals or loose-leaf paper
- pens, pencils, or laptops

Part 1: Quiet Reflection (10–15 Minutes)

Distribute the following checklist and ask participants to read each statement silently. Instruct them to place a checkmark next to any experience that resonates with them—whether they experienced it directly, witnessed it, or felt affected by it in some way.

Experience Checklist:

Place a checkmark beside any of the following if something similar has happened to you:

- □ You've scrolled through social media and have seen comments that use racial slurs or demean Black people or other racial/ethnic groups.
- □ You or your family have been labeled as "illegal" or made to feel like you don't belong by figures of authority (e.g., educators, police, or peers).
- □ You've watched a video of someone from your racial group being mistreated, harassed, or harmed—possibly fatally—based on their race.
- □ You've been the only person of your racial background in a classroom discussion about your racial group and felt pressure to represent or explain your community.
- □ Someone has touched your hair without permission while asking, "How did you get your hair like that?"
- □ Teachers or staff have expected you to excel in sports but made assumptions that you wouldn't perform well academically because of your race.

Part 2: Personal Storytelling (15–20 Minutes)

Prompt:

Choose one experience you checked and write about it in more detail. Use the following guiding questions to tell your story:

- What happened?
- How did it make you feel at the time?

- What impact has the experience had on how you see yourself or others?
- What would you want others—especially educators or peers—to understand about this moment?

This reflection can be written privately or in a journal format. Emphasize that participants should only share what they are comfortable with and that their stories belong to them.

Part 3: Group Sharing and Discussion (20–25 Minutes)

Facilitate a voluntary sharing circle or small group conversations. Begin with community agreements: confidentiality, active listening, no interrupting, and mutual respect.

Discussion Prompts:

- What patterns or themes do we notice in the stories shared?
- How do these experiences shape trust, belonging, and achievement in schools?
- As educators or peers, what can we do to reduce harm and build affirming spaces?

Closing Reflection (Optional Exit Slip):

Ask participants to respond briefly to the following on an index card or sticky note:

- "One thing I'm taking with me from today is . . ."
- "One thing I want to do differently or learn more about is . . ."

Facilitator's Note: This activity may evoke strong emotions. Be prepared to provide resources for students (e.g., school counselors, mental health services) and allow participants to opt out or pause if necessary. Ensure that facilitators are trained in culturally responsive practices.

INTEGRATING BLACK PSYCHOLOGY IN PK–5 CLASSROOM CHECKLIST

If you aim to affirm Black students, it's critical to ensure that your school or classroom integrates components of Black psychology. More than two decades ago,

Hilliard et al. provided recommendations for incorporating African and African-centered content and measures into the school curriculum. As a proponent of Black psychology, Hilliard emphasized the importance of addressing "humanity" in the classroom—treat all children as human beings. Love children and treat them as "geniuses"! Most importantly, Hilliard believed that educators should focus less on "closing the achievement gap" and more on closing the excellence gap between Black students and their potential.[13]

Not only did Hilliard advocate for incorporating the stories of Black Americans into history classes but he also insisted that the experiences of individuals of Latin American, Asian, and Native American descent be included in the curriculum. Much of this focus centered on building self-esteem among young people of color. Hilliard stressed that IQ and standardized tests are culturally biased, arguing these assessments serve to exclude rather than include. He refused to view the study of African history as a static academic subject. Instead, he worked to integrate the cultural content of the pre-enslavement African experience into contemporary social systems. Below is a checklist for educators to ensure the incorporation of Black psychological concepts (e.g., history, affirming Blackness) into PK–12 classrooms.[14]

Table 2.1 includes a *Black Student Affirmation and Inclusion Audit Tool.* It is designed to help educators, school leaders, and support staff critically reflect on how well their school environments affirm, support, and include Black students. Grounded in principles of Black psychological well-being, this tool provides indicators that assess both structural practices and daily interactions.

Integrating Black psychology into schools is crucial for cultivating inclusive learning environments that affirm the identities and lived experiences of all youth, particularly given the rise of white nationalism and anti-DEI movements. Rooted in cultural traditions, community knowledge, and a resistance to Eurocentric mental health models, this mindset provides educators with insights into how systemic oppression, racial identity development, and cultural strengths impact student learning and well-being. In essence, Black psychology posits that educators must not view Black students as lacking or problematic; instead, they should focus on healing, resilience, and self-determination. By weaving these perspectives into the curriculum, teaching methods, and school culture, educators confront racial biases, elevate student voices, and foster a more equitable and inclusive

TABLE 2.1 Black student affirmation and inclusion audit tool

Indicator	*Yes or no*
Black people and students are represented in school materials, bulletin boards, etc.	
Black students are affirmed regarding their talents in multiple and diverse ways (e.g., having speaking roles in events, receiving public affirmations, receiving high grades, receiving awards or recognition).	
Teachers "call on" Black students in class at an equal rate of their white peers.	
The history of African, Latin, Native American, and Asian cultures is taught throughout the curriculum.	
Negative language to describe students is not used by educators (e.g., "You are not smart enough to be in that class," "Are you crazy?").	
Career days include Black people in diverse occupations.	
Black parents, community members, etc., attend classroom and school events.	
Black parents and community members lead parent/school organizations (e.g., PTA).	
Black history is taught not only in February (e.g., Black History Month) but all through the school year.	
There are Black educators, school counselors, school psychologists, and other helping professionals on staff at your school.	
Black students are not disproportionately suspended or harshly disciplined.	
There are opportunities for students to receive counseling and "healing" services from trained culturally responsive counselors and psychologists.	
The library contains books illustrating Black characters with multiple identities.	
Discipline policies contain restorative justice practices, never harming the psychological state of students.	
Racism and antiracism are defined, and students are taught accurate history of anti-Black racism and other oppressive practices in the United States and globally.	

educational setting for everyone. Presented next are two case studies that demonstrate the application of Black psychology in today's educational settings.

THE CASE OF SYDNEY: A CULTURALLY AFFIRMING PERSPECTIVE INFORMED BY BLACK PSYCHOLOGY

Sydney is a thirteen-year-old Black girl in the seventh grade who lives in a suburban community in the southeastern United States. She has demonstrated strong academic potential, maintaining a pattern of B and C grades since the fourth grade. Recently, however, teachers have noted that Sydney appears increasingly disengaged and off-task in class. Despite this, she remains socially connected and well regarded among her peers, especially other Black students, who describe her as funny, caring, and dependable.

Sydney's school has a diverse student population: 22 percent Black, 70 percent White, 5 percent Asian, and 3 percent multiracial. Most families, including Sydney's, work at a local tire manufacturing plant and fall within a working- to middle-class income bracket. Her parents, who recently separated, share a household income of $90,000. As the eldest of three children, Sydney takes on significant responsibilities at home, helping care for her nine-year-old brother and seven-year-old sister after school.

After Sydney accumulates several absences, the school's attendance coordinator contacts her family. During the conversation, her mother shares that Sydney has been struggling emotionally since the separation. Sydney has expressed that she no longer enjoys school, feels disliked by her teachers, and is considering transferring to an all-Black school near her grandmother. The mother believes Sydney may benefit from a learning environment that better affirms her racial identity. The attendance coordinator, a Black woman, refers Sydney to the school's only counselor—who is white—for further support. Notably, there are no Black mental health professionals on the school staff.

Traditional (Deficit-Based) Counselor Response

In their first meeting, the counselor focuses primarily on Sydney's attendance, warning that if she misses more than twenty days, she will fail the seventh grade. The counselor emphasizes the social consequences, stating, "You won't go to high school with your friends, and I know how important your popularity is." She then asks, "How's your home life?" to which Sydney responds briefly, "It's okay. Can I go back to class now?" The counselor, unsure how to proceed, writes a pass. She does not follow up again.

This approach frames Sydney as a problem to be managed rather than a whole person to be understood. The conversation lacks cultural awareness, relational depth, or acknowledgment of Sydney's racialized experiences, which are key components of effective engagement with Black youth.[15]

Culturally Responsive Response Informed by Black Psychology

In a reimagined approach rooted in Black psychology, the counselor begins by warmly welcoming Sydney and acknowledging her presence and strength. She affirms Sydney's past academic success and intelligence, stating, "*You are clearly a smart and capable young woman, and I'm really glad you're here today.*"

Drawing from White's call for a psychology that centers Black youth's cultural and lived experiences, the counselor avoids pathologizing Sydney's behavior.[16] Instead, she recognizes the broader context: Sydney is navigating family separation, racial stressors, identity development, and adult responsibilities—all while receiving little affirmation from her school environment.

The counselor opens the conversation with culturally sensitive, strength-based questions:

- "How are you feeling about everything going on at home and at school?"
- "What's been hard for you lately?" or "What's brought you happiness and joy lately?"
- "Are there times at school where you feel like your voice or your feelings aren't being heard?"

As Sydney begins to share, the counselor listens without judgment and affirms her emotions, validating her frustration with school and her perception that teachers don't like her. Instead of dismissing these feelings, the counselor explores them. She recognizes that the disconnection Sydney feels may be linked to racial microaggressions or a lack of cultural responsiveness in her learning environment.

The counselor also introduces future-oriented support, inviting Sydney to co-create a plan that affirms her identity and supports her wellness. This might include:

- creating space for Sydney to engage in racial identity-affirming activities (e.g., a cultural affinity group or Black literature project)
- collaborating with trusted adults (possibly the Attendance Coordinator or a teacher of color) to serve as mentors
- exploring ways to reduce family burdens through school support (e.g., after-school programs or mental health referrals)

Importantly, the counselor ensures ongoing connection and follow-up. She closes the conversation by saying, "*I see you, Sydney. Let's keep talking and work together so school becomes a place where you feel strong and supported.*"

Sydney's case illustrates the importance of culturally grounded mental health support for Black students navigating racialized school environments. A framework rooted in Black psychology prioritizes affirmation over discipline, inquiry over assumption, and healing over compliance. In doing so, it opens space for students like Sydney not only to survive school but to thrive in it.

THE CASE OF JAVONNE: RACIAL TRAUMA, BLACK PSYCHOLOGY, AND HEALING IN SCHOOLS

JaVonne is a seventeen-year-old Black male high school junior in a midsized Midwestern city. Standing at 6 feet, 1 inch and weighing approximately 250 pounds, JaVonne is often perceived as older and more threatening than his peers.

Recently, JaVonne was racially profiled by local police officers who suspected him of committing a burglary. Although he was at home with his grandmother at the time, the police chased him one day outside his house based on his physical appearance and his presence in the neighborhood. The encounter escalated physically when JaVonne, terrified and overwhelmed, reacted by kicking and punching the officers during their attempted arrest. Although the burglary charges were later dropped, JaVonne was charged with assaulting a police officer and spent a night in juvenile detention before his grandmother posted bail.

When JaVonne returned to school the next day, he appeared withdrawn, angry, and uncooperative. He refused to speak with teachers or administrators about the incident. However, he showed a willingness to talk to Coach Gary, a Black male coach and mentor who has built a trusting relationship with him.

Affirming Response

Rather than viewing JaVonne through a disciplinary lens, Coach Gary adopts a caring approach. Drawing from the principles of Black psychology, which emphasize racial identity, community, historical context, and resilience, Coach Gary creates space for JaVonne to name his pain, affirm his humanity, and begin the process of healing.

Coach Gary meets with JaVonne regularly, using culturally relevant discussions about the history of police violence, the adultification of Black boys, and systemic racism to help JaVonne process what happened. He also shares his own experiences with racial profiling, offering both empathy and strategies for navigating unjust systems. This relationship represents a key tenet of African-centered psychology: *the power of community, intergenerational wisdom, and cultural connectedness as healing forces.*

Understanding the depth of JaVonne's trauma, Coach Gary works with school leaders to advocate for additional support. He recommends a referral to a Black male community-based counselor with training in racial trauma and adolescent mental health. The counselor, grounded in the radical tradition of Black psychology, prioritizes cultural pride, emotional regulation, and narrative therapy that recenter JaVonne's dignity and power.

Guiding Discussion Questions

- How can this case serve as a model for transforming school culture to prioritize care, community, and cultural responsiveness?
- How might JaVonne's encounter with the police have affected his sense of identity, safety, and trust in institutions, including school?
- In what ways does adultification bias play a role in how Black boys like JaVonne are perceived and treated by both police and educators?
- Which principles or schools of thought in Black Psychology (traditional, reform, radical) are most relevant in this case?
- Why is it important that Coach Gary shares his own lived experience with racial profiling?
- How can schools foster relationships in which intergenerational storytelling and community wisdom are part of the support ecosystem?
- What does it mean to restore a student's dignity? Who should be involved in that process—teachers, counselors, administrators, families, or others?

CONCLUSION

Black psychology is a deeply rooted, evidence-based psychological framework that affirms the lived experiences, cultural knowledge, and collective resilience of Black communities. As this chapter has shown, African-centered psychological approaches offer practical tools for enhancing the mental, emotional, and academic well-being of Black students. Grounded in research, these frameworks challenge deficit narratives and replace them with culturally congruent approaches toward healing, identity development, and self-actualization.

Black psychology offers a roadmap for educators and mental health professionals committed to justice. For schools seeking to truly support Black students, Black psychology principles provide the foundation for trauma recovery and sustained empowerment. When educators embrace Black psychology, they not only support Black children but also transform their classrooms to become places where Black joy, genius, and well-being are not the exception but the expectation.

Chapter Reflection Questions

1. How might African-centered concepts such as *communalism*, *spirituality*, and *interconnectedness* be integrated into school responses?
2. The Clarks' Doll tests revealed the harmful impact of racism and segregation on Black children's self-worth. What kinds of assessments or reflective tools might we develop today to assess how Black youth perceive themselves? Should schools use such tools to better understand students' psychological experiences? Why or why not?
3. Reflect on the wisdom of Wade Nobles (1990): *"Most mainstream American educators and scholars have rendered the relevance of culture to education as, at worst, the 'something' which is really irrelevant to the task of education and should be disregarded (i.e., I don't see color, we should just teach children, etc.)."*[17]

   - How does this statement reflect education today?
   - What would it look like for your school or district to operationalize Black psychology principles?

Chapter Reflection Questions

PART 2

Interventions That Uplift Black Students' Well-Being

You may not control all the events that happen to you, but you can decide not to be reduced by them.

—*Maya Angelou, poet*

CHAPTER 3

Centering Strengths to Affirm Black Students

Shana, a twelve-year-old Black student newly enrolled in a predominantly white suburban school, endures daily ridicule about her dark skin. One afternoon, after her classmate, Tara, a white student, passed her and muttered a racial slur under her breath, Shana reacted emotionally by shouting, "What did you say? Say it again!" The principal says that she reacted too "aggressively" and suspended her. The principal also implied that Shana's response was "expected" because of her background (clearly a micro-aggression!). Shana's response is misunderstood and is not rooted in aggression but in accumulated racial trauma and pain from countless microaggressions.

Jamar, a fifteen-year-old Black boy at a private school, is expelled after refusing to cut his hair locs. A new school policy banning "nontraditional" hairstyles targets cultural expression under the guise of professionalism. For Jamar, his hair is his identity and pride. The institution sees only his defiance.

These two events are not isolated incidents. They are everyday examples of how Black children are often punished for their Black identities. When schools respond to students like Shana and Jamar with judgment rather than care, they ask the wrong question: "What's wrong with you?" The right question is: "What happened to you?" This question recognizes context, strength, and possibly trauma.

In an era in which diversity, equity, and inclusion (DEI) initiatives are being removed from classrooms, educators must still support Black youth. A strength-based approach provides a way forward. Although the concept seems so simple, the strengths of Black students are often overlooked. Historically, Black individuals have demonstrated exceptional brilliance, resilience, and innovation in various sectors, including science, medicine, philosophy, and education. From Benjamin Banneker's astronomical calculations in the eighteenth century to Dr. Katherine Johnson's vital mathematical contributions to NASA's space missions (as depicted in the movie "Hidden Figures"), Black excellence has significantly influenced the development of contemporary systems.[1] Influential figures such as W.E.B. Du Bois, Anna Julia Cooper, and Carter G. Woodson have advanced sociological and educational discourse that remains crucial today. Nonetheless, these contributions are frequently downplayed or excluded from mainstream narratives, creating a false impression that Black genius is an anomaly. To foster a more equitable and truthful educational system, we must actively challenge these myths and acknowledge the broad array of strengths possessed by Black students.

DEFINING A STRENGTH-BASED APPROACH

A strength-based education model focuses on identifying and amplifying what students can do, rather than fixating on what they can't do. Drawing on the foundational work of positive psychology, strength-based practice emphasizes traits such as resilience, creativity, leadership, emotional intelligence, and purpose.[2] For Black students, this approach counters deeply ingrained deficit narratives. Strength-based approaches recognize the brilliance in every child, especially those whose brilliance has been historically ignored. This approach is consistent with the principles of Black psychology, emphasizing cultural identity, intergenerational strength, and the significance of community, spirituality, and historical awareness in wellness and development.

In racially hostile environments, strength-based approaches serve as more than pedagogical strategies; they act as tools for building protective factors for Black students. Research indicates that students who feel affirmed in their strengths and identity exhibit greater motivation and persistence in school.[3] Among Black students in STEM fields, culturally responsive mentorship and affirming environments have been linked to increased performance and retention.[4] These findings confirm the importance of using strength-based practices and ultimately creating a strength-based, student-centered school. In a nutshell, when Black students are valued, they thrive.

Table 3.1 illustrates what a strength-based approach *is* and *is not.*

TABLE 3.1 Strength-based approach

Is	*Is not*
Rooted in cultural humility and the belief that all students and their families bring valuable assets	A refusal to name or address racism, oppression, or inequality
Focused on student potential, joy, and resilience	Excusing or minimizing valid expressions of anger or frustration
Centered on collaboration with families and communities	Imposing dominant cultural norms or "respectability" as the standard
About recognizing and amplifying what works in academic settings	Avoiding data that reveal racial inequities
A way to build trust and connection	A tool to label or categorize students as "exceptional" or "not at-risk"

BARRIERS TO IMPLEMENTATION OF A STRENGTH-BASED APPROACH

Despite its transformative promise, implementing strength-based approaches in schools is not without significant barriers. At the root of many of those barriers are *the bias and racism that many educators harbor and, more importantly, ridding schools of the systemic practices* that continue to pathologize Black students. Many educators are trained to view Black students through a lens of danger and deficiency.[5] Thus, when educators attempt to implement strength-based practices, it can be perceived as "wrong" or "inappropriate." Educators may even be penalized for resisting the deficit status quo. Take for instance, Ms. Ayala, a sixth-grade teacher in a majority-Black and Latino public school, who believed deeply in the power of affirming students' identities and centering their cultural wealth in the classroom. As a result, she redesigned her classroom management and lessons to include collaborative projects that highlighted students' home languages, family traditions, and community histories. She also integrated positive reinforcement strategies and celebrated students' leadership skills, creativity, and resilience. However, her school's culture embodied a deficit mindset. Administrators frequently described students as "bad," "worthless," or in terms of "behavioral problems." When Ms. Ayala chose not to use behavior charts or public discipline boards, believing they shamed students rather than supported them, she was rated lower on teacher evaluations and labeled as "noncompliant." A colleague later confided to Ms. Ayala, "They think you're idealistic because you actually believe these kids can thrive."

Another barrier to using a strength-based approach in schools is a lack of preparation. Educator preparation programs often lack coursework in culturally sustaining pedagogy, Black psychology, or strength-based teaching strategies.[6] As a result, even well-intentioned teachers may resort to punitive responses, such as exclusionary discipline, because they lack the tools and training to consider behavior in context or to respond with affirming alternatives.

Overcoming these barriers requires a multipronged approach that includes ongoing professional learning or development, policy revision, and exceptional leaders who understand how to transform school cultures. Shifting a school's culture from deficit-based to strength-based necessitates intentional and sustained professional development for educators, including coaching and mentoring, led by highly effective facilitators with expertise in strength-based pedagogy. Only through long-term professional development throughout one's career can harmful patterns rooted in deficit thinking be disrupted. Research supports this work, showing that culturally responsive professional development is positively associated with improved teacher attitudes and student engagement.[7] Programs such as *MyTeachingPartner*, developed at the University of Virginia, and other video-based feedback tools assist teachers in adjusting their practice from a deficit approach to a more strength-based approach. Studies have shown these coaching strategies enhance classroom interactions and increase teacher sensitivity to student needs. Notably, some coaching models that center equity and self-awareness foster psychological safety for teachers to examine their own biases and confront racism in practice.[8]

School leaders also need to promote strength-based initiatives in a direct and unapologetic manner. When principals and other leaders adopt a strength-based framework for evaluating teachers and educators, they convey to staff that affirmation practices are both valued and anticipated. Similarly, leaders who foster community partnerships with Black mental health professionals, family leaders, and culturally affirming organizations demonstrate to school staff the strengths of Black communities and cultures. These collaborations also help alter perceptions regarding who possesses knowledge and authority. A strength-based perspective repositions Black students as knowledgeable, capable, and resilient individuals. It interprets behaviors not as defiance but as a form of communication, and it contextualizes identity as a source of cultural wealth rather than as a liability. In this way, strength-based practice is a profound act of resistance and repair, rooted in Black psychology, cultural affirmation, and the belief that healing begins when we choose to see students fully.[9]

To sustain a strength-based practice, educators must engage in continuous reflective practice, which is a critical process of examining one's values, assumptions, and interactions with students. This means asking or interrogating oneself: *Whose knowledge is valued in my classroom? Who gets disciplined most often—and for what? Whose culture is seen as the "norm"?* Without reflection, even well-meaning educators risk reinforcing power imbalances that marginalize Black students and families. For instance, take the example of hair policies that often reflect white middle-class norms and penalize behaviors or expressions associated with Black culture. Reflective educators question those norms and seek to build classrooms that value cultural difference as a strength, not a disruption. In this way, strength-based approaches are inseparable from racial equity work, even if they are framed differently in this era of anti-DEI surveillance.

STRATEGIES FOR TAPPING INTO BLACK STUDENTS' STRENGTHS

Affirming the strengths of Black students requires educators to move beyond surface-level recognition and toward culturally responsive, strength-based pedagogy. Black students possess rich cultural knowledge, resilience, creativity, and social insight that are often overlooked in school environments. Educators must create spaces that center on students' identities and lived experiences as foundational to learning, starting with intentional classroom practices rooted in validation and trust. Below is an activity that can be used to determine or "tap into" Black students' strengths.

Activity: The Story of My Name

Purpose: Build identity awareness, voice, and cultural appreciation through storytelling.

This activity invites students to reflect on and share the meaning behind their name, either their first, middle, last, or nicknames. Students are encouraged to share family stories, cultural meanings, or personal associations with their names.

For the inclusivity of students who don't know the history of their names, a teacher might add:

- What does your name mean to you today?
- Do you have a nickname or another name you go by?
- If you could choose any name for yourself, what would it be and why?

This activity not only promotes literacy and social-emotional learning (SEL) but also affirms students' identities and narratives as valid sources of knowledge.[10] In classrooms where cultural topics are politically restricted, educators can frame this as a communication or narrative-building exercise, emphasizing language development, self-expression, and belonging.

Prompting questions

- Who named you, and why?
- Does your name have cultural, religious, or historical meaning?
- Have you ever changed how you introduce yourself? What led to that decision?
- How do people respond to your name, and how does that make you feel?

This activity normalizes diverse identities while giving educators insight into students' cultural worlds.

Strength-Based Reflection Prompts

Helping students articulate their strengths builds confidence and disrupts deficit-based assumptions. The following prompts can be used for journaling, small groups, check-ins, or SEL sessions to support self-awareness and future-oriented thinking:

- Describe a challenge you overcame. What inner strength helped you through?
- What's something you love to learn about or teach others?
- Who believes in you, and how do they show it?
- What is something your family or community values in you?
- When do you feel most confident, creative, or free at school?

- What is something you're proud of, big or small?
- Picture your future. What kind of life are you working toward?

These reflections align with research showing that culturally affirming spaces promote resilience, motivation, and academic engagement among Black students. Educators can collect responses to build "strength portfolios" or "learning identity profiles," which guide personalized instruction and foster long-term relationships with students.

CENTERING STUDENT STRENGTHS IN CLASSROOMS AND SCHOOLS

The following classroom, counseling, and schoolwide activities are designed to help educators identify, affirm, and build upon students' existing capabilities. These strategies are rooted in culturally responsive pedagogy and positive youth development research, which emphasize that identity-affirming, strength-based practices enhance student motivation, well-being, and academic achievement. Whether implemented in one-on-one counseling sessions, whole-class discussions, or family-teacher conferences, each activity offers an opportunity to shift the narrative from what students lack to what they offer. Importantly, these activities also invite students to reflect on their own stories, values, and aspirations. Educators support academic growth and self-efficacy by encouraging students to see themselves as strong, creative, and worthy, two powerful foundations for long-term success.

Individual Projects

- **"This Is Me" Slideshow**

  Students create a personal slide show using images, words, and music that reflect their strengths, values, and identity.
- **Personal Storyboards**

  Students draw or digitally design a visual timeline of five key moments that have shaped who they are.
- **"Strengths Grid" Conversations**

  Use VanDenBerg and Grealish's strengths grid to guide reflective conversations with students about their capabilities in school, home, and community settings.[11]

Classroom Activities

- **Class Strengths Survey**
  Use anonymous surveys to gather information about students' interests, talents, and learning preferences to inform instruction and build classroom culture.
- **Shared Story Circles**
  In small groups, have students respond to prompts such as "A time I felt powerful was" or "Something people don't know I'm great at is."
- **Weekly Strength Spotlight**
  Feature a different student each week, highlighting their unique strengths as nominated by peers or teachers.

Schoolwide Activities

- **Identity Day (also called "Who We Are" Day)**
  Students present on a dimension of their identity, such as their family traditions, hobbies, or languages spoken, to foster schoolwide appreciation for diversity.
- **Family or Caregiver Strength Conferences**
  Begin parent-teacher meetings by inviting caregivers to name three things their child excels in or enjoys. This reframes the conversation to position families and caregivers as co-authors in the student's learning journey.

STRENGTH-BASED COUNSELING APPROACHES

School counselors, as mental health experts, are increasingly adopting *strength-based approaches.*[12] This shift moves counselors away from pathologizing and diagnosis toward more recognition of what is *right* with young people, their talents, lived experiences, and resilience. Within PK–12 settings, strength-based counseling creates a foundation for empowerment and affirmation, especially for Black students who have historically been subjected to deficit-based assumptions and lowered expectations. This framework challenges dominant counseling narratives that focus on "fixing" students to focusing on students' cultural wealth, helping them see themselves as capable contributors to their communities and schools.

Established Strength-Based Counseling Models and Frameworks

One widely used strength-based counseling approach is *solution-focused brief therapy (SFBT)*, which emphasizes goal setting and envisioning a "preferred future." It helps students recognize exceptions to problems and the resources (e.g., strengths) they already possess to solve them.[13] SFBT's practical, collaborative nature is ideal for school settings, and it has been found effective in improving students' emotional well-being, self-efficacy, and classroom behavior. With Black students, this approach can be particularly powerful in reframing identity, validating experiences of perseverance, and offering actionable steps forward, without pathologizing their reality.[14]

Narrative therapy, similarly strength-centered, allows students to externalize problems and re-author their own stories with agency and pride.[15] By exploring dominant narratives in their lives and replacing them with affirming ones, students, especially those navigating racial trauma, can see themselves not as victims of systems but as resilient actors within them. For Black students whose stories are often misinterpreted or invisible in school contexts, narrative therapy provides space to name racism and oppression while still affirming identity and power.

Another highly effective strength-based counseling approach for school settings is *motivational interviewing (MI)*. Originally developed in the field of addiction counseling, MI is now widely used across clinical and educational contexts because of its emphasis on collaboration, autonomy, and personal empowerment.[16] At its core, MI is a student-centered counseling style that helps individuals resolve ambivalence and tap into their intrinsic motivation to change. School counselors can use MI to guide students in setting academic, behavioral, or emotional goals by emphasizing personal choice and affirming their existing values and capabilities. Unlike directive approaches that prescribe solutions, MI begins with listening and validating the student's voice. Then, the counselor elicits the student's reasons for change. In this way, MI supports the development of self-efficacy and personal agency, which are key protective factors in both academic achievement and mental health.

MI is particularly effective with adolescents because it respects their need for autonomy while guiding them toward positive decision-making. For Black youth, MI's affirming and nonjudgmental stance can create a powerful sense of psychological safety.[17] For instance, a Black student navigating repeated disciplinary action might be invited, through MI, to explore how their behavior aligns or misaligns with their goals, values, or future aspirations. Instead of being punished or labeled, they are empowered to reflect and make changes based on their own vision for success. This approach honors students' lived experiences, avoids imposing adult-centric solutions, and strengthens the counselor-student relationship. MI also complements other strength-based strategies such as SFBT and narrative therapy, and it can be especially useful in brief school-based interventions, restorative justice processes, or academic coaching. Its core techniques, such as affirmations, reflective listening, and eliciting change talk—are not just methods; they are tools for cultivating student-centered environments where motivation grows from within.

I^3 Relationships Framework: Inclusive, Inspiring, Insightful Developed by the author of this book, the I^3 Framework provides a practical and strength-based, relational foundation for school counselors seeking to engage meaningfully with students, particularly students from historically marginalized backgrounds. At its core, the I^3 Framework (fig. 3.1) affirms that strong, caring relationships are the

FIGURE 3.1 The I3 Framework

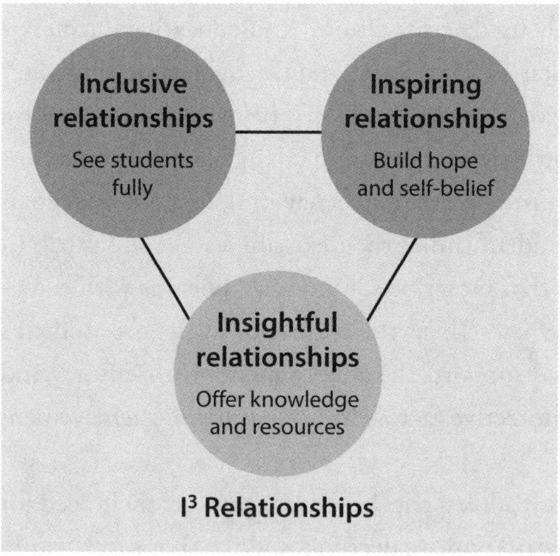

Source: Author's own theory and rendering.

foundation of student success. For Black students, who have too often experienced harm in schools, relationships rooted in *care, authenticity, and respect* are transformative.

The I^3 Framework consists of three interrelated dimensions of relationship-building that counselors and educators can cultivate: *Inclusive, Inspiring, and Insightful* relationships. The I^3 Framework is a reminder that every meaningful relationship between an educator and a student holds the potential to affirm identity, unlock strength, and ignite possibility. For school counselors, these relationships are not ancillary to the work—they *are* the work.

1. *Inclusive relationships: Inclusive relationships recognize and affirm the full humanity of each student, including their race, culture, gender, religion, language, and lived experience. Counselors who build inclusive relationships see students as they are and validate their value.*

How to cultivate inclusive relationships:

- Learn and pronounce students' names correctly—names carry cultural and personal meaning.
- Normalize and celebrate diverse cultural expressions, language patterns, and communication styles.
- Validate a full range of emotions, including anger, sadness, and joy.

Guiding belief: Inclusion is not *color-blindness,* it's about seeing students clearly and choosing to value what you see or who the student is.

2. *Inspiring relationships: Inspiring relationships cultivate hope, belief, and motivation. These are the relationships in which students begin to believe in their own capacity for success and growth.*

How to cultivate inspiring relationships:

- Offer authentic, specific praise (e.g., "Your insight during the discussion showed real depth and perspective").
- Share your own stories of struggle, resilience, and learning.
- Challenge students with high expectations, paired with warmth, not control.

Guiding belief: Inspiration doesn't come from being inspirational—it comes from helping students feel inspired by themselves.

3. *Insightful relationships: Insightful relationships offer students access to knowledge, resources, and tools that empower them to dream, plan, and act.*

How to cultivate insightful relationships:

- Connect students with mentors, networks, and community resources.
- Teach students how to navigate systems such as college applications, financial aid, advocacy, and internships.
- Say, *"I'll walk with you as you go through the application process,"* instead of only saying, *"I'm cheering for you."*

Guiding belief: Insight fuels agency. It helps students not only imagine what's possible but also take the steps to achieve it.

Culturally responsive counseling frameworks further enhance strength-based approaches by ensuring interventions are not just affirming but also relevant to students' cultural and racial identities. Yosso's concept of "community cultural wealth" emphasizes the importance of the unique social, linguistic, and familial strengths that Black students contribute.[18] Culturally responsive counselors understand that identity plays a crucial role in resilience, using students' backgrounds as a bridge to provide support. For instance, starting a counseling session by acknowledging the significance of family or spiritual life can serve as a grounding and empowering approach for Black students. These practices affirm students' worldviews and help establish safe, supportive therapeutic relationships.

Overall, mental health is deeply linked to academic performance. Students who are anxious, depressed, or stressed often struggle to concentrate, complete tasks, or perceive themselves as successful learners. This reality is particularly pressing for Black students, who may encounter multiple layers of racialized stress both inside and outside of school. Strength-based counseling improves mental health by fostering hope, self-efficacy, and resilience, all of which contribute to stronger academic outcomes.[19] Students who feel seen and supported are more likely to participate actively in class, pursue leadership opportunities, and build trusting relationships with adults. Over time, these positive developments compound, resulting in better academic achievement and long-term personal growth. The following are case studies that illustrate the importance of strength-based approaches to interacting with Black students in educational settings.

CASE STUDY: MOTIVATIONAL INTERVIEWING

Student Profile

An eighteen-year-old Black student who identifies as queer reports heavy alcohol use and expresses feelings of being a disappointment to their family.

Traditional Advising Approach (Directive)

"You need to stop drinking, or it will ruin your life."

Motivational Interviewing Approach (Collaborative, Strength-Based)

Rather than issuing ultimatums, the school counselor uses reflective listening and empathy to build rapport, validate the student's experiences, and gently explore ambivalence about drinking.

Counselor:

"I hear you saying that alcohol helps you cope with the pain of not feeling accepted by your family. That makes a lot of sense. You've been carrying a lot emotionally. But I'm also hearing that you might want something different for yourself."

Student:

"Yeah . . . I just don't know how to get there."

Counselor:

"If that pain felt lighter or less constant, what might be different in your life? What would it feel like to have support without needing to drink?"

Through ongoing MI sessions, the student begins to reflect on how their alcohol use conflicts with their personal goals, such as going to college, repairing family relationships, and feeling more in control of their future.

Rather than being judged or told what to do, the student feels empowered to explore their own values and strengths.

Outcome

The counselor helps the student develop a sense of agency and intrinsic motivation. Together, they identify small, manageable steps toward change (e.g., reaching out to a supportive addiction counselor, reducing drinking in social settings, exploring identity-affirming spaces). The counseling relationship centers respect, curiosity, and hope, not shame.

CASE STUDY: REFRAMING THE NARRATIVE AT BAYVIEW MIDDLE SCHOOL

Context

Bayview Middle School, a diverse public school serving a predominantly Black and Latino student population, had been experiencing an increasing number of behavioral referrals, declining academic performance, and low parent engagement. Teachers often described the school culture as "apathetic," and staff meetings frequently centered on what students "lacked": motivation, home support, and basic skills.

Intervention

The new principal, Ms. Serrano, introduced a strength-based initiative. She told teachers that they would be focused less on remediation and more on strengths. More specifically, she told them to ask themselves daily: *What strengths do our students already possess, and how can we build on them?* Key school actions included:

- *Schoolwide strength mapping:* Teachers and staff identified each student's strengths, such as leadership, creativity, humor, and community activism, and shared them during team meetings.
- *"Spotlight Fridays":* At this weekly Friday assembly where peers and teachers nominate students for demonstrating strengths such as

empathy, critical thinking, and resilience, teachers ensured every student in school was spotlighted.

- *Family Asset Interviews:* At fall parent/caregiver conferences, caregivers were asked to name three things their child excelled at inside or outside of school. These insights were incorporated into student goal setting.
- *Curricular redesign:* Teachers integrated student voice and cultural relevance into units, inviting students to explore their identity, heritage, and goals.

Outcomes

Within a semester, suspension rates dropped by 40 percent, and staff reported improved classroom climate and student engagement. Teachers began using strength-based language in lesson planning and feedback. One teacher reflected, "I used to focus so much on what my students couldn't do. Now I see them differently—and they see themselves differently, too."

Lesson

A strength-based lens at the school level can shift entire school cultures. It affirms student identity, cultivates pride, and fosters a collective sense of purpose rooted in possibility.

CASE STUDY: JAYLEN'S DILEMMA

Context

Jaylen is a tenth-grade Black student at a large urban high school. He's known for his charisma and humor, often making classmates laugh and bringing energy into any room. Teachers also describe him as "distracting" and frequently refer him to the office for talking out of turn, making jokes during lessons, and not completing homework. Recently, Jaylen was suspended for three days after walking out of class and muttering, "Nobody cares anyway."

The school counselor, Mr. Hart, meets with Jaylen after his return. During the session, Jaylen shares that he feels like teachers notice him only when he's in trouble. He admits he's struggling to keep up with assignments but doesn't want anyone to think he's "dumb." He also reveals that he helps take care of his younger siblings every night while his mom works a night shift. When asked what he enjoys, Jaylen says he loves rap and wants to be a YouTuber or screenwriter one day.

Challenge

Instead of labeling Jaylen as "defiant" or "unmotivated," Mr. Hart wants to respond in a way that aligns with a strength-based approach. He can easily see that Jaylen's sense of humor, verbal skills, leadership in peer groups, and sense of responsibility at home are all strengths. If you are Mr. Hart, how might *you* respond?

- How would you affirm Jaylen's strengths while helping him navigate school expectations?
- What might you say or do to help Jaylen see school as a space where his talents matter?
- How could you help shift how adults in the building perceive and interact with Jaylen?
- What would a traditional response look like? How would a strength-based approach be different? What resources, relationships, or opportunities could support Jaylen's growth?

CONCLUSION

In an educational climate increasingly shaped by fear, censorship, and the dismantling of equity efforts, strength-based approaches offer a path forward. They provide a framework for educators to uplift rather than merely remediate. For Black youth, who continue to navigate the compounded harms of racialized trauma, systemic neglect, and cultural erasure, strength-based practices are essential. This chapter asserts that supporting Black students goes beyond removing damaging labels or reducing punitive measures. It challenges us to rethink the questions we pose and the ways we interact with Black students. We should view our students through a perspective of brilliance rather than brokenness. By embracing a commitment to care, we can ensure Black students' strengths are both recognized and truly valued.

Chapter Reflection Questions

1. What does it mean to truly "see" and "hear" Black students?
2. How has deficit thinking shown up in your own practice or school community, even unintentionally? Consider moments when Black students were labeled, tracked, or disciplined in ways that did not reflect their full humanity. What might have looked different if a strength-based approach had been used?
3. In what ways are Black students already demonstrating strength, resilience, and brilliance in your school or community?
4. How do systems of discipline, grading, and curriculum design either suppress or amplify Black students' strengths?
5. What role do relationships play in a strength-based approach, particularly for Black students who may carry negative experiences of mistrust in teachers and school, in general?
6. Discuss how strength-based counseling and teaching is a "resistance" strategy for diminishing anti-Blackness in schools.
7. What does it look like to center Black families and communities in the strength-based work of schools? Why might others see this as a problem?
8. How are strength and healing connected for Black students navigating racial stress or trauma?
9. What are you willing to reimagine or unlearn to adopt a truly strength-based approach with Black students?

CHAPTER 4

Building Self-Efficacy to Affirm and Empower Black Students

What happens if I don't think I can do it?

This question, often unspoken, sits at the core of many Black students' educational journeys. In a society saturated with anti-Black messages, the erosion of self-belief can be one of the most insidious effects of systemic racism. Even when Black parents nurture and uplift their children, the subtle and overt messages that Black children receive about their capabilities in schools and classrooms are daunting. Over time, these repeated signals can chip away at a student's confidence in their own potential. The result is not just disengagement but internalized doubt that compromises learning, motivation, and, ultimately, academic success.

Developing self-efficacy is not merely a soft skill. Rather, it serves as a protective force for all children, particularly Black children. Rooted in Albert Bandura's social cognitive theory, self-efficacy refers to an individual's belief in their ability to perform a specific task or meet a challenge successfully.[1] For students, it is one of the most powerful predictors of academic motivation, resilience, and achievement.[2] For Black students who frequently navigate bias and racist beliefs, low expectations, and underrepresentation, fostering self-efficacy becomes an act of resistance and educational advocacy for justice.

A strong sense of self-efficacy can help Black students persist through academic difficulties and foster a sense of capability and worthiness for success. Conversely, research has shown that when students perceive themselves as academically incapable, they are more likely to disengage, avoid challenging tasks, and internalize societal narratives of inferiority.[3] This chapter centers on self-efficacy as a critical equity strategy. This chapter draws on Bandura's four foundational sources—mastery experiences, vicarious experiences, verbal persuasion, and physiological/emotional states—to explore how educators can intentionally cultivate a sense of capability in Black students. Each source can be leveraged to counteract racialized messaging and offer Black students new narratives of possibility. When educators understand self-efficacy as a lever for racial equity, they can create classrooms where Black students are affirmed and empowered to thrive.

UNDERSTANDING SELF-EFFICACY

Albert Bandura identified four sources from which self-efficacy develops: mastery experiences, vicarious experiences, verbal persuasion, and emotional or physiological states (see fig. 4.1). Each of these sources plays an important role in how students come to believe in their capabilities. When applied intentionally, these sources can be leveraged to counteract negative, racialized messages and to nurture resilient, self-affirming learners.

FIGURE 4.1 Bandura's four sources of self-efficacy

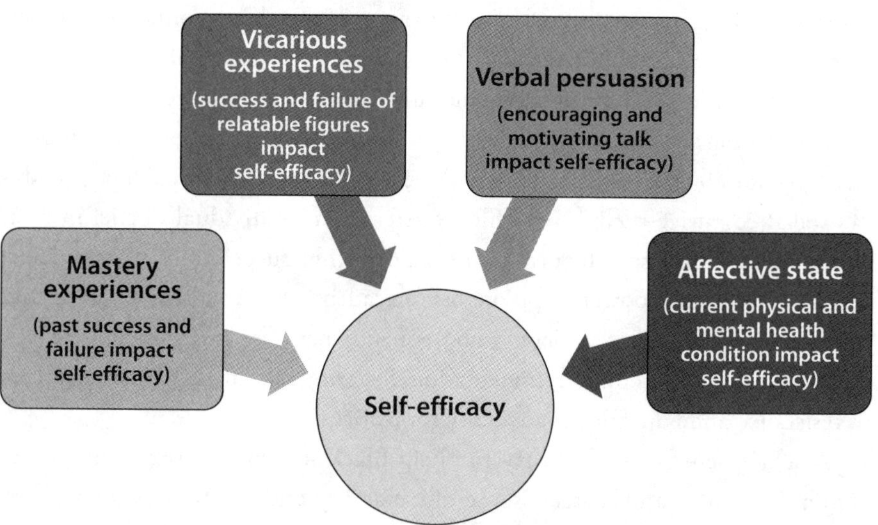

Source: Figure created by author (with AI assistance) based on Albert Bandura, *Self-Efficacy: The Exercise of Control* (W. H. Freeman, 1997).

Mastery Experiences: Creating Opportunities for Success

Mastery experiences are moments or experiences when students succeed at tasks they once doubted they could do. They are the most powerful source of self-efficacy. Yet, many Black students may not encounter these experiences in academic settings, often because of racist and biased beliefs about their capabilities. Research shows Black students are less likely to be placed in advanced courses, but they are also less likely to request placement in those courses because of a lack of positive academic experiences.[4] Here's a short example of how increasing mastery experiences can increase Black students' academic self-efficacy:

> Zaria, a seventh-grade student in a predominantly white school, doubted her math ability despite consistently earning average to above-average math grades. Her teachers rarely acknowledged her strong math skills, reinforcing her internalized doubts about her abilities, particularly those related to her aspirations to be a doctor. After a school counselor collaborated with teachers to intentionally recognize and celebrate STEM ability among girls of color, Zaria began to receive more frequent and meaningful feedback. Over time, her confidence increased, and she eventually enrolled in a summer STEM program. Her participation was the result of a changed sense of self-efficacy.

To increase Black students' self-efficacy, educators can create intentional, scaffolded opportunities for students to achieve success. These experiences must be designed not only to facilitate success but to ensure students recognize their own effort and perseverance in reaching it. When mastery is coupled with affirmation, students internalize the message: *"I did this. I can do more."*

Vicarious Experiences: Seeing Possibility in Others

Another powerful influence on self-efficacy comes from observing others succeed. When Black students see role models who share their racial or cultural identity engaging in unfamiliar tasks or roles, it signals that they, too, are capable. This is particularly important in fields where Black representation is limited. Yet representation alone is insufficient. The context and framing of vicarious experiences must be culturally responsive. Simply inviting a successful Black guest speaker to a school assembly without structured dialogue does little to support students' belief formation. What matters is how educators facilitate reflection: discussing the obstacles the role model faced, exploring how their identity shaped their journey, and connecting that journey to students' lived realities. Take into account the following story about Theo:

> Theo, a twelfth-grade student at an urban high school, has long struggled with ADHD and low self-efficacy regarding attending college. Despite meeting graduation requirements, he often tells his school counselor, "College just isn't for people like me." With no family or community examples of college attendance, Theo views higher education as unattainable for students with disabilities. The school counselor organizes a College Awareness Day, featuring a college fair and a speaker series highlighting Black college graduates. One speaker, Alix, a Black male engineer who grew up on Theo's street, shares his journey through having dyslexia and then going to college and achieving career success. His story resonates with Theo's own experiences. Following the event, the counselor meets with Theo to reflect. Theo recalls Alix's story vividly and says, "He's from where I'm from. If he did it, maybe I can too." For the first time, Theo expresses interest in the colleges Alix mentioned and begins exploring options.

Research by Witherspoon et al. and by Zimmerman underscores the importance of these experiences in shaping motivation and belief, particularly when students identify with the model.[5] Thoughtful planning of mentoring programs, field trips, and collaborative partnerships with community members can provide sustained exposure to role models who reflect students' identities and aspirations.

Verbal Persuasion: The Power of Encouraging Words

Verbal persuasion is another powerful factor in developing self-efficacy. It refers to the encouragement and affirmation from trusted individuals whom one regards as credible and caring. Although providing verbal persuasion seems straightforward, students do not receive it as frequently as one might expect. Teachers, principals, counselors, and peers are well-positioned to enhance students' self-efficacy through verbal persuasion. However, research indicates that Black students receive disproportionately negative feedback in schools, often stemming from bias, fear, and low expectations.[6]

When educators communicate high expectations and provide specific, actionable feedback, they reinforce belief in the student's potential. Consider Michael's case:

> Michael, a Black student at MIT, credits a fifth-grade teacher for helping him believe in his STEM abilities. The teacher's consistent message, "You can do this.

TABLE 4.1 Self-affirmation phrases

Self-affirmation phrase	*How to use it (verbal persuasion strategy)*
You are capable of doing hard things.	Say during moments of student frustration to build persistence.
Your ideas matter and deserve to be heard.	Use when a student hesitates to speak or share in class.
Mistakes are how we grow—you're learning.	Reframe moments of failure as growth opportunities.
You belong here, just as you are.	Repeat especially for students expressing isolation or self-doubt.
Your effort today shows real strength.	Offer after a student works through a challenge or takes initiative.
You have what it takes to succeed in this subject.	Use to counter self-doubt in difficult subjects like math or science.
You are a problem-solver and a critical thinker.	Acknowledge when a student tries new approaches or thinks deeply.
You've improved a lot—keep going!	Provide after showing a student's improvement with evidence.

Nothing is too hard for you" deeply impacted Michael's self-efficacy. That message stayed with him through the racial challenges he faced in college, offering him an inner resource rooted in his perceived ability to succeed.

However, this form of persuasion is not merely about offering praise. Generic affirmations such as "Good job" or "You're smart" lack the specificity needed to guide students' self-perceptions. Feedback must be precise and connected to effort, strategy, and growth. As Yeager et al. found in their study on "wise criticism," Black students respond more positively when feedback includes both high standards and belief in their ability to meet them.[7] Table 4.1 provides examples of affirmations educators can use to build students' self-efficacy.

Affective State: Emotion and Self-Efficacy

Black students often experience ongoing stress because of life circumstances that stem from racism, exclusion, and identity suppression. These emotional challenges can significantly impact their self-efficacy. When they feel anxious or unsafe, they may interpret these emotions as evidence of their incapacity.

Therefore, fostering self-efficacy among Black students requires prioritizing emotional wellness as a vital first step.[8]

Emerging research supports the importance of joy, wellness, and affirmation in the lives of Black students. Love, a Black author and educator, argues that joy is a form of resistance and a necessary component of justice-oriented education.[9] To counteract racial trauma, educators must cultivate school cultures that promote belonging, elevate positive racial identity, and dismantle punitive, deficit-based approaches. In classrooms, affirming Black students' emotional wellness requires more than surface-level inclusion; it means embedding culturally sustaining practices into the daily rhythm of school life. This might look like starting each day with a check-in circle that encourages emotional expression, integrating Black history and cultural pride into academic content, and explicitly teaching students to identify and regulate stress responses. These practices are grounded in the understanding that emotional safety is foundational to academic and psychological success. The following case illustrates the influence of affective state on a Black student's self-efficacy:

> Malik, a seventh-grade Black student, has recently stopped participating in science class and scored poorly on a quiz he normally would've done well on. His teacher, Ms. Ramirez, checks in and learns that Malik is dealing with stress at home. He discloses that his mother and stepfather lost their jobs. "I just don't think I'm good at math anymore," he says. Ms. Ramirez creates a calm space for Malik to work during lunch, and she gives him smaller science tasks to rebuild his confidence. Over time, Malik begins to re-engage, and his self-efficacy improves, proving that emotional support can reignite academic confidence.

BUILDING SELF-EFFICACY THROUGH COLLABORATIVE LEARNING

Collaborative learning offers another rich context for developing self-efficacy. When students work together, they benefit from vicarious learning and verbal persuasion. Surr et al. found that collaborative learning environments positively impacted the academic performance of Black students, particularly when tasks emphasized interdependence and shared success.[10] Likewise, instructional scaffolding, or providing structured support while gradually increasing student independence, is another powerful tool for building self-efficacy, especially for Black students navigating inequitable learning environments. Rooted in Vygotsky's (1978) sociocultural theory and his concept of the zone of proximal development (ZPD), scaffolding ensures students are supported as they engage with tasks that are just beyond their current level of competence.[11] When implemented thoughtfully, scaffolding helps students experience incremental mastery—one success at a time—which is a key condition for the development of self-efficacy.

Effective scaffolding practices include breaking complex tasks into manageable components, providing guided practice, offering timely feedback, and using cues or prompts that foster autonomy. For Black students who may have internalized doubts about their abilities, these strategies provide critical moments of affirmation. For example, Jamila is a fourth-grade Black student who struggles with writing assignments. When given a prompt, she often stares at a blank page and says, "I'm not a good writer." Her low self-efficacy related to writing prevents her from even trying. To support her, Jamila's teacher, Ms. Johnson, employs scaffolding techniques. First, they brainstorm ideas together using a graphic organizer. Next, Ms. Lopez models how to write an opening sentence. Jamila then attempts to write just one sentence at a time with feedback along the way. Positive reinforcement is provided for each step completed. With each success, Jamila's confidence grows. After a few weeks, she begins starting assignments on her own and says, "I think I can do this." Over time, Jamila internalizes the belief that she is a capable writer.

Scaffolding serves as a strategy for increasing students' self-efficacy in academic settings. It reflects the belief that every student can engage in advanced thinking and learning regardless of their background. When scaffolding effectively incorporates students' cultural and linguistic strengths, it demonstrates both care and high expectations. For Black students, merging this belief with support and intellectual challenges can significantly contest deficit-based views and cultivate a sense of success.

NEAR-PEER MENTORING: LEARNING FROM THOSE JUST AHEAD

Near-peer mentoring refers to support relationships in which mentors are only slightly older or more advanced than their mentees—for example, college students mentoring high school students, or high school seniors mentoring freshmen. These relationships are uniquely powerful because they align with Bandura's theory of self-efficacy: mentees gain confidence by observing relatable role models succeed, hearing affirming messages, and receiving guidance grounded in shared experience. For Black students in particular, near-peer mentors can counter messages of inferiority by modeling what is possible, sharing culturally relevant coping strategies, and offering emotional support that affirms both identity and potential.[12]

In addition to academic guidance, near-peer mentors can offer authentic and culturally grounded tools for resilience. They often help mentees navigate college applications, manage stress, and build self-regulation skills, reinforcing verbal persuasion, vicarious learning, and emotional stability, all key sources of self-efficacy. When embedded into school structures, near-peer mentoring becomes "a mirror and a map," allowing Black students to see themselves reflected in success and be equipped to reach it.

Research emphasizes that mentors who have "made it" through similar challenges can effectively inspire their mentees.[13] In practice, near-peer mentors often come from the same communities as their mentees and understand the barriers (academic, financial, social) that Black students face, enabling them to offer culturally responsive guidance and encouragement. These mentors serve as living proof that the mentees' goals are attainable: "If I can do it, you can too," which boosts the mentees' confidence and aspirations.

Notably, near-peer programs provide dual benefits: they support younger students while also empowering the mentors themselves. Unlike traditional adult mentoring, near-peer relationships foster a unique bond of trust and comfort.[14]

College readiness and enrollment outcomes are a major focus of near-peer programs in high school and college preparatory settings. Because many Black students and other first-generation learners lack familial experience with college, near-peer mentors fill a critical gap by guiding them through the complex college application process. For example, the College Advising Corps (CAC) is a successful program that embeds recent college graduates in high schools as full-time near-peer college advisors.[15] The near-peer mentors help students navigate filling out financial aid forms, meeting application deadlines, and finding fee waivers. Near-peer advisors demystify the path to college and raise college-going expectations in schools. In practice, this leads to tangible gains. One analysis found that high schools with a near-peer college mentorship program saw completion rates for the Free Application for Federal Student Aid (FAFSA) jump to 35 percent from 28 percent in similar schools without the program. This seven-point increase means hundreds more low-income students accessed aid, directly enabling college enrollment. Additionally, fourteen hundred students in the mentored schools secured roughly $13 million more in federal grants they may have otherwise missed. Early application rates and scholarship awards also improved. Although long-term college enrollment data are still being collected, these early indicators (more applications, financial aid, and post-secondary plans) strongly correlate with higher college matriculation.[16]

Beyond college and career readiness, near-peer mentoring profoundly impacts Black students' social-emotional development. Unlike distant authority figures, near-peer mentors form friendships and offer "constructive reinforcement," showing younger students that someone like them can thrive academically. High school mentoring programs have documented numerous SEL benefits for mentees, including increased self-esteem, confidence, and motivation. The trusting near-peer relationship allows mentees to candidly discuss fears or setbacks and receive encouragement from mentors who have overcome similar hurdles. This fosters a growth mindset and resilience. Mentees begin to internalize their mentors' messages. For example, a once disengaged Black student decides to take challenging courses because their slightly older Black mentor convinced them, "You are capable of this." Such boosts in self-confidence translate into greater classroom participation and leadership among Black youth mentees.

CASE STUDY: MASTERING THE MOMENT

Aasha is a bright, creative sixth-grade student who enjoys reading and storytelling but often freezes up during math class. Her previous teacher described her as "capable but lacking confidence." In math assessments, Aasha performs below grade level despite strong verbal skills and engagement in other subjects. She often says things like, *"I'm just not a math person,"* and avoids participating in math lessons.

Mr. Thompson, a new teacher trained in culturally responsive and strength-based practices, decides to focus on building Aasha's *math self-efficacy* using Bandura's four sources:

- *Mastery experiences:* He breaks down math problems into scaffolded steps and ensures Aasha experiences small wins—first in one-on-one settings, then in small groups. He celebrates her first independently solved long-division problem with a class "shout-out," which boosts her confidence.

- *Vicarious experiences:* Mr. Thompson pairs Aasha with Amari, an eleventh-grade Black girl at the local high school who once struggled but now excels in math. Amari shares how she got better by practicing each day. Watching Amari succeed helps Aasha reframe her own narrative.
- *Verbal persuasion:* Mr. Thompson regularly affirms Aasha's progress: *"You're not only doing math—you're thinking like a mathematician."* He also invites her to help lead a group game focused on multiplication facts, reinforcing her identity as someone who can do math.
- *Affective state:* Aasha often became anxious before math tests. Mr. Thompson teaches breathing techniques and offers flexible seating and low-stakes assessments first. This lowers her anxiety and shifts her perception of math as threatening.

By spring, Aasha's math scores have improved significantly, but more importantly, her *belief* in herself has transformed. She now approaches challenges with persistence and even volunteers to lead warm-up problems. When asked about math at a parent-teacher night, she says with a smile, *"I like it now. It's kind of fun when you figure it out."* Aasha's shift shows how deliberate, equity-driven applications of self-efficacy theory can help Black students move from avoidance to empowerment.

Discussion Questions

1. Peer mentoring is a proven strategy to increase Black students' self-efficacy. What steps would you take to design a mentoring program that centers cultural identity and resilience?
2. During the COVID pandemic, Black students faced heightened stress and barriers to virtual learning. What is the relationship between self-efficacy, academic performance, and racialized stress? How can educators be better prepared for future crises?

3. Consider the case of Trinity, an eleventh-grade Black student who feels disrespected by her teachers and is struggling academically while living in unstable conditions. As her teacher or counselor, how would you apply self-efficacy theory to support her success and well-being?

CASE STUDY: POTENTIAL UNLOCKED?

Student: Marshall, tenth grade
Setting: Suburban high school where Black students make up less than 10 percent of the population

Marshall is a quiet, thoughtful student with a strong interest in science. He dreams of becoming an engineer but is currently struggling in Honors Chemistry. His teacher, Ms. Carlson, has noted that, although Marshall's written work shows promise, he rarely asks questions or participates in labs. He recently failed a major exam and now says he wants to drop the class. In a meeting with his counselor, Marshall admits, *"I don't see people like me doing this. Maybe I'm not meant for it."*

Marshall has internalized doubts about his ability to succeed in advanced STEM courses. He's receiving little affirmation from teachers and is often the only Black student in his classes. His parents are supportive but don't have backgrounds in science and are unsure how to help.

You are Marshall's teacher, counselor, or school leader. What steps would you take to help Marshall and other Black students stay in Honors Chemistry and move toward their engineering goals? Which of the four sources of self-efficacy would you activate first, and how? What role might peer or near-peer mentoring play in changing his beliefs about belonging in the Honors Chemistry class? How could his science teacher create an environment that affirms Marshall's identity and potential?

CONCLUSION

Self-efficacy is a catalyst for liberation. For Black students, whose confidence and self-efficacy are too often undermined by systemic racism, bias, and exclusionary practices, fostering self-efficacy is both an academic imperative and an act of justice. This chapter has demonstrated that when educators intentionally build students' belief in their own capabilities through mastery, modeling, encouragement, and emotional safety, they create conditions for real and lasting success. Black students do not lack ability; they lack environments that reflect and reinforce their brilliance. By leveraging Bandura's four sources of self-efficacy within culturally affirming frameworks, educators can reframe schooling as a space where Black students are supported to thrive. The question is not whether Black students can succeed, but whether schools will commit to practices that make that success inevitable.

Chapter Reflection Questions

1. How can mastery experiences be intentionally designed in classrooms serving Black students, particularly in environments that have historically denied them opportunities for academic success?
2. Consider how curriculum, feedback, and instructional scaffolding contribute to or hinder a student's ability to feel capable.
3. In what ways do vicarious experiences, such as exposure to same-race role models or success stories, shape the self-efficacy of Black students? Are these experiences equally powerful in predominantly white or under-resourced schools?
4. Affective states such as stress or anxiety can drastically impact self-efficacy. How might educators recognize and respond to these emotional barriers in real time, especially in high-stakes environments such as testing or disciplinary moments?
5. Reflecting on Bandura's theory as a whole, what are the limitations of applying the theory of self-efficacy without considering structural and systemic factors, such as racism, sexism, and so on, that shape the experiences of Black students?

CHAPTER 5

A Discipline Alternative—Restorative Justice

Addressing bias and racist beliefs associated with school discipline is crucial for the well-being of Black students. The disciplinary frameworks in US schools have historically mirrored the structures of the criminal justice system. Rooted in retributive ideals of control and punishment, the trends of who are the recipients of punishment in schools have also reflected patterns of poverty, power, and anti-Black beliefs. The racism underlying these attitudes can be traced back to chattel slavery and carceral ideologies, meaning that Black people were to be "controlled," not "nurtured." And thus, for Black children, school discipline is frequently shaped by educators' perceptions of danger rather than empathy.

For generations, harsh school discipline practices have disproportionately harmed Black students, including exclusionary methods such as suspensions and expulsions.[1] Zero-tolerance policies and reactive disciplinary strategies have been central to what many scholars identify as the school-to-prison pipeline. These policies often criminalize Black students' behavior, fuel racial inequities in school discipline, and, in many cases, retraumatize students who are already navigating racism outside the school walls.[2] The result is a crisis in belonging and emotional safety, eroding students' confidence and capacity to thrive.

At the heart of punitive school discipline also lies a retributive logic asserting that wrongdoing deserves severe punishment. Schools often enforce harsh penalties under the belief that such sanctions will deter future behavior. However, this assumption overlooks the influence of implicit bias and racist ideologies. The labeling of Black students often reflects what educators believe about students, and those labels are attached to Black students—labels such as disruptive, defiant, or dangerous, even when exhibiting the same behaviors as their white peers.[3] This racialized interpretation of behavior contributes to a cycle of exclusion and harm, with far-reaching consequences, including lost instructional time, diminished academic performance, damaged relationships with educators, and an increased risk of entanglement with the criminal legal system.[4]

In response to these systemic inequities in discipline, restorative justice (RJ) has emerged as a transformative approach. Unlike traditional discipline, RJ does not begin with punishment. It begins with a set of questions rooted in empathy and community: What happened? Who was harmed? What are their needs? Who is responsible for meeting those needs? What can be done to make things right? RJ centers relationships, healing, accountability, and collective care. This chapter examines the potential of RJ in transforming school culture and promoting the well-being of Black students. Through research, narratives, and practical implementation strategies, this chapter illustrates why RJ is not just an alternative to discipline—it is an alternative to injustice.

THE ROOTS OF HARSH DISCIPLINE FOR BLACK STUDENTS

To fully grasp the urgency and need for restorative justice, educators must address the persistent historical legacy of Black criminalization in the United States. As discussed in previous chapters, the legacy of harm and criminalization stems from the slave patrols that enforced labor to the Black Codes and Jim Crow laws that aimed to penalize and control daily Black life. Such criminalization of Black people has deep and painful historical roots.

Today, this legacy persists in schools, where disciplinary policies and surveillance systems reflect a culture of control and exclusion. Black students face disproportionate punishment and policing that mirror the long-standing societal expectations of controlling Black people through the adult criminal justice system (fig. 5.1). However, as the Clarks' Doll Tests illustrated, these harmful processes impact students' perceptions. More specifically, these experiences shape how Black students see themselves. Repeated criminalization in school settings fosters internalized beliefs of inferiority, leading to self-hatred, decreased academic motivation, and acceptance of low expectations. Scholars like Woodson long ago warned of the dangers of miseducation, where students learn to doubt their own worth.[3] More recently, research in Black psychology and trauma studies confirms that

FIGURE 5.1 The roots of harsh discipline for Black students

Black students—particularly Black boys—are disproportionately punished and policed. This mirrors a broader legacy of Black criminalization.

Black laws and codes
From slave codes to Jim Crow, laws were used to restrict the lives of Black Americans.

Mass incarceration
Starting in the 1970s, the criminalization of Black life led to the expansion of the criminal legal system.

Inequities in school discipline
Today, Black students face punitive discipline at rates far higher than their peers.

- Black students account for 38% of suspensions.
- Schools with more Black students are more likely to have police.
- Among all girls, Black girls face more and harsher forms of discipline.
- Schools with more Black students tend to use exclusionary discipline tactics.
- Black males face more office referrals for minor infractions.

Source: Figure created by author (with AI assistance) based on data and analysis from D. J. Losen, C. L. Hodson, M. A. Keith II, K. Morrison, and S. Belway, *Lost Opportunities: How Disparate School Discipline Continues to Drive Differences in the Opportunity to Learn* (UCLA Center for Civil Rights Remedies, Civil Rights Project at UCLA, 2020), and Tiffany Ferrette, "The Roots of Discipline-Induced Trauma for Black Children in Early Childhood Settings" (Center for Law and Social Policy, February 2021).

such systemic criminalization can damage identity formation, lower self-efficacy, and increase psychological distress.[5]

For many years, the criminalization of Black people has been a primary stance for many politicians. For instance, during the 2020 presidential debate, President Donald Trump declared, *"I am the law-and-order candidate."* This phrase, though not new, carries significant historical implications. The phrase "law and order" has historically signaled to voters the intention to implement policies and practices that disproportionately impact Black communities through heightened policing, mass incarceration, and surveillance, rather than changing policies that increase opportunities for people to thrive.[6] The intention of the rhetoric was frequently employed in the wake of Black Lives Matter protests and nationwide protests that followed the deaths of unarmed Black persons (e.g., George Floyd, Breonna Taylor) at the hands of police officers.[7]

These dynamics of overpolicing and control are reflected in schools every day. According to data from the US Department of Education's Office for Civil Rights, Black students represent about 15 percent of the public school population, yet they account for 38 percent of all out-of-school suspensions.[8] Black boys, in particular, are suspended at nearly four times the rate of white boys. Black girls, often overlooked in discussions of school discipline, are also disproportionately punished, facing higher rates of suspension than any other group of girls. These disparities begin as early as preschool. Black preschoolers are 3.6 times more likely to be suspended than their white peers.[9]

These statistics are not solely the result of individual bias; they are rooted in racist beliefs and policies that equate Blackness with danger. Research shows that schools with higher percentages of Black students are significantly more likely to have law enforcement officers, metal detectors, surveillance systems, and zero-tolerance policies.[10] These highly punitive environments clearly denote that Black students are to be controlled and watched rather than nurtured or understood. Moreover, the disciplinary responses Black students receive are often harsher than those given to their white peers for identical behavior. In one notable study, Skiba et al. found that Black students were more likely to be referred to the principal's office for subjective offenses, such as defiance or disrespect, whereas white students were more often referred for objective infractions, such as smoking in the hallways.[11] Zimmerman further observes that teachers, including Black teachers, are more likely to adopt an authoritarian stance when addressing Black male students' behavior, employing control rather than care as the dominant disciplinary framework.[12]

Racial disparities in discipline practices lead to significant consequences. Exclusionary disciplinary practices correlate with reduced academic success, higher dropout rates, and an increased risk of involvement in the juvenile justice system.[13] Instead of fostering safety or love, these policies perpetuate existing cycles of inferiority, punishment, and racial trauma. Reversing the dynamic in schools requires a fundamental redesign of school culture. Restorative justice provides a constructive way forward as a critique of the racialized systems of discipline that have historically dominated our schools. Ridding schools of policies that perpetuate excessively harsh punishments and criminalize typical adolescent behavior is a first step. Zero-tolerance policies, which enforce strict and often severe penalties for certain offenses, are particularly damaging. They offer little flexibility in decision-making and disproportionately affect Black students, who face disciplinary action for more subjective behaviors like "defiance" or "disrespect." The use of suspension and expulsion, particularly for minor, nonviolent infractions, worsens racial inequalities by removing students from their educational settings, raising the risk of academic failure and involvement with the justice system.

Additionally, the presence of police (e.g., school resource officers) and surveillance-based security measures tends to be concentrated in predominantly Black schools. This often leads to a punitive culture where students are policed rather than supported. For instance, schools with heavy security and policing measures report lower academic performance, increased absenteeism, and reduced student engagement.[14] Essentially, metal detectors and police presence often serve as early points of entry into the criminal justice system. Researchers call this the "school-to-prison pipeline," where schools are funneling students, especially Black and Latino students, into carceral systems. And, in terms of the Black students' well-being, research indicates that the presence of armed officers and metal detectors can lead to increased stress, anxiety, and feelings of being criminalized, particularly among Black students.[15]

Over the last two decades, mass school shootings or incidents leading to multiple deaths have mainly occurred in schools with predominantly white student bodies. Key instances include the Columbine High School shooting (1999), the Sandy Hook Elementary shooting (2012), and the Marjory Stoneman Douglas High School shooting (2018). Although comprehensive data on the racial demographics of schools affected by mass shootings are scarce, available records suggest that these tragic events are less frequent in majority Black schools. Nonetheless, institutions serving largely Black and Hispanic students often enforce stricter security protocols compared to their predominantly white counterparts. Research indicates that the likelihood of a school implementing various security measures increases as the percentage of Black and Hispanic students enrolled rises. These security measures may include metal detectors, surveillance cameras, and the involvement of school resource officers.[16]

Why Restorative Justice for Black Students?

Restorative justice is a disciplinary philosophy rooted in healing, dignity, and relationship-building. RJ shifts the focus from punitive discipline to discipline with accountability, empathy, and community engagement. Rather than asking, "What rule was broken and how should we punish?" educators using RJ will ask, "Who was harmed, what do they need, and how can we make things right?"[17] This framework directly challenges the punitive systems that have historically oppressed Black students. Restorative justice interrupts these criminalization patterns by creating school environments where students can be heard, understood, and empowered to repair harm in a supportive setting. For Black youth, whose behaviors are often misinterpreted through racialized lenses, RJ provides a platform that values responsibility, historical context, emotion, and cultural expression.

A growing body of research supports RJ efficacy. Gregory et al. found that schools implementing restorative approaches experienced reduced discipline disparities and improved student-teacher relationships, particularly in racially diverse settings.[18] Additionally, in the Oakland Unified School District, a flagship site for RJ implementation, the number of suspensions of Black students dropped by 47 percent over three years, while academic engagement and perceptions of school safety improved. Similarly, Gonzalez demonstrated that RJ implementation led to improved academic outcomes and reduced exclusionary practices for students of color.[19]

Restorative justice closely aligns with key tenets of Black psychology and self-efficacy theory. The RJ process, which enables students to share their experiences, collaborate on problem-solving, and rebuild trust, promotes self-efficacy by fostering mastery, affirmation, and social recognition. Simultaneously, RJ reflects principles from African-centered or Black psychological frameworks by emphasizing communal responsibility, cultural integrity, and the holistic development of the individual.[20] These frameworks reject deficit-based views of Black students and instead highlight their resilience, creativity, and leadership potential. Furthermore, restorative practices provide a context for positive racial identity development. As Black students experience affirmation, fair treatment, and authentic accountability, rather than disproportionate punishment, they are more likely to internalize messages of worth, competence, and belonging. This not only improves academic performance and mental health but also creates conditions where Black students can thrive rather than merely survive.[21]

The promise of RJ depends on culturally responsive and racially conscious implementation. Studies warn that when RJ is introduced without training, consistency, or attention to systemic inequities, its impact is diluted or misused.[22] Evans and Vaandering emphasize that educators' beliefs about race, racism, behavior, and student potential shape how restorative practices are delivered and whether they genuinely affirm students or replicate existing biases.[23] In sum, RJ holds the potential to disrupt cycles of harm and criminalization. RJ can affirm the full humanity of Black students when grounded in culturally relevant frameworks and strength-based approaches. RJ can serve as both a shield and a pathway, protecting students from systemic punishment while guiding them toward healing, connection, and empowerment. Table 5.1 provides research on the effectiveness of RJ on Black student outcomes.

The research on RJ in rural schools is limited. Emerging studies and case reports suggest that, when thoughtfully implemented, RJ can benefit Black students in rural areas, particularly by fostering a student-centered approach to discipline. RJ's emphasis on relationship-building and community healing offers a valuable counterbalance to feelings of isolation. For example, rural schools have begun integrating RJ practices to reduce suspensions and enhance culturally responsive dialogue. Although most data focus on general populations, reports indicate that Black rural students experience disproportionate discipline similar to their urban peers, making RJ a promising approach (see fig. 5.2 for suspensions in US southern states). Further research is needed to assess the long-term effects of RJ in rural contexts, particularly when intersecting with issues of race, geography, and limited resources. However, when adapted with cultural humility and strong community buy-in, RJ holds potential as a healing-centered model for affirming and uplifting Black students in rural schools.[24]

IMPLEMENTING RESTORATIVE JUSTICE IN SCHOOL CONTEXTS

As previously stated, implementing RJ in schools requires a fundamental shift in school culture. This shift moves schools from a paradigm of rule enforcement to one rooted in relationship-building, healing, and care. It challenges educators to rethink their traditional responses to behavior and discipline and to center their students' humanity.

When implemented with fidelity, RJ leads to improved student-teacher relationships, reduced suspension rates, and enhanced school climate. This

TABLE 5.1 Effectiveness of RJ on Black student outcomes

Study	*Population/context*	*Key findings*
Gregory et al. (2016)[1]	Small city high schools with racially diverse populations	Reduced racial discipline disparities and improved teacher-student relationships.
Gonzalez (2015)[2]	Urban secondary school (Denver) implementing RJ schoolwide	Decreased suspensions and improved academic performance for students of color.
Jain et al. (2014)[3]	Oakland Unified School District (OUSD)	47% reduction in office referral of Black students, 63% increased conflict resolution.
Anyon (2016)[4]	Denver Public Schools implementing RJ	Four essential strategies of RJ: principal vision, staff buy-in, professional development, and full-time coordinator.
Augustine et al. (2018)[5]	Multiple schools in Pittsburgh, PA	Mixed results; Black students' suspension rates decreased but academic outcomes did not improve.
Evans and Vaandering (2016)[6]	Theoretical and practical analysis in PK–12 settings	Educator beliefs and school culture significantly affect RJ implementation outcomes.

Sources:

[1]Anne Gregory, Kathleen Clawson, Alycia Davis, and Edison G. Gewirtz, "The Promise of Restorative Practices to Transform Teacher–Student Relationships and Achieve Equity in School Discipline," *Journal of Educational and Psychological Consultation* 25, no. 1 (2015): 1–29.

[2]Thalia González, "Socializing Schools: Addressing Racial Disparities in Discipline Through Restorative Justice" (January 24, 2015); Thalia González, "Socializing Schools: Addressing Racial Disparities in Discipline Through Restorative Justice," in *Closing the School Discipline Gap: Equitable Remedies for Excessive Exclusion*, Daniel J. Losen ed., 2014, available at SSRN: https://ssrn.com/abstract=2728960.

[3]Sonia Jain, Henrissa Bassey, Martha A. Brown, and Preety Kalra, "Restorative Justice in Oakland Schools: Implementation and Impacts" (Data in Action, Sept. 2014).

[4]Yolanda Anyon, "Taking Restorative Practices School-Wide: Insights from Three Schools in Denver" (Denver School-Based Restorative Practices Partnership, 2016), https://socialwork.du.edu/sites/g/files/lmucqz281/files/2018-10/taking_restorative_practices_school-wide.pdf.

[5]Catherine H. Augustine, John Engberg, Geoffrey E. Grimm, Emma Lee, Elaine Lin Wang, Karen Christianson, et al., *Can Restorative Practices Improve School Climate and Curb Suspensions? An Evaluation of the Impact of Restorative Practices in a Mid-Sized Urban School District* (RAND Corporation, 2018).

[6]Katherine R. Evans and Dorothy Vaandering, *The Little Book of Restorative Justice in Education: Fostering Responsibility, Healing, and Hope in Schools* (Good Books, 2016).

FIGURE 5.2 Black suspension rates in Southern states

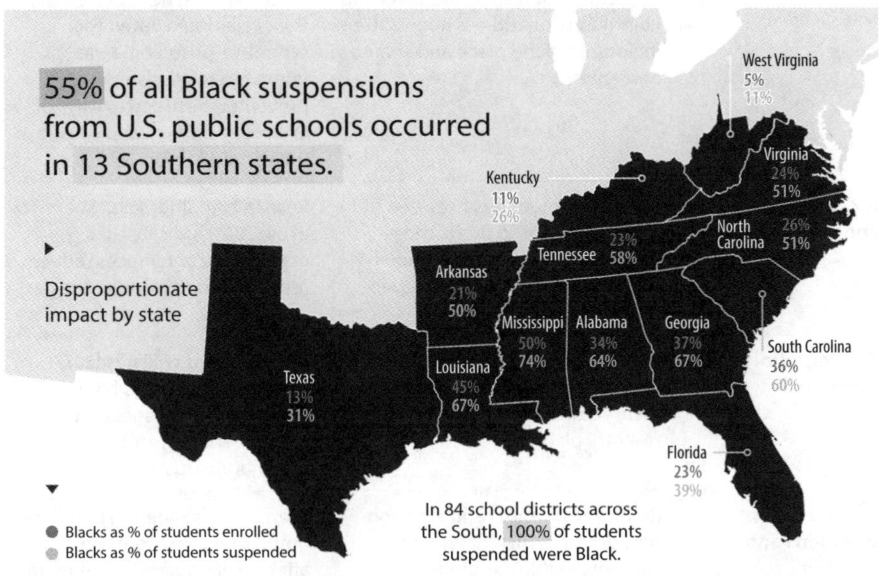

Source: Adapted from E. J. Smith and Shaun R. Harper, *Disproportionate Impact of K–12 School Suspension and Expulsion on Black Students in Southern States* (Center for the Study of Race and Equity in Education, University of Pennsylvania, Philadelphia, 2015).

section explores core restorative justice strategies and techniques that have been successfully implemented in schools. The strategies outlined here are especially critical in disrupting biased disciplinary patterns. When implemented with fidelity and care, restorative justice strategies create school spaces for truth-telling and reconciliation. Table 5.2 outlines restorative justice strategies that have been most effective in practice. Below are brief descriptions of restorative justice strategies.

Restorative Circles

Restorative circles are structured, intentional dialogues that bring students together affected by a specific conflict or community disruption. Grounded in the values of equity, empathy, accountability, and mutual respect, restorative circles provide a space where students can speak honestly, listen deeply, reflect on the impact of what has happened, and collaboratively identify steps for healing and

TABLE 5.2 RJ strategies

Restorative strategy	*Description*	*Evidence of effectiveness*
Restorative circles	Facilitated group dialogues used proactively or responsively to build community or address harm. Often include a talking piece and shared agreements.	Ortega et al. (2016) found that participants in RC reported that the circles interrupted the school-to-prison pipeline, improved relationships, prevented destructive ways of engaging conflict, and caused meaningful dialogue.[1]
Restorative conferences	Structured meetings between those who caused harm, those affected, and others to acknowledge impact and develop repair plans.	Research findings (e.g., Shem-Tov et al., 2024) indicate that restorative conferences reduce repeat offending and rearrests.[2]
Reintegration meetings	Meetings to welcome students back from suspension or absence, focused on support, reflection, and re-entry planning.	Winslade and Williams (2017) found that meetings help students reclaim agency, prevent repeat behavior, and strengthen community trust within schools.[3]
Restorative questions and affective statements	Reflective prompts and emotion-based statements that guide students to think about their behavior and its impact.	Evans and Vaandering (2016) noted that consistent use of affective language built empathy and de-escalated conflicts.[4]
Peer mediation and student RJ councils	Trained student leaders resolve minor conflicts or facilitate circles, often increasing youth leadership and school engagement.	Fronius et al. (2016) highlighted that peer-led RJ programs are associated with reduced suspensions, fewer racial discipline disparities, improved school climate, and greater student voice and agency.[5]
Daily check-ins and check-outs	Brief daily routines where students share feelings and experiences, fostering trust and early intervention for distress.	Darling-Hammond et al. (2020) reported that check-ins increased emotional regulation and connection, especially for minoritized youth.[6]

Sources:

[1]Lilyana Ortega, Mikhail Lyubansky, Saundra Nettles, and Dorothy L. Espelage, "Outcomes of a Restorative Circles Program in a High School Setting," *Psychology of Violence* 6, no. 3 (2016): 459–68, doi:10.1037/vio0000048.

[2]Yahav Shem-Tov, Johanna Lacoe, Ryken Grattet, Brandon Martin, and Steven Raphael, *Can Restorative Justice Conferencing Reduce Recidivism? Evidence from the Make-It-Right Program* (California Policy Lab, Jan. 2024), https://www.capolicylab.org/wp-content/uploads/2024/01/Can-Restorative-Justice-Conferencing-Reduce-Recidivism-Evidence-from-the-Make-it-Right-Program-1.pdf.; Lawrence W. Sherman, Heather Strang, Daniel J. Woods, Sarah Bennett, Nova Inkpen, Dorothy Barnes et al., *Are Restorative Justice Conferences Effective in Reducing Repeat Offending?* (Campbell Systematic Reviews National Institute of Justice, 2015), https://nij.ojp.gov/library/publications/are-restorative-justice-conferences-effective-reducing-repeat-offending.

TABLE 5.2 (*Continued*)

[3]John M. Winslade and Michael J. Williams, "Re-Entry Conversations: A Restorative Narrative Practice for Student Reintegration," *Narrative and Conflict: Explorations in Theory and Practice* 6, no. 1 (2017): 32–53, doi:10.13021/G8ncetp.v6.1.2017.1906.
[4]Katherine Evans and Dorothy Vaandering, *The Little Book of Restorative Justice in Education: Fostering Responsibility, Healing, and Hope in Schools* (Good Books, 2016).
[5]Trevor Fronius, Hannah Darling-Hammond, Sean Persson, and Jon West, *Restorative Justice in U.S. Schools: An Updated Research Review* (WestEd Justice & Prevention Research Center, 2016), https://jprc.wested.org/wp-content/uploads/2016/02/RJ_LiteratureReview_2016_FullReport.pdf.
[6]Linda Darling-Hammond, Channa M. Cook-Harvey, and Livia Lam, *Educating the Whole Child: Improving School Climate to Support Student Success* (Learning Policy Institute, 2020).

repair. Restorative circles can be used proactively to build community in response to harm and as reintegration tools when students return from suspension or extended absences. They are especially powerful in schools for:

- building trusting relationships among students and staff
- addressing conflict and harm without exclusionary discipline
- supporting students in processing trauma, grief, or schoolwide incidents
- reinforcing shared values and expectations in the classroom

Circles can be used in advisory periods, classroom settings, staff meetings, or facilitated one-on-one sessions. Participants typically sit in a circle to symbolize equality and pass around a "talking piece" to signal each participant's opportunity to talk.

Research has shown that restorative circles contribute to reduced suspension and expulsion rates, improved student-teacher relationships, and increased feelings of school connectedness. A 2020 randomized control study in *The American Economic Review* found that restorative practices like restorative circles reduced suspensions by 44 percent and improved perceptions of school climate, particularly for Black students.[25] Gregory et al. discovered that implementing restorative circles in high school classrooms improved classroom management and reduced racial discipline disparities.[26] Wachtel emphasized that the consistent use of proactive circles builds a foundation of trust, making students more willing to engage in difficult conversations when conflict arises.[27] The following is an example of a restorative circle:

Ms. Gonzalez noticed growing tension between two students in her eighth-grade classroom. The students, Marcus and Tyla, experienced a disagreement after a group project, and the conflict escalated into name-calling. Rather than send them to the office, Ms. Gonzalez invited them to participate in a restorative circle with a facilitator. Seated in a circle with a talking piece, the students took turns sharing how they experienced the conflict, how it made them feel, and what they needed to do to move forward. Marcus admitted he felt "dissed" by Tyla, and Tyla shared that she was frustrated and embarrassed by how he talked to her. Together, they developed an agreement to check in before future collaborations and committed to respectful communication. Their relationship improved, and so did the classroom climate.

Restorative Conferences

Restorative conferences are structured, facilitated meetings that address serious incidents of conflict, harm, or misconduct. Unlike informal restorative circles, these conferences are typically used in response to more significant events, such as bullying, physical altercations, or property damage, and they involve a thorough preparation process. Restorative conferences are often employed in school settings as an alternative to suspension or expulsion, particularly for behavior that would normally trigger exclusionary discipline. They are also used when reintegrating a student after a disciplinary removal or school absence as a result of suspension or hospitalization. Conferences can occur in administrator offices, school counselor offices, or restorative spaces, and they are most successful when follow-up support is provided.

The conference brings together the person who caused harm, those who were harmed, and supporters or community members from both sides. With the help of a trained facilitator, participants explore what happened, who was affected, and what can be done to repair the harm. The goal is to restore relationships, reintegrate the individual who caused harm, and reaffirm shared values within the school community. Restorative conferences are grounded in principles of accountability, healing, and voluntary participation. They are most effective when all parties feel safe, heard, and supported throughout the process.

Numerous studies support the efficacy of restorative conferences in reducing recidivism, improving student outcomes, and transforming school culture. David Karp and Beau Breslin found that 91 percent of participating victims and 89 percent of offenders in school-based restorative conferences felt the process was fair and satisfactory, indicating high levels of engagement and perceived justice.[28] A meta-analysis by Strang et al. concluded that restorative conferences are significantly more effective than traditional discipline in reducing repeat offending and increasing satisfaction for both victims and offenders.[29] Morrison and

Vaandering emphasized that restorative conferences promote ethical engagement, reduce power imbalances, and support the reintegration of youth into the school community. The following is an example of a restorative conference[30]:

> *After a hallway fight between two high school students, Malik and Jordan, the vice principal considered suspending them. Instead, they were invited to a restorative conference facilitated by the school's RJ coordinator. Before the meeting, each student and their parents/caregivers met with the facilitator to understand the process and clarify their intentions. During the conference, Malik shared that he felt provoked by a social media rumor, while Jordan described feeling caught off guard and embarrassed in front of peers. Both acknowledged how the fight disrupted the school day and upset their classmates. With support from their families and teachers, the students crafted a restitution plan that included a joint service project, peer-led presentations on conflict resolution, and ongoing check-ins with their counselors and a mentor. The conference not only repaired the immediate harm but also helped re-establish community trust.*

Reintegration Meetings

Reintegration meetings are a restorative justice practice designed to welcome students back into the school community following a suspension, expulsion, incarceration, or extended absence resulting from trauma or crisis. These meetings acknowledge the harm or disruption caused by the absence and aim to re-establish trust, connection, and clear expectations for moving forward.

In contrast to traditional reentry protocols that typically concentrate on academic recovery or behavior management, reintegration meetings prioritize relational healing and community responsibility. These meetings feature a structured dialogue among the student, a staff facilitator (often a school counselor, RJ coordinator, or administrator), key educators, and occasionally family members. The objective is to reflect on the reasons for the absence or incident, reaffirm the student's importance and role within the school community, identify the necessary supports for the student's success, and collaboratively develop a reentry plan that encompasses both academic and social-emotional elements.

Although reintegration meetings are often underutilized, studies show that when implemented effectively, they contribute to a stronger school attachment and reduced recidivism. For instance, González highlighted reintegration circles as vital in maintaining dignity for youth returning from expulsions and in reducing the likelihood of repeated infractions.[31] And Jain et al. found that reintegration meetings helped transform punitive school cultures by centering student voice, building empathy, and reducing feelings of alienation.[32]

Step-by-Step Approach to Utilizing Reintegration Meetings in Schools

1. Schedule a meeting before the student returns or on the first day back.
2. Invite participants who have supported or impacted the student's school experience (e.g., teachers, counselors, administrators, family members).
3. Create a welcoming space, avoiding punitive tones or physical layouts that reinforce power imbalances.
4. Facilitate with care, using guiding questions such as:
   - What has happened since you've been gone?
   - What do you need from us to feel supported and successful?
   - How can we work together to prevent similar challenges in the future?
5. Document an action plan that includes social, emotional, and academic supports, as well as regular follow-up.

Here's an example of a reintegration meeting:

> *After serving a five-day suspension for coming to math class intoxicated, tenth grader Jasmine was invited to a reintegration meeting facilitated by the school's restorative justice coordinator. Her math teacher, school counselor, and aunt joined the meeting. Jasmine expressed anxiety about school and the influence of some of her friends on her drug use and drinking. Her math teacher acknowledged her anxiety but emphasized her belief in Jasmine's math potential. The school counselor offered assistance with her potential addiction. Together, they developed a reentry plan that included daily check-ins, counseling both in school and outside of it, and a quiet space Jasmine could use when feeling overwhelmed. The meeting enabled her to return with support and dignity.*

Restorative Questions and Affective Statements

Restorative questions and affective statements are foundational tools for effective communication in RJ. They help build emotional literacy, accountability, and mutual understanding by inviting reflection rather than blame. These approaches center on language that promotes connection over correction, helping to shift school culture from punitive to relational. *Restorative questions* are open-ended prompts designed to guide conversations following harm. They help individuals reflect on their actions, understand their impact, and identify ways to repair relationships. *Affective statements* are "I" statements that express emotions and describe the effect someone's behavior has had on another person. They model healthy emotional expression and signal respect and care. These questions are versatile and can be used in a wide range of settings:

Core Restorative Questions

- *During conflict resolution or discipline situations* (e.g., instead of "Why did you do that?" say "What were you thinking at the time?")
- What happened? What were you thinking and feeling at the time? Who has been affected by what you did? What do you think you need to do to make things right?

Examples of Affective Statements

"I felt disrespected when you walked away while I was talking."
"I'm really proud of how you handled that situation."
"It hurt me to see you treat your classmate that way."

Restorative questions and affective statements have been shown to increase student self-awareness, enhance teacher-student relationships, and decrease reliance on exclusionary discipline. McCluskey et al. found that the use of affective language and restorative questioning contributed to creating calmer school environments and led to more meaningful resolutions of conflict.[33] Vaandering emphasized that these tools support an ethic of care and foster authentic dialogue in schools, particularly when addressing power dynamics and racial inequities. Educators who disclose feelings and affect send a message of shared vulnerability to the student.[34] According to the International Institute for Restorative Practices (IIRP), the consistent use of restorative language enhances student engagement and fosters relational trust, both of which are crucial for sustained behavior change. Here's an example of using restorative questions and affective statements[35]:

> *During a classroom disruption, a teacher pauses instruction and approaches the student calmly. Then, the teacher asks for a short conference at her desk after the lesson. Instead of sending the student out, the teacher, while in conference with the student, says, "I felt really disrespected when you interrupted me several times while I was speaking. What was going on for you at that moment?" The student, surprised but relieved, admits to feeling overwhelmed after a difficult morning. They talk briefly about how*

to communicate better next time and agree on a plan for support. The situation is resolved without punishment, without embarrassing the student in front of other students, and with restored connection.

Peer Mediation and Student Restorative Justice Councils

Peer mediation is a conflict resolution process in which trained student mediators assist their peers in navigating disagreements within a safe, structured, and supportive environment. Rather than enforcing discipline, mediators facilitate dialogue that enables participants to share their perspectives, express feelings, and collaboratively develop solutions. Peer mediation is rooted in principles of empathy, neutrality, and confidentiality.

Similar to peer mediation, Student RJ Councils are school-based entities comprising students trained in restorative practices who serve as facilitators, advisors, and advocates for RJ initiatives within their schools. These councils may:

- facilitate restorative circles or conferences
- help mediate peer conflicts
- provide input to administrators and teachers on school climate and discipline policies
- promote a culture of inclusion and care

Both models position students as leaders in shaping school culture and contributing to a more relational, strength-based learning environment. Peer mediation and RJ councils have been associated with improvements in school climate, reductions in disciplinary referrals, and increased student agency. Burrell found that schools using peer mediation reported significantly fewer suspensions and a measurable increase in students' ability to resolve conflicts independently.[36] According to the National Center for Restorative Justice, student-led RJ initiatives foster a greater sense of belonging and significantly improve peer relationships, particularly in racially and culturally diverse schools.[37] Morrison et al. documented that peer mediation programs reduce repeat conflicts and empower minoritized students who often feel voiceless in traditional discipline systems.[38] Additionally, a study by Zion et al. in urban schools found that students who served on RJ councils developed leadership skills and demonstrated a deeper understanding of justice, fairness, and community responsibility.[39] An example of peer mediation follows:

At Dunbar Middle School, three eighth-grade students, Kendra, Simone, and Danielle, had an argument that escalated into a public argument in the school cafeteria. Instead of sending them to the assistant principal, the school's RJ coordinator referred the case to the Student RJ Council. Two trained student mediators facilitated a session where each girl shared how the conflict affected her. Through structured dialogue, they discovered the disagreement stemmed from a misunderstanding. The mediators helped them develop a written agreement about communication and boundaries. Afterward, the young women reported feeling more respected and supported and their friendship was healed or saved.

Daily Check-Ins and Check-Outs

Daily check-ins and check-outs are simple yet powerful restorative practices that provide consistent, structured opportunities for educators and students to connect and reflect on how students are feeling. These brief routines typically occur at the beginning and end of the school day (or class period) and serve as a relationship-centered alternative to behavior tracking or punitive surveillance. Check-ins invite students to express how they feel, set goals, or identify what they need for a successful day. Check-outs create space to reflect on how the day went, what went well, what could have been improved, and whether the student feels ready for the next day. Check-ins and check-outs can be facilitated one-on-one (e.g., between a student and a counselor or trusted adult) or in small groups in class. They can be verbal, written, or digital, and they work well in classrooms, advisory periods, or counseling sessions. Educators often use simple prompts such as "What's one word to describe how you're feeling today?" "What's something you're looking forward to or worried about?" "Did anything happen today that you want to talk about?" When used consistently, these routine checks help students regulate emotions, anticipate challenges, and celebrate growth. They are especially beneficial for students returning from disciplinary actions, those experiencing trauma or instability, or students who need extra connection and predictability.

Research indicates that daily check-ins and check-outs support emotional regulation, relational trust, and reductions in disciplinary incidents. Brackett et al. found that consistent emotional check-ins help students become more aware of their feelings and reduce disruptive behavior by fostering self-regulation.[40] Morrison and Vaandering identify check-ins and check-outs as essential components of a restorative school climate, contributing to positive student-teacher relationships and stronger classroom communities.[41] In another study of RJ implementation in a large urban district, researchers reported that schools using regular check-ins saw measurable improvements in student attendance, engagement, and overall school connectedness.[42] Here is an example of using check-ins:

> *At Jefferson Middle School, Mr. Hall begins each homeroom with a five-minute check-in. Students use a color-coded "feelings thermometer" to indicate how they're feeling that day. Green means "I'm ready to learn," yellow means "I'm stressed or distracted," and red means "I'm overwhelmed and not ready to learn." Mr. Hall takes note and follows up privately with any students who mark their work with a red pen. At the end of the day, students write one sentence on a sticky note answering, "How did your day go?" or "What are you proud of today?" Over time, students report feeling more connected and more confident in asking for help. One student, Malcolm, who had previously struggled with behavior referrals, now checks in every morning and says it helps him "before things go wrong."*

BARRIERS TO EFFECTIVE RESTORATIVE JUSTICE IMPLEMENTATION

One of the most difficult aspects of implementing RJ programs in schools is achieving consistent, culturally responsive, and schoolwide integration, particularly in schools and school systems still heavily shaped by punitive discipline norms and racial bias. RJ requires educators to move away from traditional punishment-based responses and adopt an empathy-based, strength-focused approach and prioritize relationships of care. This shift is especially challenging in schools where staff have been trained to prioritize compliance over connection. Research shows that educators' attitudes toward discipline, especially implicit bias against Black youth, can undermine RJ efforts if not intentionally addressed.[43] Additionally, research has shown that when RJ is not integrated throughout the entire school, it often becomes a standalone intervention used only in response to conflict. Without full integration into the school's culture, policies, and daily routines, RJ will not replace harmful practices and can feel superficial or performative to students. Appendix B includes a sample letter template to explain the restorative justice philosophy to parents.

Facilitating restorative practices (e.g., circles, conferences, reintegration) requires time, skill, and emotional labor. Many schools underestimate the need for ongoing professional development, coaching, and opportunities for educators to reflect. Inadequate investment in ongoing training and evaluation leads to inconsistent execution and poorly facilitated processes that can retraumatize students.[44] Additionally, RJ programs that overlook racism, hierarchical power dynamics, and historical trauma often fail to meet the needs of Black students. For RJ to be effective for Black students, it must affirm cultural identity, acknowledge systemic racism and the harm it has caused to Black communities, and elevate community-defined practices of healing and justice. This includes resisting colorblind implementation and avoiding a one-size-fits-all approach. Overall, successful RJ programs require courageous leadership, deep cultural humility, and a sustained commitment to equity at every level of the school system.[45]

Best Practices for Supporting Black Students Through Restorative Justice

As previously discussed, implementing RJ effectively for Black students requires more than just employing a set of strategies. Educators working with Black students must strongly believe in racial equity and justice. Too often, RJ is deployed as a tool for behavior management without interrogating the deep racialized harm that discipline systems have historically caused. When grounded in equity, however, RJ becomes a powerful mechanism for affirming Black students' identity and resisting systemic injustice in schools. Figure 5.3 contains best practices for supporting Black students through RJ.

Below are five interrelated best practices to guide educators, schools, and districts in ensuring that RJ works with Black students:

1. Center Racial Equity Restorative justice must be explicitly linked to racial justice. This means identifying how disciplinary policies have disproportionately harmed Black students and ensuring that RJ is not a neutral process. Restorative justice must be used to affirm Black identity, elevate student voice, and promote agency and belonging. Educators must be trained to understand racial trauma and how restorative practices can serve as healing-centered interventions.

2. Invest in Whole-School Training True culture change requires that all educators and adults in schools (e.g., custodians, bus drivers) receive foundational training in RJ philosophy, language, and application. Schools should adopt a tiered model of support:

- **Universal (Tier 1):** Proactive community-building circles for all students
- **Targeted (Tier 2):** Small-group or one-on-one circles for students with recurring conflicts
- **Intensive (Tier 3):** Conferences or reintegration plans after serious incidents

FIGURE 5.3 Best practices for supporting Black students through restorative justice

1. Center racial equity

Restorative justice (RJ) must be explicitly linked to increasing racial justice. This means naming how disciplinary policies have disproportionately harmed Black students. RJ must be used to affirm Black identity, to elevate student voice, and promote agency and belonging across all groups of students (Evans & Vaandering, 2018).

2. Invest in whole-school training

True culture change requires that all adults—teachers, counselors, custodians—receive foundational training in RJ philosophy and application. Schools should adopt a tiered model of support.

- Universal (Tier 1): Proactive community-building circles for all students
- Targeted (Tier 2): Small-group or one-on-one circles for students
- Intensive (Tier 3): Conferences or reintegration plans after serious incidents

A shared understanding across the school building creates consistency and reduces the risk of racialized implementation gaps.

3. Embed Black cultural frameworks

RJ strategies are strengthened when rooted in African-centered values such as interdependence, communal care, healing, and the power of oral storytelling, drawing from the work of scholars like Shawn Ginwright (2018) and Linda James Myers (1992).

4. Integrate student leadership

Black students should not only participate in the restorative process but also lead it. Training Black youth to cofacilitate circles, serve on RJ councils, and influence policy builds self-efficacy, community accountability, and belonging. Leadership roles also allow students to challenge injustice within the system and reshape school culture on their own terms.

Source: Figure created by author (with AI assistance) using data from Julia Anyon et al., "Restorative Interventions and School Discipline Sanctions in a Large Urban School District," *American Educational Research Journal* 53, no. 6 (2016): 1663–97, and Catherine H. Augustine et al., *Can Restorative Practices Improve School Climate and Curb Suspensions?* (RAND Corporation, 2018).

A shared understanding across the building creates consistency and reduces the risk of racialized implementation gaps.

3. Embed Black Cultural Frameworks RJ strategies are strengthened when grounded in African-centered values such as interdependence, communal care, and the power of oral storytelling. Drawing from the work of scholars like

Ginwright and Myers, schools can transcend Eurocentric disciplinary frames and integrate traditions of collective responsibility, spirituality, and resilience that reflect Black students' cultural heritage.[46]

4. Integrate Student Leadership Black students should not only participate in restorative processes but also lead them. Training youth to co-facilitate circles, serve on RJ councils, and influence policy fosters self-efficacy, community accountability, and a sense of belonging. Leadership roles also allow Black students to challenge injustice from within the system and reshape school culture on their own terms.

5. Monitor and Respond to Equity Outcomes Data must guide RJ implementation. Schools should disaggregate RJ participation, outcomes, and satisfaction by student demographics to ensure inclusive practice. Questions that educators should ask are: *Are Black students being referred to RJ practices as often as white peers? Are all genders participating in RJ practices? Are students' voices being respected, and are outcomes just and fair?* If disparities persist, implementation must shift accordingly.

Again, RJ requires a fundamental shift in mindset from rule enforcement to relationship-building and student healing. This shift challenges educators to confront personal biases, reimagine the purpose of discipline, and prioritize healing over punishment. A review by Augustine et al. through the RAND Corporation emphasized that sustained educator training, leadership investment, and schoolwide buy-in are essential for successful and sustainable implementation.[47] RJ is not a quick fix. Schools must dedicate time, resources, and vision to cultivate restorative environments where Black students feel seen, safe, and powerful.

CASE STUDY: RESTORING CONNECTION—RASHAD AND MS. HEMPHILL

Rashad, a seventh-grade Black student, had been frequently late to school. One morning, after a tense exchange with Ms. Hemphill, the school secretary, Rashad responded with profanity and stormed away. Under the school's prior discipline model, this would have led to an immediate suspension. However, the school had recently committed to a restorative justice approach. Instead of punitive action, Rashad was invited to participate in a facilitated restorative circle. A trained RJ coordinator met with Rashad privately first, learning that his family was facing eviction and was currently living in a motel. He was visibly overwhelmed and exhausted. The coordinator also met with Ms. Hemphill, who admitted feeling disrespected but was open to understanding more.

In the circle, Rashad and Ms. Hemphill were joined by the facilitator and Rashad's counselor. Rashad explained his circumstances, and for the first time, he felt seen and not judged. Ms. Hemphill shared her own stress about managing multiple front-desk responsibilities and acknowledged that she had not paused to ask what was going on. Together, they co-created a plan: Rashad would check in with a counselor each morning before going to class, and Ms. Hemphill would greet him by name and smile. The school counselor helped connect Rashad's family to housing resources.

The circle reshaped a relationship. Rashad's behavior improved, his attendance stabilized, and he began to participate more in class. Ms. Hemphill reported feeling greater empathy and increased her use of reflective questioning when conflicts arose with other students. The school noted this as a model case of restorative practice grounded in racial understanding, empathy, and shared accountability.

CASE STUDY: TWO PATHS, ONE DISTRICT

Two middle schools in the same small-city district faced similar challenges: high suspension rates and racial disparities in discipline. At School A, a zero-tolerance policy governed behavior. Students could be suspended for verbal disrespect, dress code violations, or repeated tardiness. At this school, Black boys constituted 30 percent of the population but accounted for 65 percent of all out-of-school suspensions. Black families reported feeling targeted. Tensions between staff and students were high, and trust was eroding.

At School B, a restorative justice model had been in place for two years. The principal allocated time for weekly restorative circles, invested in staff-wide RJ training, and hired a full-time RJ coordinator. When students acted out, they were guided through reflection, reparation, and reintegration rather than exclusion. Black students served on the peer RJ council, and families were invited to participate in restorative conferences. Since implementation, School B has seen a 45 percent decline in suspensions, increased parent engagement, and improved school climate ratings. Teachers reported feeling more connected to their students and better equipped to manage conflict.

Now, School A is considering a shift. After another high-profile discipline case involving a Black student and a staff member, the district has proposed piloting RJ practices in School A. The staff is divided. Some see it as a chance to transform relationships; others worry it won't "hold students accountable."

- If you were leading School A, how would you begin to introduce restorative justice in a way that addresses staff skepticism and affirms Black students' needs?
- How might the use of student voice and family involvement transform the school's culture around discipline?
- What specific training or mindset shifts are needed to ensure implementation is not just procedural but also culturally responsive?
- What barriers do you anticipate—logistical, emotional, or cultural—and how would you address them in your implementation plan?
- How would you ensure that Black students are not just recipients of RJ but also architects of it?

CONCLUSION

Restorative justice represents more than a set of tools; it is a transformative vision for what schools can offer to Black students. It challenges us to dismantle entrenched systems of criminalization, exclusion, and punishment that have significantly harmed Black students. It requires us to view Black children as valued members of the community who deserve dignity, care, and opportunities.

At its core, RJ is a practice of remembering the humanity of every student, acknowledging the ancestral traditions of healing and accountability, and recognizing the collective responsibility we share in creating learning environments rooted in justice. For Black students, this approach can be especially powerful.

It affirms their identity, honors their voice, and cultivates a sense of belonging in systems that too often marginalize or erase them.

Chapter Reflection Questions

1. Draft a one-page letter or FAQ for families explaining the goals and benefits of restorative justice.
2. Do restorative justice practices conflict with traditional American ideas of justice? What historical or cultural narratives shape our understanding of discipline, accountability, and safety?
3. How can your school or district implement RJ in a way that centers racial equity and equality? Describe in detail.
4. Where in your current school practice or classroom management do you see opportunities to shift from punitive responses to restorative approaches?
5. What kinds of harm are often left unacknowledged or unresolved in your school community?
6. What supports do educators need to implement RJ with fidelity and racial consciousness?
7. What would a school rooted in restorative justice feel like for Black students, families, and staff?
8. Reflect on a time when you witnessed or participated in a disciplinary moment that could have been approached restoratively.

CHAPTER 6

Empowering Black Families and Communities

For far too long, a myth has existed among some educators claiming that Black parents don't care about their children. This harmful myth dismisses Black parents' deep love for and advocacy on behalf of their children. This deficit narrative, rooted in anti-Black racist beliefs, persists in schools despite substantial research demonstrating that Black parents want the best for their children and eagerly seek collaboration with schools when given the opportunity. A recent study by Anderson, funded by the United Negro College Fund, highlights what many in Black communities have long recognized: Black parents are deeply concerned about educational quality and equity, and they want to be engaged, serving as co-creators of their children's educational experiences. Yet, schools often ignore or marginalize Black voices, justifying exclusion through racialized assumptions about family interest and capacity.[1]

Drawing from Black psychology and strength-based approaches, educators must shift toward a radically different paradigm, in which the cultural strengths, historical resilience, and communal agency of Black families are acknowledged. Black psychology teaches us that optimal development is rooted in self-determination, interdependence, and spiritual wholeness.[2] When schools align with Black families based on these principles, they not only empower Black families but also create conditions that are conducive to the success of Black students.

This chapter examines strategies that demonstrate how to genuinely engage Black families through policy, pedagogy, and everyday school culture. Schools as anchors in Black communities require educators to transition from transactional parent engagement approaches (e.g., attending parent nights) to transformative partnerships that distribute power and foster collective efficacy.

BLACK FAMILY EMPOWERMENT AND SOCIAL CAPITAL

The myths surrounding Black families and education are misleading. Research has shown that, when accounting for socioeconomic status, levels of parental engagement are similar across racial groups.[3] Nevertheless, the contributions of Black families often remain invisible because school systems evaluate engagement through white, middle-class norms such as volunteering to be a "room parent" or attending all-school events.[4] This framing marginalizes Black families and frequently fosters mistrust and frustration among Black parents and families.

But this framing has been in place for hundreds of years. The Black family in the United States has endured centuries of systemic trauma and mistreatment, beginning with the institution of slavery. Enslavement not only exploited the labor of Black people but actively sought to dismantle family structures. Parents were sold away from children, marriages were not legally recognized, and family bonds were routinely severed to advance the slave economy. Historian Herbert Gutman has documented how, despite these brutal conditions, many enslaved people fought to maintain kinship networks and cultural traditions, resisting the dehumanizing effects of slavery in whatever ways they could.[5] Still, the legacy of that era left deep scars in the collective memory of Black families and laid the groundwork for ongoing structural challenges.

Today, educators have documented that Black student achievement increases when schools embrace culturally sustaining and community-responsive strategies that center Black identity, family leadership, and collective wellness.[6] At the heart of these approaches is empowerment as a transformative practice. Empowerment is the process through which individuals and communities gain the skills, resources, authority, and confidence to influence the conditions of their lives.[7] Conger and Kanungo further emphasize that empowerment enhances self-efficacy by removing institutional barriers and giving people real influence over systems.[8]

Helping Black families feel empowered requires redistributing power within schools. Parents, community members, and educators share this power. This process encompasses structural change and involves co-creating policies, honoring lived experiences, and building relational trust between schools and families.

Empowerment in this context is a collective, political act and an assertion that Black families are powerful and needed in the education of their children.[9]

HISTORICAL ROOTS OF DISEMPOWERMENT OF BLACK FAMILIES

Again, to grasp the importance of empowerment, educators must first recognize the historical factors that have disempowered Black families. Over the decades, racialized housing policies and school segregation have undermined the material and political strength of Black communities. The Home Owners' Loan Corporation (HOLC) maps from the 1930s and 1940s classified Black neighborhoods as "high risk" for investment, severely limiting homeownership and the potential for long-term wealth.[10] As a result of this disinvestment, schools became under-resourced, social networks with institutional influence diminished, and generations were systematically excluded from decision-making roles in education.

Black family empowerment focuses on building the skills and knowledge of Black parents and family members to achieve their family goals and aspirations. After schools racially integrated following the 1954 *Brown v. Board of Education* US Supreme Court case, many Black families were systematically denied access to information about schooling and postsecondary opportunities that white middle-class families used to influence school policy, secure educational opportunities, and navigate bureaucratic systems.[11] Consequently, the lack of information and understanding of schooling, or social capital, became a significant factor in structural educational exclusion. Despite these barriers, Black families have developed alternative forms of capital—what Yosso calls "community cultural wealth"—including navigational, resistant, and familial capital, which support survival, resistance, and success in hostile systems. Empowerment means recognizing wealth," including navigational, resistant, and familial capital, which supports survival, resistance, and success in hostile systems.[12] Empowerment means recognizing and building on these familial strengths while also working to dismantle the structures that deny access to dominant forms of social and institutional power.

Social Capital and Educational Access

Social capital, as defined by Pierre Bourdieu (1986), refers to the resources and benefits accessible through networks of trust, mutual obligation, and social connection.[13] In schools, this includes everything from knowing how to appeal a disciplinary action to understanding how to enroll a child in advanced coursework or on a college track. For families, social capital offers a gateway to educational access, institutional navigation, and systemic influence.[14] However, Black families often lack access to social capital or these networks due to:

- *historical exclusion* from homeowner associations, PTAs, country clubs, and elite private schools
- *lower representation* in decision-making bodies such as school boards
- *mistrust* created by decades of punitive schooling practices and surveillance of Black children and families
- *information gaps* caused by inconsistent or nontransparent school communication

Lack of access to social capital is not due to a lack of interest or involvement on the part of Black parents. In fact, it is quite the opposite. The lack of social capital stems from the gatekeeping mechanisms that prevent Black families from leveraging the same informal channels of influence available to white, affluent parents.[15] For instance, school counselors might provide college information only to high school students in AP, gifted programs, or advanced courses, thereby excluding all other students from essential details about college. When racial inequities are deeply embedded in these courses, information is disseminated unequally and inequitably.

Schools and districts must act intentionally to build networks for Black families to gain access to information, influence, and power. This involves cultivating both bonding capital (within-community ties) and bridging capital (connections to institutional players). Effective strategies include parent mentoring networks that pair parents based on their experiences navigating the school system; community-led policy forums where parents shape school priorities, budgets, and discipline policies; cultural knowledge exchanges that recognize Black family traditions, advocacy models, and intergenerational wisdom; and parent leadership institutes focused on advocacy, school law, and equity-centered organizing.[16] These efforts are effective not only in predominantly white schools, where Black families may face racial isolation and invisibility, but also in majority Black schools, where representation does not always equate to empowerment. Even in majority Black schools, families may confront disempowering systems, including scripted engagement efforts, exclusion from budgetary decisions, or a school culture that treats Black parents as liabilities rather than partners. True empowerment requires that schools become accountable to the communities they serve, not just in theory, but in terms of power and structure. It means shifting from outreach to solidarity.

Conger and Kanungo describe empowerment as enhancing self-efficacy by removing barriers to power through both formal structures and informal strategies. Furthermore, Black family empowerment is crucial as it enhances Black families' power to act on behalf of their students. When schools invest in the agency, cultural wealth, and leadership of Black families, they affirm students' identities, transform institutional dynamics, and advance racial justice. By understanding both the historical roots of disempowerment and the transformative potential of social capital, educators can begin to dismantle barriers and build communities where Black families are not only welcomed but also powerful. Empowerment, in this context, involves more than providing information or involving parents in school events; it also includes fostering a sense of agency, advocacy, and collective leadership.[17]

Empowerment strengthens the capacity of Black communities to organize and demand changes in education systems. Community organizing and protests illustrate the transformative power of collective action and empowerment. These movements have historically emerged in response to inequities seen through the media or publicized to the extent of catalyzing educational improvements.[18] Educators must recognize the "power" of Black family empowerment if change is desired.

For Black families, access to social capital has historically been hindered by systemic racism, school segregation, and exclusion from decision-making structures.[19] These limitations are not rooted in any cultural deficit but in the deliberate marginalization of Black communities from dominant networks of influence and institutional trust. Building social capital for Black families is a matter of equity. When schools intentionally cultivate relationships and expand community-based networks, they help dismantle these historic exclusions. The following are four actionable ways educators and schools can enhance Black families' access to social capital: launching family or parent mentoring programs, organizing community-led roundtables, providing capacity-building workshops, and forming trusting cultural liaisons.

1. Launching Family or Parent Mentoring Programs Family peer mentoring connects families who have successfully navigated the school system with those who are newer to or less connected with the system. This model creates intergenerational and intracommunity learning opportunities, enabling parents to share information about school choice, advocacy for discipline, access to honors or special education services, and college readiness. Mentoring programs enhance parents' self-efficacy, reduce feelings of isolation, and empower them to advocate for their children.[20] These programs are particularly effective when mentors share cultural and community ties with mentees. In Montgomery County, Maryland, the Black and Brown Coalition for Educational Equity has created a parent ambassador program, in which experienced caregivers serve as mentors to parents navigating Individualized Education Program (IEP) meetings and the gifted program enrollment process. This grassroots, culturally responsive initiative builds trust and reduces institutional intimidation.[21]

2. Organizing Community-Led Roundtables Community roundtables are intentional spaces where families and educators engage in two-way dialogue about school policy, curriculum, and student needs. Unlike typical parent nights, these events are co-designed and co-facilitated by families and community leaders. They enable Black families to shape decisions, share experiences, and challenge inequities directly. In Oakland, California, the district's Office of Equity sponsors quarterly "Family Listening Circles," in which Black parents discuss issues of school climate, discipline, and curriculum access directly with administrators. Their feedback has led to changes in hiring practices and the expansion of restorative justice programs.[22] Such initiatives align with the community cultural wealth model, which honors the navigational and resistant capital of historically marginalized groups. These roundtables generate collective agency and foster institutional accountability.[23]

3. Providing Capacity-Building Workshops Workshops can serve as powerful spaces for Black families to learn about topics ranging from special education advocacy and college admissions to financial aid navigation, school board engagement, and immigration protections. However, these must be co-created with communities and families. Here's a case of a capacity-building workshop in action: At Barack Obama High School, local educators partnered with a community-based organization to offer a "Parent Power Series." The series included sessions on school law, restorative justice, leadership training, and ways to give public testimony at school board meetings. It led to increased parent participation in school improvement planning. Workshops that foster self-advocacy and systems literacy increase parental involvement, especially when conducted in culturally safe environments.

4. Forming Trusting Cultural Liaisons Cultural liaisons can serve as bridges between schools and their surrounding communities. These hired school roles can be parent leaders, school staff, or community organizers trained to engage with sensitivity, consistency, and trust. In Minneapolis Public Schools, the Family Engagement Liaison Program features Black liaisons who regularly visit homes, interpret school policies, and assist parents in preparing for meetings. This program has led to measurable increases in parent-teacher communication and attendance among Black students.[24] Additionally, Black families report higher satisfaction and trust when they have consistent, culturally affirming relationships with someone in the school who shares their background or understands their community.[25] These roles are especially critical in under-resourced schools where mistrust of institutions may be significant.

COMMUNITY ACTIVISM AS EMPOWERMENT

Activism has always been a fundamental element in empowering the Black community. From the Black mothers who helped establish Freedom Schools during the civil rights movement to modern educators and parents who challenge book bans and the presence of police in schools, Black activism remains a crucial force in combating educational inequities. Although some may perceive community activism as a reactive stance, it necessitates educators to convene allies and co-conspirators to assert the vision of Black children and families. As understood through Black psychology, community-based activism serves as a spiritually and psychologically restorative practice, fostering a sense of purpose, collective efficacy, and historical ties.[26]

Educators should view themselves in solidarity with advocates and activists in Black communities. This does not mean they must attend community protests. However, it does require courageous leadership and a steadfast commitment to the well-being of Black students. Educators can express their activism in schools by opposing unfair policies and practices, such as the excessive discipline of Black students and the exclusion of Black perspectives and histories from the curriculum. Their role also includes supporting grassroots initiatives that promote culturally relevant curricula, equitable funding for schools, and the hiring and backing of Black educators. Activism thrives when educators partner with community organizations that assist Black youth and families, collaborating with established community advocacy efforts. When educators recognize their role as co-liberators with families and communities, schools can evolve from places of harm into centers of change.

INTERVENTIONS THAT EMPOWER BLACK FAMILIES

Empowering Black families involves recognizing their agency, cultural richness, and history of resistance. Grounded in the principles of Black psychology, which emphasize self-definition, interdependence, and resilience, empowerment interventions affirm the dignity, leadership, and strengths of Black caregivers. As previously stated in this chapter, educators must move beyond simple transactional engagement and foster liberatory partnerships that uplift Black families as co-educators and change agents. The following are interventions that promote Black family empowerment.

Narrative Shifting: From Deficit to Dignity

Historically, post-integration schools have often viewed Black families through a deficit lens, focusing on what is "lacking" rather than on what is powerful and present. Narrative shifting means replacing these harmful assumptions with affirmations of Black family and parental leadership, advocacy, and cultural knowledge. Educators must actively recognize and acknowledge the wisdom, care, and commitment Black parents and caregivers bring. Here's an example:

> *Instead of framing a student's late assignment as a sign of parental neglect, an elementary school teacher in Atlanta took the time to speak with the student's grandmother, who was raising him. The teacher reframed the conversation around the family's dedication, asking how she could better support the grandmother, her schedule, and her commitment to the student. This shift built trust and led to a more collaborative learning plan.*

Racial Acknowledgment: Honoring Identity and History Racial acknowledgment involves intentionally uplifting the histories, traditions, and experiences of Black communities. It requires educators to view Blackness not as something to "overcome," but as something to affirm. This includes integrating the contributions of Black leaders, thinkers, and cultural practices into the curriculum, schoolwide events, and conversations about justice. Here's an example:

> *A middle school in a northeastern suburb began hosting "Family Heritage Nights" co-led by parents. At these events, families shared traditions, music, and resistance stories from across the African diaspora. The events helped students and caregivers feel seen, validated, and included in the school's cultural narrative.*

Access to Data: Equipping Families to Advocate Providing families with data on student performance and outcomes serves as a powerful advocacy tool. When families obtain detailed information about discipline disparities, advanced course enrollments, gifted and talented programs, special education, and other achievement metrics, they are empowered to advocate more effectively for their children and ensure accountability within the educational system. For instance:

> *At a high school in a midwestern city, the administration launched a "Data Equity Night" where families could see dashboards disaggregated by race and learn how to use that data to advocate for AP placement, mental health supports, and policy change. Black parents led follow-up sessions to share strategies and push for reforms.*

Culturally Responsive Communication: Building Respectful Relationships Schools often unintentionally isolate families by using complex language, impersonal outreach methods, or neglecting cultural norms. Culturally responsive communication involves incorporating the languages present in the community, respecting names and titles, actively listening, and ensuring consistent follow-up. Communication must validate identity rather than undermine it. For instance:

> *A rural district in North Carolina trained all staff to avoid jargon in communications and ensured that all school messages were available in accessible formats. All families, including Black families, reported a significant increase in understanding, satisfaction, and willingness to attend meetings after feeling more respected in how they were approached and messaged.*

Parent Education Programs: Empowering Through Knowledge Empowerment also includes supporting families beyond the classroom. By offering educational programs in financial literacy, homeownership, health equity, and entrepreneurship, we acknowledge the connection between education, economics, and overall well-being. For example:

In a suburban school district, a community school partnered with a Black-owned, community nonprofit to offer weekend workshops on financial planning and home buying. Parents expressed feeling more hopeful and confident about supporting their children's education but also about building generational stability.

Policy Advocacy: Building Capacity to Influence Systems True empowerment happens when families transition from simply receiving policy decisions to becoming co-creators of policy. Schools can clarify policy processes, educate parents on advocacy, and support them in attending school board meetings and legislative hearings. For instance:

A coalition of Black parents, with the backing of school leaders, effectively testified before the State Senate to prevent proposed changes to the school curriculum that would eliminate Black History Month and other essential Black historical content. Thanks to their efforts, the Senate vote was notably closer, and the legislation was successfully stopped.

Emotional Support: Centering Culturally Competent Healing Considering the racialized trauma that Black families frequently encounter, it is essential for schools to provide culturally relevant emotional support. This involves hiring Black mental health professionals who are attuned to the lived experiences of both students and their families, creating affirming environments conducive to healing. Here's an example:

A middle school in a small city created a "Wellness Room" led by a Black clinician trained in trauma-informed and Afrocentric wellness practices. Students and parents could access drop-in sessions that provided both counseling and cultural affirmation.

Community Forums: Co-Creating School Culture Community forums offer Black families a platform to express their priorities, propose solutions, and co-lead school transformation. These are not one-off town halls but ongoing, relational spaces where families influence the school's agenda. Here's an example:

A majority Black charter school hosts monthly "Parent Power Hours," where caregivers drive the conversation. Topics have included school safety, Black Studies curriculum, and school climate. Their input has directly shaped hiring practices and educator professional development offerings.

Strength-Based Black Parent Consultation Consultation with Black families should always begin with trust, respect, and an understanding of the historical trauma experienced by Black people. As Harry and Gibbs emphasize, educators must resist deficit assumptions and instead build relational partnerships when implementing parental consultation.[27] Effective consultation affirms the family's knowledge, frames concerns within the family and community contexts, and invites collaboration rather than correction. Here's an example:

> *When Ms. Rogers received a call from her daughter Jordan's counselor, the conversation began with affirmations of Jordan's leadership, creativity, and potential. Rather than opening with the counselor's concern about Jordan's recent grades, the counselor asked how the school could better support Jordan. Ms. Rogers shared her worries about homework completion. Together, they co-created a plan including a tutoring referral and a more flexible homework deadline, grounded in respect and partnership. This approach defused defensiveness and modeled how educators can support students while honoring the family's strengths and context.*

All the above interventions correspond with fundamental aspects of Black psychology, which include safeguarding and promoting cultural identity, prioritizing community, and striving for liberation via collective empowerment. Schools implementing these practices recognize and elevate Black families as crucial leaders in their children's educational journeys.

BLACK PARENTING PRACTICES, HISTORICAL CONTEXT, AND THE BALANCE OF EMPOWERMENT AND PROTECTION

Black parenting practices in the United States are deeply intertwined with a long legacy of resistance, protection, and community support. From the time of enslavement to today, Black caregivers have had to raise their children in a society that frequently criminalizes their existence and pathologizes their behavior. Consequently, Black parenting often embodies what scholars term a "racial socialization imperative" or the deliberate preparation of children to navigate and endure racism while fostering pride in their identity.[28] Historically, Black parents have had to parent defensively. During enslavement, Black parents had no legal authority over their children. Under Jim Crow, Black families had to train their children in strict codes of deference to avoid violence. In more recent history, Black parents have taught their children how to survive police encounters, discriminatory classrooms, and biased disciplinary systems. These realities have shaped parenting styles that emphasize respect, resilience, and self-protection, traits often misunderstood by educators unfamiliar with the cultural or historical context.[29]

Yet, despite these challenges, Black parenting is characterized by empowerment, warmth, and an aspirational vision. It is infused with oral tradition, communal values, spirituality, and a profound sense of responsibility to ensure that children thrive. However, schools often misinterpret Black parenting norms through a white middle-class lens. Assertive communication, strict discipline at home, or cultural parenting values are sometimes flagged as "inappropriate," leading to disproportionate reporting of Black families to child protective services.[30] These actions can erode trust, disrupt family units, and reinforce historical trauma. At the same time, schools are legally obligated to report suspected abuse or neglect. This responsibility is essential for protecting all children, including Black children, from harm. The challenge and opportunity lie with educators in building relationships with Black families and not relying on biased assumptions.

Educators and mandated child welfare reporters must undergo training on the cultural context of Black parenting. Culture is grounded in shared storytelling, collective values, spirituality, and a deep sense of responsibility to ensure that children are safe. Although no form of harm or abuse is ever acceptable, it is crucial for educators and mandated reporters to differentiate between harmful behavior and culturally rooted disciplinary practices or communication styles. Too often, schools misinterpret Black parenting norms through a white, middle-class lens. Assertive communication, firm discipline at home, or culturally based expressions of care are sometimes wrongly labeled as "inappropriate," leading to disproportionate reporting of Black families to child protective services.[31] Understanding cultural context is a vital step toward achieving equity and justice in school-family partnerships. Training should be ongoing, nuanced, and informed by experts in Black family systems and child development. To support both the empowerment of Black families and educators' legal duty to protect students, educators must approach child welfare with care, cultural awareness, and relational integrity. When concerns arise, educators should begin with collaborative interventions whenever it is safe and suitable. They can hold family conferences, refer families to community-based support services, or involve culturally responsive counselors and mental health professionals in school lessons and activities. These early steps help preserve the family's dignity while addressing concerns in a constructive manner.

In many cases, involving cultural liaisons or community advocates in child abuse cases is essential. These trusted figures can mediate difficult conversations, clarify misunderstandings, and advocate for solutions that honor both family realities and student well-being. Their presence affirms the importance of cultural context in child welfare decisions. Furthermore, when a formal report is required, schools must approach the process with transparency and care. Educators should explain the rationale for the report, clarify the subsequent steps, and communicate the rights of families within the system. Reporting should never be used punitively or coercively; it must be framed as a legal mandate that does not preclude ongoing support and collaboration. When handled with respect and honesty, even mandated actions can preserve a foundation of trust and partnership between schools and families.

Remember, Black families have long been forced to protect their children not only from physical danger but also from the psychological harm inflicted by systems that do not value their lives. Schools must honor the resilience and strength of Black parenting while fulfilling their legal obligations to protect students. This requires cultural understanding, partnership, and a commitment to empowerment rather than punishment.

CASE STUDY: REFRAMING THE NARRATIVE—MS. JOHNSON AND THE READING GROUP

Ms. Johnson, a Black mother of three, had always been deeply involved in her children's education. At her daughter Taylor's new elementary school, however, she quickly noticed a pattern. Taylor, despite reading well above grade level, had not been placed in the school's accelerated reading group. When Ms. Johnson raised the concern during parent-teacher conferences, the teacher responded with vague comments about "classroom behavior" and "group dynamics." Ms. Johnson felt dismissed and unseen. Drawing from the advice of the community education liaison, Ms. Johnson scheduled a meeting with the teacher, school counselor, and community liaison. She came prepared with Taylor's reading assessments, report cards, and a list of books Taylor had read independently.

During the meeting, the liaison helped reframe the conversation. Instead of focusing on Taylor's personality and behavior, the discussion centered on Taylor's strengths, love of reading, and missed opportunities for enrichment. The teacher expressed her concerns about Taylor's "attitude";

however, she admitted that Taylor should be in the advanced reading group. The group discussed what the teacher perceived as a negative attitude, whereas Ms. Johnson stated that if Taylor "sucks her teeth again," to let her know. Taylor was placed in the advanced group the following week, and the school counselor launched a teacher professional development series on equity in literacy instruction.

What Worked

- Ms. Johnson's *social capital* gave her both the confidence and tools to navigate the system.
- The school used the moment as an opportunity to learn, not defend.
- The presence of a *cultural liaison* helped foster understanding and accountability.

Discuss if this approach could work in your school setting. Why or why not?

CASE STUDY: WHO GETS TO LEAD?—MR. BENTON AND THE PARENT COUNCIL

Mr. Benton, a Black father of a seventh grader named Isaiah, was excited to join his child's new school community. As a former PTA president at a previous school, he looked forward to contributing his time and leadership. When he learned the school had a "Parent Engagement Council," he attended an open meeting and volunteered to help lead an upcoming event.

Over the next few weeks, however, Mr. Benton noticed subtle patterns that troubled him. His ideas were often overlooked, while suggestions from white parents were implemented more quickly. He was asked to "help out" but was not invited to shape agendas. When he raised a concern about the need for more culturally inclusive events, another parent responded, "Let's not make everything about race."

Mr. Benton left the last meeting frustrated and questioning whether his voice truly mattered. He wanted to stay engaged for Isaiah's sake but was unsure how to proceed. The school principal, who had been copied on several email threads, had yet to reach out.

Reflection Questions

1. How might Mr. Benton's experience reflect broader patterns of exclusion in parent leadership spaces?
2. What assumptions might be at play in how Mr. Benton's ideas were received or ignored?
3. What are some immediate steps the school could take to build trust and meaningfully re-engage Mr. Benton?
4. What role could a cultural liaison, affinity space, or principal intervention play in this context?
5. Have you witnessed or experienced similar dynamics in your school or community? What was the outcome, and what would you do differently now?

CONCLUSION

Historically, Black parents and communities have fought relentlessly for access to quality education, often in the face of institutional exclusion and racialized harm. From the clandestine teaching of enslaved children to the Freedom Schools of the civil rights movement, Black family engagement has always been a force of resistance and hope. It is rooted in a profound understanding that education is not just about academic success; it is also about survival and liberation.

Yet even today, the full contributions of Black families are too often rendered invisible in educational spaces shaped by white middle-class norms. Schools continue to interpret involvement through narrow metrics rather than honoring the many ways Black families support, advocate for, and protect their children outside of formal school structures. This disconnect is the product of systemic barriers that limit access to information, influence, and decision-making power. Uplifting Black youth means uplifting their families. Uplifting Black families means investing in their voices, leadership, and dreams. In doing so, we move closer to an education system worthy of every child.

Chapter Reflection Questions

1. How have historical systems of oppression (e.g., redlining, school segregation, child welfare policies) shaped contemporary relationships between Black families and schools?
2. What dominant assumptions about parent engagement exist in your school or district? Who defines what "engaged" looks like, and how might these definitions exclude Black families?
3. How does your school currently affirm the leadership and expertise of Black parents?
4. How do race and class influence access to social capital in your school community?
5. Consider a time when a Black caregiver raised a concern or advocated for their child. How was their advocacy received? What dynamics were at play, and what could have been done differently?
6. What are the risks of failing to empower Black families, and what are the transformative possibilities when we do?
7. If you could redesign one structure, practice, or policy in your school to better empower Black families, what would it be and why?

PART 3

Changing Systems of Oppression

The opposite of poverty is not wealth. In too many places, the opposite of poverty is justice.

—*Bryan Stevenson, lawyer, activist, author, and founder of the Equal Justice Initiative (EJI)*

CHAPTER 7

Dismantling Policies That Traumatize Black Youth

The policies shaping America's education system have never been race neutral. School policies are the formal guidelines and rules to promote an effective learning environment. These policies cover a wide range of areas, including attendance, discipline, dress codes, grading systems, curriculum standards, student rights, teacher conduct, and parental involvement. School policies, however, have shaped the uneven schooling process for Black students. From the criminalization of Black literacy during slavery to today's racialized school funding formulas, Black students have navigated educational policies that have resulted in the racial trauma discussed in this book. They manifest in the over-policing of Black students, the erasure of Black history from the curriculum, the routine silencing of Black cultural expression, and the systematic denial of access to information, gifted programs, and advanced course offerings.

Grounded in the norms of US society, including white supremacist logic, education policies have normalized educational harm against students considered to be "other." What might appear to be "standard policies," such as zero-tolerance discipline or regulating curriculum content, are often policies cloaked in the language of order and rigor but result in exclusion, fear, and identity-based trauma for Black students. The result is an educational landscape in which Black students are too often "pushed out" and erased from the perception of excellence.

Black families, educators, and advocates have long pushed back against harmful policies. Building on this tradition of advocacy, researchers such as Iruka and colleagues have published reports such as "The National Agenda for Black

Children," which calls for bold and systemic policy changes, including child tax credits and antidiscrimination legislation in schools.[1] This chapter focuses on five school policy areas that reflect historical patterns and drive contemporary disparities and trauma:

1. school policing and hardening, which have criminalized Black students under the guise of safety
2. hair discrimination, which targets Black identity through punitive dress code enforcement
3. gifted and talented education, which often excludes Black learners through biased criteria
4. curricular restrictions, which erase Black histories and limit students' right to learn
5. special education services, which are needed in Black communities but are often disproportionate and inappropriate

Dismantling or reframing these policies is crucial for prioritizing the well-being of Black students. Achieving this requires a fundamental shift from compliance-driven policy to one grounded in cultural affirmation, racial equity, and collective care. As we explore each of these areas, we must ask: *What would policy look like if it were designed to protect Black children's joy, genius, and future?*

POLICING AND SCHOOL HARDENING: TRAUMA BY DESIGN

For Black youth, schools are often not the safe havens they should be. Instead, they can feel like surveillance zones or spaces where discipline, compliance, and control are prioritized over care, connection, and cultural affirmation. Policies aimed at majority Black schools and set for "safety reasons" have historically translated into increased policing, metal detectors, surveillance cameras, and other punitive infrastructure. These measures not only fail to prevent violence but disproportionately criminalize Black students. According to the US Department of Education Office for Civil Rights, Black students account for 31 percent of school-based arrests, despite comprising only 15 percent of total public school enrollment.[2] This disparity is worsened by adultification bias, in which Black children are perceived as older and more threatening than their white peers.[3] In practice, this leads to Black students being punished more harshly for typical child and adolescent behavior, contributing to trauma, alienation, and the perpetuation of the school-to-prison pipeline.

Although over-policing in urban schools has received national attention, recent research has shown that rural schools are increasingly adopting similar "hardening" strategies, often without the public scrutiny or community oversight found in larger districts. Recent national data show that schools—including many in rural locales—are channeling safety budgets into sworn security personnel and security technologies (e.g., cameras, controlled access, and threat-reporting systems). At the same time, research finds that intensified surveillance and policing practices disproportionately expose Black students and other students of color to harm, reinforcing racialized disparities in discipline and school climate. Although these communities are often portrayed as less diverse, the presence of Black students and students of color in rural areas is growing and so too are the risks they face under racially biased surveillance systems.[4]

Furthermore, data from the Urban Institute indicate that schools serving higher percentages of Black students (urban and rural) are three times more likely to have police officers than school counselors. This dynamic sends a clear message that behavioral control is prioritized over student well-being.[5] To be clear, hardening strategies such as police presence in schools have not been shown to reduce school violence. In fact, Kupchik (2016) argues that such policies foster a culture of fear, lower academic achievement, and disproportionately harm students of color.[6]

It's important to note that Black girls are especially vulnerable in hardened environments. The National Women's Law Center and Southern Poverty Law Center (2024) reported that Black girls are more likely to be disciplined for subjective infractions such as "defiance" or "attitude," categories steeped in racial and gendered bias.[7] These punishments often stem from interactions with SROs who lack training in how to interact with students with care and humanity, which ultimately lead to unnecessary criminal referrals and long-term psychological harm. The problem is not just the presence of security, it's the absence of care.

Despite the significant harm caused by punitive school safety measures, a growing body of evidence points to more effective and humane alternatives. Schools that divest from surveillance infrastructure (e.g., metal detectors, armed officers, and rigid zero-tolerance policies) and instead invest in holistic support systems, such as restorative justice, trauma-informed care, and mental health resources (e.g., school counselors), have seen significant improvements in student outcomes. These approaches have been linked to increased student engagement, reduced disciplinary referrals, and the development of healthier school climates.[8] From a policy perspective, legislation should place clear limits on the presence and role of police in schools. Although the *George Floyd Justice in Policing Act* stalled in the Senate in 2021, it remains a model for increasing law enforcement transparency and reducing the negative impact of policing on public education. Furthermore, schools must adopt community-led safety planning practices that include Black students, parents, and advocacy organizations in the decision-making process.

Finally, transparency and accountability are foundational. Schools must regularly collect and report data on arrests, suspensions, and police referrals, disaggregated by race, gender, and disability status. These numbers are more than statistics; they are barometers of justice and equity. Without them, schools cannot be held accountable for discriminatory practices or assess the success of reform efforts.

HAIR DISCRIMINATION: CULTURAL IDENTITY UNDER ATTACK

Hair discrimination in schools is not a matter of fashion policy. Instead, it is a clear racial and psychological injustice. When Black students are punished or ostracized for wearing locs, braids, afros, or twists, it sends a clear and damaging message that their natural selves are unwelcome. This type of regulation reflects the deep roots of anti-Blackness embedded in schools and educational norms steeped in white norms.[9]

These policies of bias function as assaults on Black self-esteem and racial identity. Studies show that repeated exposure to racial discrimination, including hair-based bias, can erode self-concept, increase symptoms of depression and anxiety, and negatively impact academic achievement.[10] For Black girls in particular, hair-related discrimination can lead to internalized shame and withdrawal from school engagement. This psychological harm is cumulative, traumatic, and deeply rooted in histories of colonialism and white supremacy.[11]

Black psychology offers a vital counter-framework. Scholars such as Linda James Myers (1993) and Wade Nobles (2006) argue that cultural affirmation is an essential component of Black students' well-being. From this perspective, hair is not just hair, it is a living expression of ancestral legacy, resilience, and identity. When schools restrict Black hair or punish students for their hairstyles, they are attacking Black students' cultural heritage and psychological empowerment. A strength-based approach to education demands that we affirm Black identity. Educators and school leaders must revise dress codes that disproportionately target Black students and instead co-create inclusive policies with families and students.

Legal protections such as the CROWN Act (Creating a Respectful and Open World for Natural Hair) are essential. Passed by the US House in 2021 but stalled in the Senate, the Act seeks to prohibit discrimination based on hair texture and protective styles nationwide. In the absence of federal action, over 30 states and Washington, D.C., have enacted their own CROWN legislation as of 2024[12] (see table 7.1). However, legal policy alone is insufficient. It is incumbent upon educators to internalize the intent of such laws and implement them in their daily interactions with students.

In addition to hair discrimination, numerous studies have indicated that Black students are subjected to hair-related harassment, teasing, or bullying at school. Educators can turn this around by having students explore the topic of hair discrimination more deeply. Hearing students' thoughts on the issue can provide valuable insights.[13] Additionally, educators can diversify the books, historical and contemporary figures discussed in class, images displayed throughout the school, and the guests invited to speak. They can create opportunities to increase diverse hair representation and foster an identity-affirming environment that benefits all students.

GIFTED AND TALENTED EDUCATION: SORTING BY BIAS

For decades, gifted and talented education in the United States has been viewed as a pathway to academic rigor, enrichment, and future college and career opportunities. Yet for many Black students, that pathway has been systematically obstructed. Despite the presence of exceptionally talented Black children in every community and classroom, they remain consistently underrepresented in gifted and talented (G/T) programs nationwide. According to the US Department of Education data, Black students represent only about 10 percent of G/T enrollments, despite constituting nearly 15 percent of the total public school population.[14] These disparities are not due to a lack of giftedness but rather stem from

TABLE 7.1 States with CROWN laws

State	*Year enacted*	*Notes*
California	2019	First state to enact the CROWN Act
New York	2019	
New Jersey	2019	
Virginia	2020	
Colorado	2020	
Washington	2020	
Maryland	2020	
Delaware	2021	
Connecticut	2021	
New Mexico	2021	
Nebraska	2021	
Nevada	2021	
Oregon	2021	
Maine	2022	
Louisiana	2022	
Illinois	2022	
Massachusetts	2022	
Tennessee	2022	
Alaska	2022	
Texas	2023	
Michigan	2023	
Minnesota	2023	
Arizona	2023	Enacted via executive order
Arkansas	2023	
Vermont	2024	
New Hampshire	2024	
District of Columbia	2020	Enacted protections against hair discrimination

a legacy of exclusion rooted in racist ideology (e.g., Eugenics) and discriminatory educational policy.

The origins of G/T programming in the United States are intertwined with the Eugenics movement, which sought to measure and rank human intelligence through biased tools such as IQ tests, often with the explicit goal of proving the superiority of white, upper-class children. These tests, introduced in the early twentieth century, became gatekeepers to elite educational programs and were used to justify the segregation and marginalization of Black students. Eugenicists such as Lewis Terman, credited with advancing intelligence testing in schools, believed that Black and immigrant children were inherently less capable, which is a belief that shaped early gifted identification protocols and continues to haunt the field today.[15] As a result, gifted programs became not only academic accelerators but also social and economic sorting mechanisms, offering access to advanced curriculum, experienced teachers, and leadership development for some, while denying it to others.

To this day, many school districts rely on teacher referrals or standardized test scores to determine giftedness. However, brilliance exists everywhere. When schools fail to recognize the cultural, linguistic, and intellectual diversity of giftedness, they perpetuate a system of educational gatekeeping. A truly equitable education system must reject the remnants of Eugenic thinking and embrace universal screening, culturally responsive pedagogy, and community-informed definitions of giftedness. The genius of all children should be reflected in gifted and talented programs.

States are not federally required to offer or equitably fund gifted education, resulting in significant disparities. Despite similar test scores and grades, Black students are frequently overlooked. Policies that maintain strict test-based criteria or fail to use universal screening replicate educational tracking that *Brown v. Board of Education* sought to dismantle. Recommendations from the National Association for Gifted Children and researchers like Ford and Moore call for detracking, culturally responsive assessments, and multiple pathways for identification to ensure equitable access to gifted programs.[16]

Donna Ford, a nationally renowned expert in gifted education and equity, has spent her career calling out the systemic racism embedded in G/T identification and programming.[17] Her work is grounded in the belief that giftedness exists in every racial and socioeconomic group, but traditional identification methods, rooted in bias and deficit-thinking, routinely deny Black students access to enrichment and opportunity. Ford's scholarship offers a concrete, research-driven roadmap for transforming G/T education into policies that ensure a more inclusive and just system. The following are her ideas for transforming gifted programs through policy changes.

1. Universal Screening for Giftedness

Ford argues that relying on teacher referrals perpetuates racial bias. Instead, she champions universal screening policies that test all students rather than only those recommended, to uncover giftedness in underrepresented groups. Research indicates that universal screening significantly increases the identification rates of students who are Black or Latino.[18] This method ensures that brilliance is not filtered through teacher bias or narrow conceptions of intelligence.

2. Culturally Responsive and Valid Assessment Tools

Ford consistently critiques the cultural bias inherent in traditional IQ and achievement tests. She advocates for policies that require multidimensional assessments, including nonverbal tests, dynamic assessment, and portfolios that reflect diverse forms of intelligence. These tools more effectively capture the potential of students from historically excluded backgrounds.

3. Teacher Training in Equity and Cultural Competence

Without explicit anti-bias training, educators often misinterpret the behavior, language, or learning styles of Black students. Ford emphasizes the need for policies that include professional development focused on cultural competence, implicit bias, and recognizing giftedness through a cultural lens. Teachers must be taught to see cultural differences as a strength, not a deficit.

4. Strength-Based Mindsets and High Expectations

A recurring theme in Ford's work is the rejection of deficit-based narratives. She urges educators to view Black students through a strength-based framework, recognizing cultural wealth, resilience, creativity, and leadership as markers of giftedness. This reframing aligns with Black psychology's emphasis on self-efficacy and the affirmation of racial identity.

5. Accountability for Equity in G/T Enrollment

Ford calls for policies that require systemic data tracking to hold districts accountable for racial disproportionality. She recommends conducting equity audits, disaggregating G/T enrollment data by race and socioeconomic status, and revisiting identification policies annually to ensure they do not restrict access.

6. Community and Family Engagement

Engaging families is essential for building trust and identifying giftedness within a cultural context. Ford encourages schools to partner with Black families, honor their insights, and involve them in program development and advocacy efforts. Policies that require family-informed gifted identification result in more accurate, inclusive outcomes, which are key to dismantling faulty gifted practices.

7. Diversifying the Gifted Education Workforce

Ford also underscores the importance of representation. Black teachers are more likely to recognize giftedness in Black students, yet they remain underrepresented in G/T roles and leadership. Recruiting and retaining educators of color is a key step toward dismantling systemic bias in the gifted process.

CURRICULUM CENSORSHIP AND BOOK BANS: A THREAT TO TRUTH AND EQUITY

Since 2020, the United States has experienced a significant rise in efforts to dismantle diversity, equity, and inclusion (DEI) programs and policies. These attacks were formally initiated with Executive Order 13950, issued by President Donald Trump in September 2020.[19] The order banned any federal training that promoted what the administration deemed "divisive concepts," including discussions of white privilege, systemic racism, or critical race theory.[20] Although Executive Order 13950 was rescinded by President Biden in 2021, the ideological momentum behind it continues to shape anti-DEI legislation and curriculum bans across dozens of states. At its core, the order sought to recast historical truth-telling as indoctrination, reframing conversations about racism as "divisive" while reifying white comfort over factual education. This aligns with long-standing white supremacist ideologies that seek to erase the histories of harm to Black Americans.[21]

The resurgence of this ideology has reemerged with the second Trump administration vowing to "eliminate DEI across the federal government" and prosecuting schools and universities that promote what his administration calls "woke" education.[22] Figure 7.1, which presents a timeline of recent book bans, illustrates how these broader political attacks on DEI intersect with escalating censorship in schools. This rhetoric has emboldened efforts to dismantle DEI offices, restrict inclusive curricula, and prohibit teacher preparation programs from addressing systemic racism or equity-based practices.[23] In February 2025, the US Department of Education issued a *Dear Colleague Letter* clarifying how Title VI applies to DEI efforts in schools. The letter signals a

FIGURE 7.1 Timeline of book banning and curriculum restrictions

- 2024: Over 500 legislative proposals introduced: 75% target race, gender, identity
- 2023: Book bans extend to public libraries, curriculum gag orders expand
- 2022: Book bans surge; PEN America reports 1,648 titles banned in one year
- 2021: Wave of anti-CRT legislation; over 100 bills introduced
- 2020: George Floyd protests prompt surge in antiracist book purchases and visibility
- 2017: Book bans increase post-Trump election, with early anti-CRT rhetoric emerging
- 2014: Renewed focus on diversity in education after Ferguson protests
- 2010: Rise of Tea Party-era curriculum challenges targeting "liberal bias"
- 2003: Early challenges to books like *The Bluest Eye* in conservative districts

Source: Timeline created by author (with AI assistance) using data from *PEN America*, "Banned in the USA: the Growing Movement to Censor Books in Schools," 2022–2024, https://pen.org/banned-in-the-usa/; American Library Association, "State of America's Libraries Reports," 2021–2024, https://libguides.ala.org/librarystatistics; Southern Poverty Law Center, "Year in Hate and Extremism Reports," 2016–2023, https://www.splcenter.org; The Education Trust, "CRT and Book Banning Policy Trends," 2021–2023, https://edtrust.org; Meira Levinson, "Curricular Challenges and Civic Education," *Harvard Educational Review*, 2017.

significant shift in the Office of Civil Rights enforcement priorities—one that chills DEI efforts at PK–12 and higher education institutions. Despite that the letter is framed as "guidance" and not law, the fear and threats of retribution continue to silence educators and endanger the well-being of Black students.

These bans and directives are not merely political theater; they are deeply harmful to all students, including Black students and families. Black psychology teaches us that identity development, self-efficacy, and well-being are shaped by cultural affirmation and historical grounding. When schools remove books and curricula that address Black history and the Black experience, they send a message to Black youth that their stories are not valid, their struggles are not real, and their brilliance is not recognized. This is a form of psychological violence, which is a denial of truth that undermines students' sense of agency and belonging. Efforts to erase or distort history are not neutral acts. They are aligned with the goals of white supremacy, which seeks to control not just political and economic systems but also cultural narratives and collective memory. As W. E. B. Du Bois warned over a century ago, *"What is the object of education if not to know the truth and to tell it?"*[24]

RECOMMENDATIONS FOR ADVOCATING AGAINST ANTI-DEI POLICIES

Throughout history, Black communities have responded to oppression with strategic and powerful forms of resistance. From teaching in secret during slavery to founding Freedom Schools during the civil rights movement, Black educators and families have always affirmed the right to learn and to teach truthfully. In this moment of escalating curriculum bans and anti-DEI legislation, educators must draw on that same legacy of courage, community, and collective action.

Educators and school leaders must boldly affirm the right to teach truthful history, including the full scope of Black experiences, resistance movements, and systemic oppression. Silence in the face of censorship is complicity. As Black activists did in the past, educators today must organize and educate. This includes building coalitions with families, civil rights organizations, student groups, and professional associations to resist the erasure of Black knowledge.

Districts should conduct equity audits to examine textbooks, library collections, and course syllabi for racial bias, omissions, and exclusions. Just as past generations reviewed segregated school policies and advocated for desegregation, current leaders must scrutinize educational content to ensure it reflects diverse voices and truths.

Students and families can lead school-based resistance by following in the footsteps of the 1960s student walkouts, parent boycotts, and Black PTA activism. Today, this might involve organizing Banned Books Week events, creating student-led curriculum committees, and testifying at school board and legislative hearings. Youth organizers have always been at the forefront of movements—from the Student Nonviolent Coordinating Committee (SNCC) to today's youth-led protests for racial justice—and they must be supported, not silenced. Legal and advocacy organizations such as the ACLU, the NAACP Legal Defense Fund, and the African American Policy Forum offer toolkits, litigation support, and policy guidance for challenging unconstitutional censorship. These modern efforts echo the legal battles of Thurgood Marshall and Constance Baker Motley, whose work ensured that educational access and justice were pursued in the courts as well as communities.

Ultimately, educators can collaborate with community members, cultural centers, and Black historians to preserve and promote truth-telling in education. Storytelling circles, public art projects, and oral history programs can help preserve narratives that formal curricula often omit. The following is a short list of books that have been banned in states with anti-DEI policies. The list was retrieved from PEN America's Index of School Book Bans (2024).[25] Appendix C includes a longer list of banned books by Black authors or about Black characters. Consider reading these books as a way to oppose book-banning policies:

- *Ruby Bridges Goes to School: My True Story* by Ruby Bridges
- *Mae Among the Stars* by Roda Ahmed
- *The Undefeated* by Kwame Alexander
- *Go Tell It On the Mountain* by James Baldwin
- *Roots: The Saga of An American Family* by Alex Haley
- *Crown: An Ode to the Fresh Cut* by Derrick Barnes
- *The Bluest Eye* by Toni Morrison

Special Education Services: Essential but Equitably Distributed?

The history of special education in the United States is intricately tied to racial inequalities. Since formal special education services began in the 1970s, Black students have been disproportionately referred to and enrolled in such programs, not necessarily due to actual disabilities but largely because of systemic biases and cultural misunderstandings.[26] Significant laws, including the Education for All Handicapped Children Act (1975) and its reauthorization as the Individuals with Disabilities Education Act (IDEA), aimed to ensure appropriate and equitable services for all children with disabilities.[27] Yet, these protections haven't prevented the over-identification of Black students for specific disability categories, namely emotional disturbance (ED) and intellectual disability (ID), which often come with stigmatizing labels and restrict access to rigorous academic opportunities.[28] Despite the intent of IDEA to ensure free and appropriate education for every student, Black students are still more likely than their white peers to be referred for special education services in ways that reflect implicit bias rather than need. Studies have found that Black children are more likely to be disciplined, suspended, or labeled with behavioral disorders, contributing to the school-to-prison pipeline.[29] In contrast, white students are more often granted 504 plans under Section 504 of the Rehabilitation Act, which provide accommodations such as extended test-taking time, help with organization, and college prep supports.[30] These accommodations are framed in empowering ways and are less stigmatizing than traditional special education classifications.

This discrepancy reveals a troubling duality: although Black students are disproportionately placed in restrictive special education environments, white students often receive support plans that enhance their academic performance and college readiness. Furthermore, obtaining a 504 plan frequently depends on parental advocacy, medical documentation, and navigating the school system—areas in which systemic inequities in access and information can disadvantage Black families. Thus, Black students are over-identified in some contexts and underserved in others.

As a point of information, 504 plans are formal accommodations designed to support students with disabilities in PK–12 schools, as mentioned earlier, under Section 504 of the Rehabilitation Act of 1973, a federal civil rights law.[31] These plans are intended for students who have a physical or mental impairment that substantially limits one or more major life activities, such as learning, reading, concentrating, or communicating, but who do not necessarily qualify for special education services under the Individuals with Disabilities Education Act (IDEA). Unlike an individualized education program (IEP), which involves specially designed instruction and is more comprehensive, a 504 plan provides equal access to education through reasonable accommodations. These may include:

- extended time on tests and assignments
- preferential seating
- modified classroom environments
- permission for breaks or movement
- assistive technology or tools
- behavior support plans
- reduced homework load or modified testing conditions

These 504 plans are not intended to give students an advantage but rather to level the playing field, allowing students with disabilities to access the same educational opportunities as their peers. Schools are legally obligated to implement 504 plans once they are established, and parents have the right to be involved in the development and monitoring of the plan. Although they don't require as many procedural safeguards as IEPs, 504 plans are enforceable under civil rights law, meaning schools can be held accountable for failing to provide the necessary accommodations.[32] To ensure equal access to special education services, schools in all neighborhoods and communities must review and address their practices and biases and guarantee access to 504 plans for all families.

How can educators correct the bias in special education? First, educators must acknowledge the historical and systemic biases embedded in the special education referral and placement policies. Professional development in culturally responsive assessment and anti-bias training should be a foundational requirement for all school personnel involved in identifying students for special education services. Second, educators must be trained to distinguish between cultural differences in behavior and true indicators of disability. This requires a shift from deficit-based thinking, where behaviors outside white, middle-class norms are seen as problematic, to a strength-based approach that recognizes the cultural assets of Black students. Additionally, schools should implement multitiered systems of support and response to intervention frameworks, emphasizing both fidelity and equity. These approaches guarantee that prior to any special education referrals, children receive access to evidence-based, tiered support aimed at addressing academic and behavioral issues without preemptively labeling them. Consistent progress monitoring and culturally relevant screening instruments can help ensure that referrals are genuinely based on data rather than subjective perceptions.[33] Last, educators are essential in promoting equitable access to 504 plans and IEP accommodations. All families must have access to both special education options for interventions. Schools can organize informational sessions, offer translated resources, and designate trained advocates or liaisons to help families navigate these complex systems. Ultimately, correcting these injustices requires a commitment to systemic policy change where educators view families and caregivers as partners in determining student interventions and policies that do not perpetuate racial disparities in learning outcomes. By doing so, educators can help build a system where all students, regardless of race, receive the academic services and opportunities they deserve.

CASE STUDY: DISRUPTING INEQUITY IN GIFTED AND TALENTED IDENTIFICATION

Springhill School System, a small district in a northwestern state, has a G/T identification policy requiring that students are screened in grades 2 and 7 based on teacher recommendations and scores from standardized tests, such as the Wechsler Intelligence Scale for Children or the PSAT. In seventh grade, students must be recommended by at least two teachers, and all testing is conducted in English only. Although parents can submit private test scores, there are no documented outreach efforts to explain this process to non-English-speaking or underserved families.

This policy, though seemingly neutral, creates multiple barriers for Black students and other minoritized youth. First, teacher referral systems have been shown to be biased due to unconscious beliefs about race, class, and behavior. As research shows, Black students are under-referred for gifted services even when their test scores are comparable to their white peers. In relying on subjective teacher nominations, the policy introduces gatekeeping mechanisms that disproportionately exclude Black students, particularly boys.

Second, standardized intelligence tests such as the Wechsler and PSAT perpetuate the racial bias present in psychometrics, a legacy stemming from the Eugenics movement when IQ testing was utilized to misrepresent Black intelligence.[34] These evaluations are known to be culturally and linguistically biased, placing students from nondominant backgrounds at a disadvantage. Furthermore, the policy's requirement for English-only testing alienates multilingual learners and students from Afro-Caribbean, African immigrant, or nondominant linguistic families.

Finally, there is no mention of holistic or culturally responsive assessments, such as portfolio evaluations, performance tasks, or alternative indicators of giftedness that may align more closely with Black students' strengths in creativity, leadership, and problem-solving. To correct this policy and create equitable access to G/T programs, the school district implemented a multipronged, culturally responsive identification policy and system grounded in best practices:

1. Universal Screening with Multiple Measures

Every student will be screened for giftedness using multiple tools, including culturally responsive nonverbal tests (e.g., *Naglieri Nonverbal Ability Test*),[35] performance assessments, portfolios, and student interviews. This approach helps to disrupt referral bias and widens the identification net.

2. Equity Audits and Disaggregated Data Reviews

The school system will conduct an annual review of G/T enrollment data disaggregated by race, gender, socioeconomic status, and language background. If Black students are underrepresented, district leaders must revise practices and provide targeted support.

3. Bias and Equity Training for Teachers

Educators will receive mandatory professional development on culturally responsive gifted education, anti-Black bias, and how to recognize giftedness in students from underrepresented backgrounds

4. Parent Advocacy Workshops

Schools must offer accessible parent workshops (with interpretation if needed) to inform families about their rights, the gifted identification process, and to encourage family participation in program design.

5. Community-Sourced Definitions of Giftedness

Schools will collaborate with Black families and communities to co-define giftedness beyond test scores—drawing on cultural knowledge, resilience, leadership, and critical consciousness as valued traits.

The reform of the G/T policy at Springhill Elementary was presented as a justice issue. Giftedness should not be exclusive to the privileged. By acknowledging the talent of Black and other minoritized children and reconstructing systems to support inclusivity rather than segregation, schools can achieve education's fundamental goal: opportunity.

CASE STUDY: DISCIPLINE WITHOUT RESTORATION—A MISSED OPPORTUNITY FOR JUSTICE

At Lincoln Middle School, located in a racially diverse school district, a new school discipline policy was adopted following a high-profile student fight that went viral on social media. The school board, facing pressure from parents and community members, passed a "zero-tolerance safety resolution" to address growing concerns about behavior and safety. The policy mandates automatic suspension for any physical altercation, regardless of context or severity. A three-strike rule applies to verbal conflicts, leading to in-school suspension after the third incident. There is no use of restorative justice circles or peer mediation for students involved in any repeat offenses. Parental notification occurs only after disciplinary action is taken, and students returning from suspension must sign a "behavior contract" without a reintegration plan or support services. Within four months of the policy's implementation, Black students make up 22 percent of the school population but 63 percent of suspensions. Several Black students report that they were suspended for defending themselves against bullying. Black parents have expressed frustration about being excluded from the discipline process. Although white parents support the new policy because it stresses "safety and control," teachers report feeling unsupported and unclear about when they are allowed to use restorative approaches. There is no tracking of how discipline outcomes vary across racial or disability status. Despite the policy's goal of improving safety, student climate surveys show increased reports of feeling "disconnected from school" and "low engagement" particularly among Black students. Meanwhile, Black community leaders have raised concerns about the school fostering a school-to-prison pipeline culture.

Discussion Prompts

1. Analyze the policy.
   What are the key components of the zero-tolerance policy that may disproportionately affect Black students? Which aspects conflict with restorative justice and trauma-informed approaches?
2. Consider the context.
   Why might school leaders feel pressured to adopt a strict policy? What historical or social narratives influence the push for "tough-on-discipline" rules, especially in schools with higher percentages of Black students?
3. Identify equity concerns.
   How does this policy align or misalign with what research says about effective and justice-centered school discipline? What are the racial equity implications?
4. Reimagine the possibilities.
   If you were part of the school leadership team, how would you redesign the policy? What evidence-based alternatives would you propose that balance safety, equity, and student well-being?
5. Create a stakeholder plan.
   How would you engage students, families (especially Black families), and staff in co-developing a revised policy? What role should data and lived experience play in shaping discipline systems?

CONCLUSION

For too long, educational policies have adversely affected Black students by criminalizing their behavior, undermining their brilliance, and erasing their histories. Whether through exclusion from gifted programs, over-identification for special education placement, hair discrimination, harsh disciplinary actions, or the prohibition of culturally affirming literature, these policies have established a system that perpetuates unequal experiences for Black students and punishes diversity instead of celebrating it.

However, policy also holds the power to initiate change. It can transform school cultures from punitive to restorative, from biased to equitable and just, and from exclusionary to inclusive opportunities. When educators view themselves as "policy actors," they take steps to reclaim the system for equity and freedom. Educators can modify policies rooted in white supremacy and create new ones based on love, justice, and a belief in the potential of Black children.

Chapter Reflection Questions

1. Think about a school or district policy you are familiar with (e.g., discipline, gifted education, dress code, curriculum). Who benefits from this policy? Who might be unintentionally harmed or excluded?
2. What are signs that a policy may be rooted in deficit thinking, racism, or exclusion?
3. Anti-DEI efforts often claim that Black history or discussions of race are "divisive." How would you respond to this argument as an educator, policymaker, or advocate? What are the consequences of erasing historical truths in schools?
4. Consider how curriculum restrictions impact not just Black students but all students. Why is it vital for democracy to have the freedom to learn accurate history? What role should educators take in opposing censorship?
5. Educators often see themselves as rule followers rather than rule makers. In what ways can educators influence, rewrite, or resist policies that harm Black students? What actions (small or large) can you take to be a policy advocate?
6. What lessons can we learn from historical Black activism in education, such as Freedom Schools, textbook protests, or parent organizing, that inform our resistance to harmful policies today?
7. If you had the power to design a new education policy to better support Black student success, what would it be? How would it affirm identity, culture, and community?

CHAPTER 8

Mental Health Counseling and Care in Schools

In the African American community, we've been taught to tough it out, hide our suffering, but this is something none of us have ever experienced, and no one should suffer in silence.

—*Taraji P. Henson, actress*

Taraji P. Henson's powerful words illuminate the invisibility of the emotional suffering and declining mental health of Black youth. From the trauma of the transatlantic slave trade to modern-day mass incarceration, the collective psyche of Black people has endured repeated assaults. For centuries, Black Americans have carried the psychological burden of enslavement, segregation, surveillance, economic deprivation, and cultural erasure. Yet access to culturally responsive support and healing for Black people has been unavailable. This legacy of experiencing racialized trauma without treatment has left deep psychological wounds that persist across generations.

The system for providing mental health services specifically for Black students is nonexistent. For Black children, schools often become the only accessible site for psychological intervention, yet there is a continued lack of attention to their specific wellness needs. Instead of acting as centers of support, too many schools, including those predominantly attended by Black students, function as sites of discipline and control. According to the American School Counselor Association, the national student-to-counselor ratio is 424:1, which far exceeds recommended levels; this ratio is even worse in predominantly Black schools.[1] Essentially, Black students are more likely to encounter law enforcement than a licensed school counselor in their schools.[2]

This chapter examines how policy, staffing, and pedagogy can be adjusted to prioritize the mental well-being of Black youth. Guided by the principles of Black psychology and racial equity, the solution to providing mental health support for Black students is not simply to add more counselors but to create culturally responsive systems of care that affirm Black identity and prioritize holistic wellness.

UNDERSTANDING MENTAL HEALTH AND ITS IMPORTANCE

In 2021, the US Surgeon General, Dr. Vivek Murthy, issued an advisory on youth mental health due to the rising and widespread mental health concerns among young people after the COVID-19 pandemic.[3] This was one of the few instances in which the mental health of youth has been at the forefront as a significant national issue affecting school-age children. It was long overdue.

For the sake of clarity, mental health conditions include mental disorders (e.g., schizophrenia) and psychosocial disabilities (e.g., anxiety), as well as other mental states associated with significant distress, impairment in functioning, or risk of self-harm (i.e., suicide). Exposure to unfavorable environmental circumstances, such as traumatic events (e.g., violence), poverty, racism/inequality, and environmental deprivation, increases the risk of experiencing mental health disorders.[4] Mental health also refers to a person's emotional, psychological, and social well-being. It affects how individuals think, feel, and behave and determines how they handle stress, relate to others, and make decisions. Mental health is not simply the absence of mental illness. Rather, it includes positive characteristics such as the ability to manage emotions, maintain fulfilling relationships, and cope with life's challenges.[5]

Mental health risks can affect individuals at all stages of life, but they are particularly impactful during childhood and adolescence. Research on protective factors, such as social-emotional skills, positive social interactions, community cohesion, and coping strategies, indicates that Black students' capacity to endure traumatic experiences relies on enhancing these factors or skills. According to the National Institute of Mental Health (NIMH), nearly one in five adults in the United States (57.8 million people) experienced mental illness in 2021, and approximately one in six youth aged six to seventeen years experience a mental health episode each year.[6] For children and adolescents, untreated mental health issues can disrupt learning, development, and social-emotional well-being, leading to long-term consequences for physical health, academic achievement, and overall life outcomes.

Despite the widespread mental health issues facing the Black community, access to quality care has long been less equitable compared to affluent white communities. For instance, non-Hispanic Black adults are less likely than white adults to receive any mental health treatment (15.3 percent versus 23.0 percent) and are also less likely to be prescribed mental health medications or receive counseling.[7] Furthermore, disparities in mental health treatment for youth commence at an early age. A 2022 report from the CDC found that Black adolescents were more likely to experience persistent sadness or hopelessness but less likely to receive school-based or clinical interventions.[8] These disparities are not solely the result of individual choices; they are embedded in larger complex systems that often oppress the most vulnerable populations, who may be less knowledgeable about treatment options. Black youth frequently experience "racial battle fatigue," a term coined by Smith and colleagues to describe the cumulative emotional and physiological toll of navigating anti-Blackness in educational settings and society at large.[9] This chronic exposure to racialized stress, compounded by insufficient institutional support and a lack of culturally responsive care systems, exacerbates the crisis. When mental health is overlooked or criminalized, as often happens for Black children and Black educators, the outcome is harm, not healing. Recognizing mental health as a vital aspect of Black students' success requires systemic change, school-based mental health interventions, and a commitment to culturally grounded practices rooted in Black psychology.

The State of Black Mental Health Today

As previously stated, racial disparities in access to mental health treatment continue to exist. According to McLean Hospital, only 25 percent of Black Americans seek mental health treatment when needed, compared to 40 percent of white Americans.[10] The COVID-19 pandemic exacerbated this crisis. The Centers for Disease Control and Prevention (CDC) found rising mental health concerns among Black Americans, yet data revealed that Black people were less likely to receive appropriate care. Structural barriers, including the shortage of Black mental health professionals, systemic racism, and stigma within Black communities,

TABLE 8.1 Mental health treatment rates

Mental health treatment	*Non-Hispanic Black adults*	*Non-Hispanic white adults*
Received any mental health treatment in past 12 months	15.3%	23.0%
Took prescription medication for mental health	11.1%	19.1%
Received counseling or therapy from a mental health professional	8.0%	10.9%

Source: National Center for Health Statistics, "Mental Health Treatment Among Adults: United States, 2019," CDC, 2020, https://www.cdc.gov/nchs/products/databriefs/db380.htmCDC.

continue to drive these inequities.[11] Table 8.1 presents nationally representative data from the United States on mental health treatment utilization in 2019, comparing non-Hispanic Black adults *and* non-Hispanic white adults.

Mental health treatment inequities are linked to structural racism, which results in a shortage of Black mental health professionals, along with mistrust of health-care institutions and internalized stigma surrounding help-seeking. These factors contribute to a compounding effect. The CDC noted that although Black students report higher symptoms of anxiety and depression, they are significantly less likely to receive care. The table illustrates these disparities with alarming clarity.[12]

Traditional models of psychology have historically excluded, misrepresented, or pathologized the experiences of Black people. Early psychological theories, rooted in Eurocentric frameworks and influenced by eugenicist thinking, often framed Black behavior and identity as deficient or deviant. These approaches failed to consider the historical, cultural, and systemic factors shaping Black life in America, and they continue to affect how mental health is diagnosed and treated in schools and communities today. Despite the evolution of Black psychology in the late 1960s as a liberatory framework centered on the cultural realities, spiritual values, and resilience of people of African descent, traditional Eurocentric theories of psychology and counseling remain pervasive. Black psychologists like Joseph White[13] argued that Black people must be understood within their own cultural context and not measured against white norms.

Racialized trauma encompasses the ongoing emotional and psychological suffering endured by individuals as a result of both direct and indirect encounters with racism, discrimination, and systemic oppression. For Black people, this trauma is not a one-time occurrence but a continuous experience embedded in everyday life, history, and societal frameworks. The American Psychological Association (2021) states that racism acts as a persistent stressor, affecting mental health outcomes and hindering psychological resilience.[14] Symptoms of this stress can resemble those of post-traumatic stress disorder (PTSD), such as hypervigilance, anxiety, depression, and emotional numbness.[15]

The intergenerational transmission of racial trauma further compounds mental health challenges in Black communities. The work of Joy DeGruy on *Post Traumatic Slave Syndrome* highlights how the legacy of slavery, segregation, and systemic disenfranchisement continues to influence behaviors, coping mechanisms, and psychological responses among Black Americans.[16] Her framework suggests that internalized racism, community mistrust, and survival-oriented behaviors are not pathologies but adaptive responses to centuries of racial violence and marginalization. DeGruy suggests that therapy and counseling should support positive Black identity formation and utilize oral history and narrative sharing for processing generational pain and reclaiming communal healing and agency. Additionally, she advocates for culturally relevant rites of passage that instill pride, historical knowledge, and purpose in Black students. Most importantly, DeGruy draws from liberation psychology by emphasizing that therapy should not only focus on symptom relief but also on liberation from racist, oppressive systems.

Other pioneering scholars in Black psychology have long emphasized the necessity of culturally responsive frameworks to understand and address Black students' mental health. Years ago, Na'im Akbar introduced models that viewed psychological functioning through African spiritual and communal lenses, emphasizing mental health as the alignment of the self with community and purpose.[17] Wade Nobles[18] expanded this work by centering African philosophy and worldview as essential to understanding Black wellness. Similarly, Myers developed the Optimal Conceptual Theory, which connects mental health to harmony with one's cultural legacy, collective identity, and spiritual essence.[19] More recent researchers, such as Kevin Cokley, have critically examined impostorism, racial identity, and academic self-concept.[20] Parham's application of African-centered psychology, particularly the Nigrescence model, helps counselors support healthy racial identity development while addressing the impact of systemic oppression.[21] Lee champions transcultural counseling and calls on school counselors to recognize the sociopolitical realities Black students face, advocating for culturally competent, advocacy-oriented practices.[22] Building on this foundation, West-Olatunji et al. emphasizes relational-cultural theory and the healing power of connection, empathy, and affirming environments in counseling Black youth, particularly Black girls navigating STEM academic areas.[23] Together, these scholars contend that culturally responsive counseling must affirm identity, resist deficit narratives, and actively disrupt the circumstances that endanger the well-being of Black students.

To break the cycles of racialized trauma, schools, clinics, and community spaces need to integrate the work of theorists who have considered anti-Black racism as a factor in the mental well-being of Black students and families. Culturally responsive, strength-based counselors and trauma-informed practitioners who validate Black students' identities and their traumatic experiences are essential to the success of Black students. Additionally, it is crucial to consider intersectional social identities. Interventions such as healing circles, expressive arts rooted in African diasporic traditions, and community-based therapeutic models demonstrate their potential to enhance mental wellness. Most important, mental health initiatives must be paired with structural and policy changes to dismantle the racist systems that perpetuate trauma in the first place. If we do not address the root causes of mental health disruptions, such as over-policing, economic exclusion, housing segregation, and educational inequality, treatment will remain reactive and insufficient. Healing racial trauma necessitates both personal restoration and collective or community liberation.

Depression and Suicide Among Black Youth

The Office of the US Surgeon General (2021) indicates that Black youth are at a heightened risk for depression due to the combined impacts of racism, economic hardships, police violence, and limited access to health care.[24] Historically, suicide rates among Black youth were lower than those of their white and Asian peers; however, they have now exceeded those rates. From 2014 to 2022, the suicide rate among Black youth doubled, currently averaging twice as high as in many areas statewide (see Figure 8.1).[25]

A notable problem in understanding this uptick in suicide rates is the underdiagnosis of depression and the overdiagnosis of behavioral disorders among Black students in schools. Research conducted by Stevenson et al. and Mason et al.

FIGURE 8.1 Black adolescent suicides

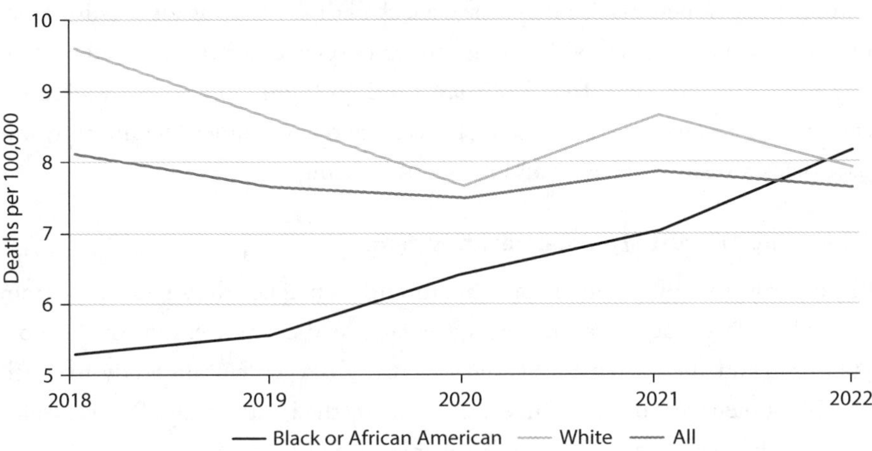

Source: D. M. Stone, K. A. Mack, and J. Qualters, "*Notes from the Field:* Recent Changes in Suicide Rates, by Race and Ethnicity and Age Group—United States, 2021," *Morbidity and Mortality Weekly Report* 72, no. 6 February 10, 2023):160–62. DOI: http://dx.doi.org/10.15585/mmwr.mm7206a4.

indicates that conduct issues in young Black children are frequently mischaracterized, resulting in missed opportunities for timely mental health assistance.[26] Depressive expressions in Black youth are often hidden, misunderstood, or disregarded. Studies show that urban Black adolescents report significantly higher levels of depression compared to their peers, yet again, their reports are not met with increased treatment.[27] Researchers from Rutgers University found that Black adolescents frequently communicate symptoms of depression through physical complaints and personal conflicts.[28] This highlights the importance of educators recognizing nontraditional indicators of emotional distress.

Bias plays a crucial role in how depressive symptoms are treated. According to the American Psychological Association (APA), Black boys are often perceived as older, less innocent, and more threatening than their peers.[29] This stereotype, coupled with a lack of awareness regarding depression in Black boys, frequently results in punitive measures rather than therapeutic interventions.

School connectedness serves as a protective factor against depression. Gale and Nepomnyaschy (2024) discovered that a strong sense of belonging and safety in the school environment is linked to fewer depressive symptoms among Black students.[30] In contrast, when students experience marginalization or a sense of powerlessness, their mental and emotional health may decline. Feelings of alienation can lead to anger, helplessness, and psychosomatic issues, such as headaches or chronic pain. When Black students feel a lack of disconnection and institutional power, they may respond with coping strategies such as defiance, withdrawal, or physical confrontations. Together, these findings highlight the urgent need for educators to reconsider how the school climate and environment significantly impact Black students' behavior and mental well-being.

Addressing Mistrust of Mental Health Systems

The mistrust that Black individuals have toward mental health systems stems from a long history of racial trauma and systematic medical abuse. One of the most publicized and unethical medical events was the Tuskegee Syphilis Study, in which 600 Black men were promised free health care by the United States Public Health Service.[31] However, the investigators never informed the subjects of their diagnosis of syphilis, even though treatment with penicillin was widely available in the late 1940s. This legacy continues to inform Black people's perceptions of medical care today. Research shows that Black Americans are significantly less likely to access mental health services than their white counterparts because of mistrust in the medical system.[32]

Another major contributing factor to Black people's mistrust of mental health providers is the perception that counselors and therapists lack a connection to Black cultural realities. Many Black families report feeling misunderstood or judged by counselors who fail to recognize the role of racism in their lives and who prematurely diagnose their behaviors as pathology rather than cultural expectations.[33] For instance, a Black mother of three is referred to therapy by her primary care provider to help manage stress and exhaustion. During a session with a counselor, she shares that she lives in a multigenerational household and relies heavily on support from her extended family, particularly her mother and aunt. Instead of recognizing this as a culturally rooted strength, the counselor tells her that she may be "too dependent" on her family and suggests that she work toward "greater individuation" from them. She leaves the session feeling judged and misunderstood. As a result of this disconnect, spirituality, community healing, and faith-based coping are often preferred avenues of support for Black people.[34]

Many Black families express skepticism about pharmaceutical treatments for their children's mental health needs. With the rising use of medications for attention-deficit/hyperactivity disorder and psychotropic drugs prescribed to children, Black parents have concerns about overmedication, misdiagnosis, and inadequate communication regarding side effects.[35] Educators who quickly recommend medication for Black students without first establishing trust or considering nonpharmaceutical interventions may alienate these families and reinforce medical mistrust. As Bryant-Davis explains, "Mental health services have often operated from a deficit model, viewing Black people as broken, needing medication, rather than as survivors of broken systems who need to be heard."[36]

To build trusting therapeutic relationships, educators and mental health providers must first validate the historical and present-day reasons for skepticism. They must approach Black families with humility, listen to community narratives, and honor alternative forms of healing, such as prayer, music, movement, and ancestral veneration. Mental health care should also be framed as a tool for empowerment and liberation, rather than just symptom reduction. Mental health programs that use culturally grounded and community-engaged approaches have demonstrated success in increasing engagement among Black students and their families. For example, the "Healing Hurt People" initiative in Philadelphia uses peer navigators and trauma-informed counseling rooted in African American cultural strengths. Participants have shown improved emotional functioning and greater trust in mental health systems.[37] In schools, this means taking the time to consider the potential risks of recommending medications, involving caregivers at every step of mental health discussions, and incorporating wellness practices that align with cultural values.

CENTERING BLACK PSYCHOLOGY IN SCHOOL-BASED MENTAL HEALTH

Mental health programs in schools that focus on Black psychology frameworks and approaches address the profound effects of racialized trauma faced by Black youth. These approaches challenge dominant Eurocentric paradigms by emphasizing healing, cultural affirmation, ancestral connection, and collective identity. However, the implementation of such approaches is hindered by a severe shortage of school-based mental health professionals in general and an even more severe shortage of professionals trained in Black psychology principles. According to the American School Counselor Association (ASCA), the national student-to-counselor ratio is approximately 385:1, far exceeding the recommended 250:1 ratio.[38] The situation is often worse in schools with high percentages of Black and low-income students, precisely the populations most affected by trauma and systemic inequities. Without access to trained counselors who understand culturally responsive care, many Black students are left unsupported, pathologized, or criminalized rather than affirmed and healed.

To effectively support the mental health of Black students, school-based programs rooted in the principles of Black psychology are successful. Unlike Western mental health frameworks that prioritize individualism and emotional detachment, Black psychology defines wellness as alignment with one's purpose, ancestry, community, and the universe. In practice, this means school mental health services must go beyond clinical interventions to include racial identity development, restorative practices, and culturally grounded care. Scholars such as Wade Nobles remind us that Black students are navigating the psychological wounds of "spirit murder" or the cultural and psychological dislocation caused by racism and erasure.[39] Healing, he argues, requires cultural reclamation, emphasizing values such as unity (*ujima*), collective responsibility, and spiritual wholeness. Schools, therefore, must become intentional sites of cultural restoration, where mental health providers and educators aren't just neutral service providers.

Additional research affirms that internalized racism and stereotype threat negatively impact Black students' mental health and academic confidence. These findings show that Black students who internalize negative racial stereotypes experience higher rates of anxiety, depression, and lower academic self-concept.[40] This underscores the need for racial socialization practices, where counselors and educators actively affirm Black identity and challenge deficit narratives to build students' psychological resilience.

Culturally Responsive School Mental Health Clinics

Given that Black students are disproportionately exposed to racial discrimination, which contributes to their elevated levels of stress, anxiety, depression, and trauma, school-based mental health programs and clinics are essential for providing immediate support for students. Many schools, particularly high schools, have opted to integrate mental health services and support into their curriculum and operations, including universal mental health screenings designed to capture the unique stressors Black students face such as racial profiling, cultural invalidation, and stereotype threat.[41] Moreover, these clinics include counselors and educators trained in racial literacy and bias recognition, enabling them to respond to student behavior with empathy rather than punishment, thereby creating conditions for healing rather than harm. Researchers such as Ginwright[42] assert that trauma-informed education for Black youth must go beyond addressing individual symptoms and work toward transforming the school climate into one that fosters joy, belonging, and radical healing.

Many Black students face barriers to traditional mental health care, including a lack of insurance and transportation.[43] School-based mental health centers and clinics remove these barriers by bringing services directly into schools. For instance, in Baltimore, the University of Maryland School Mental Health Program demonstrated success by embedding clinicians in schools across the city. Black students reported higher usage rates and more consistent care than in outpatient settings.[44] Likewise, Duong and colleagues found that school-based mental health services improved academic functioning and attendance for students of color, particularly when trust and accessibility were prioritized.[45]

Neglecting racialized trauma in schools can have serious long-term consequences. School-based mental health centers and clinics can address this by offering early identification, prompt support, and culturally appropriate interventions. By embedding mental health services within the school environment, the stigma surrounding seeking help diminishes, particularly for Black students who might otherwise be reluctant to pursue treatment.

Honoring Culturally Grounded Coping Strategies

As previously mentioned, healing within Black communities is often rooted in spiritual, collective, and embodied practices such as prayer, song, dance, ancestral reverence, and storytelling, which are culturally and historically significant. These strategies have enabled Black people and communities to endure harsh environments. Traditional mental health frameworks frequently overlook these vital practices and strategies. For instance, Western psychological models tend to emphasize individualistic traits and coping strategies, such as emotional control, self-discipline, and perseverance. One popularized concept in recent decades is "grit," as defined by Angela Duckworth. Grit is the ability to persevere in pursuit of long-term goals. Although grit has been celebrated in mainstream education for its predictive power over academic success, it has also been criticized for overlooking structural inequalities and placing the burden of overcoming adversity on the individual, often in ways that sidestep systemic racism.[46] For Black students, the cultural demand for grit can be double-edged. On one hand, many Black youth already demonstrate grit, often navigating hostile school environments, racial microaggressions, and societal bias with remarkable determination. Studies have found that grit, when combined with racial identity affirmation and a sense of community support, can serve as a coping mechanism.[47] However, when grit is valorized without acknowledgment of the external burdens Black students bear, it can become another form of racial gaslighting, suggesting that success hinges solely on effort rather than also addressing discriminatory barriers.

Culturally grounded coping strategies emphasize collective healing over individual perseverance. Practices such as peer-led healing circles, expressive arts, movement-based therapy (e.g., stepping, double Dutch, dance), and spiritual practices not only help students process trauma but also restore their identity and connection. Belgrave and Brevard found that grounded coping strategies significantly improved the resilience, emotional regulation, and sense of cultural pride of Black students.[48] Programs like the "Healing Generations Institute" and "Youth Speaks" have demonstrated that when Black students are encouraged to engage in culturally relevant expression through poetry, drumming, or community storytelling, they not only develop coping skills but also experience increased school engagement, reduced stress, and improved academic outcomes.[49]

Critically, educators and mental health providers must distinguish between coping strategies that affirm Black students and those that unintentionally burden them. Encouraging Black students to "just work harder" or "grind through adversity" without structural support may reinforce trauma rather than heal it. Instead, educators and mental health professionals should adopt a dual approach: one that empowers students with agency and perseverance (including grit, when culturally contextualized), while also validating collective, spiritual, and ancestral practices as powerful tools for survival and flourishing.

Engaging Families and Communities as Healers

Healing within Black communities has generally been based on collective traditions rather than individual care models. Families, elders, and community members serve as crucial agents of healing. Black or African-centered psychology views mental health as a communal responsibility, intertwining wellness with family, ancestors, and the larger community. Current studies show that involving family systems in counseling for Black youth enhances their outcomes in mental health, academic participation, and identity growth.[50] Traditional Western counseling approaches overlook important cultural dynamics. However, culturally responsive models acknowledge the vital roles of caregivers, extended family, and elders in cultivating the resilience and spiritual strength of Black students.

Redefining family engagement extends beyond conventional parent-teacher meetings. Educators must actively partner with caregivers by offering culturally relevant workshops, intergenerational storytelling circles, and community forums that honor Black histories, traditions, and resilience. McWayne and colleagues highlight that culturally aligned family engagement strategies—such as hosting communal gatherings, valuing oral histories, and incorporating grandparents and chosen family members—build trust and nurture more authentic relationships between schools and communities.[51]

The Role of Elders and Intergenerational Healing

In many African traditions, elders are revered not only as wisdom-keepers but also as spiritual and moral anchors for the community.[52] Engaging elders in school-based mental health initiatives can facilitate protective factors for Black youth exposed to systemic racism.[53] Elders also help transmit culturally congruent coping strategies, such as communal prayer, ritual music, and cultural pride. When educators dismiss extended family members from mental health efforts, they perpetuate the very alienation that many Black families historically experienced from educational and clinical institutions. Families, elders, and community members are critical agents of healing. Schools should actively partner with caregivers through culturally responsive parent workshops, intergenerational storytelling circles, and forums that elevate cultural wisdom. This approach aligns with Black psychological traditions that view wellness as a communal responsibility.

Who Provides Mental Health Services to Black Students?

A transformative mental health model must normalize seeking help, reduce stigma, and provide accessible, in-school services that are culturally responsive and aligned with community needs. This includes hiring more diverse counselors and mental health providers, particularly Black counselors in schools with Black students. Only 11 percent of school counselors identify as Black,[54] leaving many students without access to professionals who understand their backgrounds, or the unique stressors tied to navigating racism. Without this cultural congruence, counseling services may fail to build trust or address the full scope of students' needs.

The need for counselors in schools, rather than police, is a well-documented crisis, but it falls especially hard on majority Black schools, where students often face the dual burden of under-resourced learning environments and heightened exposure to racialized trauma and stress.[55] As stated earlier, the ASCA recommends a student-to-counselor ratio of 250:1, and the national average currently stands at approximately 376:1. Table 8.2 includes student-to-counselor ratios for each state.[56.] These ratios mask deeper disparities. In many urban districts that serve large Black student populations, ratios can exceed 500:1, and in some schools, counselors are entirely absent or unprepared. According to the Education Trust, schools serving high percentages of Black and Latino students are significantly less likely to have access to school counselors compared to predominantly white schools.[57] In fact, nearly one in five high schools with high Black and Latino enrollment do not have a single school counselor. These schools are also more likely to rely on punitive disciplinary practices instead of holistic, supportive services fueling the school-to-prison pipeline and reinforcing cycles of trauma and disengagement. Again, these disparities are harmful and increase the risk of placing Black students in positions of inopportunity and harm. Black students are often left without access to trusted adults who can support them academically, emotionally, and socially.

The absence of adequate school counseling in Black schools is a justice issue. Ensuring Black students have access to well-trained, culturally responsive school counselors must be a national policy priority. Investments in equitable staffing, improved pipeline programs for Black counselors, and trauma-informed practices rooted in Black psychology principles are essential to affirming Black students and their families.

SOCIAL-EMOTIONAL LEARNING CURRICULA FOR BLACK SCHOOL-AGE STUDENTS

The integration of social-emotional learning (SEL) curricula into educational settings has gained significant traction to foster students' mental wellness, social awareness, relationship skills, and responsible decision-making.[58] For Black

TABLE 8.2 Student-to-school counselor ratios by state (2023–2024)

State	*Ratio*	*Meets ASCA recommendation?*
Alabama	432:1	☒ No
Alaska	378:1	☒ No
Arizona	667:1	☒ No
Arkansas	347:1	☒ No
California	464:1	☒ No
Colorado	278:1	☒ No
Connecticut	320:1	☒ No
Delaware	253:1	☒ No
Florida	454:1	☒ No
Georgia	361:1	☒ No
Hawaii	249:1	☑ Yes
Idaho	391:1	☒ No
Illinois	314:1	☒ No
Indiana	348:1	☒ No
Iowa	289:1	☒ No
Kansas	296:1	☒ No
Kentucky	310:1	☒ No
Louisiana	441:1	☒ No
Maine	297:1	☒ No
Maryland	332:1	☒ No
Massachusetts	289:1	☒ No
Michigan	598:1	☒ No
Minnesota	296:1	☒ No
Mississippi	372:1	☒ No
Missouri	328:1	☒ No
Montana	291:1	☒ No

Continued

TABLE 8.2 *continued*

State	*Ratio*	*Meets ASCA recommendation?*
Nebraska	339:1	☒ No
Nevada	444:1	☒ No
New Hampshire	191:1	☑ Yes
New Jersey	329:1	☒ No
New Mexico	310:1	☒ No
New York	328:1	☒ No
North Carolina	343:1	☒ No
North Dakota	297:1	☒ No
Ohio	348:1	☒ No
Oklahoma	363:1	☒ No
Oregon	372:1	☒ No
Pennsylvania	328:1	☒ No
Rhode Island	253:1	☒ No
South Carolina	372:1	☒ No
South Dakota	328:1	☒ No
Tennessee	372:1	☒ No
Texas	444:1	☒ No
Utah	500:1	☒ No
Vermont	171:1	☑ Yes
Virginia	378:1	☒ No
Washington	339:1	☒ No
West Virginia	361:1	☒ No
Wisconsin	330:1	☒ No
Wyoming	298:1	☒ No

Note: The national average student-to-school counselor ratio for 2023–2024 is 376:1, which exceeds the recommended 250:1 ratio.

Source: American School Counselor Association, "Student-to-School-Counselor Ratio, 2023–2024," data source: U.S. Department of Education, National Center for Education Statistics, Common Core of Data (CCD), State Nonfiscal Public Elementary/Secondary Education Survey, 2023–24, v.1a. https://nces.ed.gov/ccd/.

students, the potential benefits of SEL are amplified when curricula are implemented with cultural responsiveness and an understanding of students' backgrounds. Research suggests that SEL programs, when adapted to be culturally relevant, can positively impact Black students' academic achievement, reduce behavioral issues, and enhance their overall well-being.[59] For instance, culturally adapted SEL interventions have demonstrated success in improving Black students' school experiences, particularly their examined social competence and likeliness to be involved in "aggressive" events.[60] This evidence underscores the importance of moving beyond generic SEL programs and embracing approaches that acknowledge and affirm the cultural identities and lived experiences of Black students.

However, educators must make a distinction between the principles of SEL and the tenets of Black psychology. SEL, as commonly implemented, often focuses on universal social and emotional competencies. Although these competencies are undoubtedly valuable, Black psychology is rooted in an Afrocentric worldview and emphasizes the significance of racial identity development, cultural affirmation, and understanding the impact of systemic racism and oppression on the psychological well-being of Black individuals. Black psychology posits that the psychological experiences of Black people are uniquely shaped by their historical and ongoing encounters with racism and the need to develop resilience and coping mechanisms within a society that often marginalizes them.[61] Comparing SEL with Black psychology highlights the potential limitations of a purely universal approach for Black students.

Evidence-based practices for implementing SEL with Black students necessitate a conscious effort to bridge the gap between universal SEL principles and the culturally specific insights of Black psychology. This involves adapting existing SEL curricula or developing new ones that incorporate relevant examples, scenarios, and language that reflect Black students' racial identity, their lived experiences, and the racialized trauma they experience. Furthermore, it requires training educators to understand the nuances of Black cultural experiences, the impact of racial trauma, and the importance of fostering a sense of belonging and racial pride among Black students. Research has shown that when SEL programs are implemented by educators who create Black-affirming classroom environments, Black students report higher levels of engagement and positive outcomes.[62] Therefore, the effective implementation of SEL for Black students demands a commitment to Black psychological principles, a strength-based approach, and a deep understanding of the racism that continues to impact Black students' and their families.

TOWARD A JUSTICE-ORIENTED, ANTIRACIST FRAMEWORK OF SCHOOL COUNSELING

Holcomb-McCoy's framework, presented in *School Counseling to Close Opportunity Gaps*, redefines school counseling as a justice-centered profession.[63] It challenges the notion of counselors as neutral facilitators and positions them as equity leaders committed to dismantling educational disparities. Her six functions of the school counselor's job offer a transformative framework for school counseling, one that integrates seamlessly with culturally grounded coping strategies and healing-centered engagement by centering racial identity, systemic change, and student agency. The following is a description of each function.

1. Counseling and Intervention Planning

Holcomb-McCoy emphasizes that individual and group counseling should be "culturally responsive, trauma-informed, and grounded in empathy and accountability." She also stresses the importance of utilizing strength-based counseling and applying Black psychology principles to uplift Black students' cultural, racial, and spiritual backgrounds as strengths rather than deficits.

2. Consultation

Consultation with teachers, administrators, and families must be rooted in advocacy and cultural humility. Holcomb-McCoy asserts that parent and teacher consultation is not passive; it is a form of activism when we use it to interrupt bias and push for equity. School counselors are called to challenge educators' assumptions; help dismantle deficit thinking and co-create strategies that affirm rather than pathologize Black and other marginalized students.

3. Connecting Schools and Communities

This function emphasizes the significance of linking school-based initiatives with broader community resources. Holcomb-McCoy argues that counselors should understand the ecological contexts in which students live and collaborate with families, churches, grassroots organizations, and social service agencies. These partnerships extend the influence of school counselors and enable students to access culturally relevant support systems, including elders, spiritual leaders, and healers, who are often marginalized in Western models.

4. Collecting and Using Data

Data serves as a disruptive tool when it emphasizes inequities in access, discipline, achievement, and participation. Holcomb-McCoy claims that school counselors have a crucial duty to utilize data to identify and address opportunity gaps. When counselors ignore data, they inadvertently support the continuation of inequities in schools.

5. Challenging Racism and Bias

At the heart of the framework is a commitment to antiracism. Holcomb-McCoy asserts that school counselors are ideally suited to confront racism and bias within their institutions. Although addressing colleagues' racist attitudes can be challenging, it is essential for school counselors to leverage their interpersonal skills to serve as the "voice" for antiracism. Holcomb-McCoy's emphasis aligns with healing-centered approaches that foster structural change.

6. Coordinating Student Success and Support

This final function underscores the counselor's role as the primary coordinator of student services, resources, and support systems crucial for achieving comprehensive student success. From academic assistance and college access initiatives to integrated mental health services, counselors are tasked with uniting a student services unit that affirms students' capabilities and supports them in achieving their goals. Holcomb-McCoy emphasizes that success is measured not just by grades or test results but also by identity development, well-being, and social-emotional flourishing.

Together, Holcomb-McCoy's six functions create a blueprint for school counselors to move beyond checklist advising and compliance-based models toward a justice-driven program. This framework affirms that school counselors are more than gatekeepers to postsecondary opportunities; they are also mental health providers, consultants, and, most importantly, dismantlers of anti-Black racism.

BROACHING RACISM-RELATED EVENTS WITH BLACK YOUTH

Engaging in conversations about race and racism within counseling is essential for culturally competent practice, moving beyond a "colorblind" viewpoint to acknowledge the considerable impact of race on personal experiences. It requires school-based counselors and mental health providers to consistently and intentionally address racial, ethnic, and cultural issues within the therapeutic relationship.[64] Studies show that when therapists actively engage with topics of race, it strengthens the therapeutic alliance, encourages client self-disclosure, and improves the overall effectiveness of counseling, especially for Black individuals.[65] This approach signals to students that their racial identity and experiences are acknowledged, valued, and understood in the therapy environment. The benefits of broaching are multifaceted. First, it can validate the students' experiences of racism and discrimination, which may have been previously dismissed or minimized. As previously stated, Black students and their families often navigate a world where their experiences of racial bias are questioned, leading to feelings of invalidation and isolation. By explicitly addressing race, the counselor creates a space for these experiences to be acknowledged and processed, contributing to the healing and empowerment of Black students. Second, broaching can help students explore how race intersects with other aspects of their identity, such as gender, sexual orientation, and socioeconomic status, providing a more holistic understanding of their lived reality. This intersectional lens is essential for effective counseling with clients who hold multiple social identities.

Studies have shown that people of color are more likely to perceive counselors who broach race as being effective.[66] Conversely, when therapists avoid discussing race, it can lead to a breakdown in the "therapeutic alliance." Furthermore, failing to address race can perpetuate microaggressions within the counseling session, which are subtle, often unintentional, slights that communicate hostility or negativity toward Black people. These microaggressions can have a significant negative impact on Black students' willingness to remain in counseling and their overall trust in the process.

So, how can school counselors effectively broach issues of race? It begins with self-reflection and ongoing professional development. School counselors must examine their own racial identity, biases, and privilege to understand how these factors may influence their interactions with students. It is also crucial to develop cultural humility, recognizing that they are always in the process of learning and that Black students are the experts on their own experience. Broaching should be an ongoing process, not a one-time event. Counselors can use open-ended questions to invite students to share their experiences with race, such as "How has being Black influenced your experiences at school?" or "What has it been like for you, as a Black student, at this school?" Furthermore, it is important to listen actively, validate the student's feelings, and create a safe and nonjudgmental space for them to explore their thoughts and emotions related to race.

All in all, addressing race and racism in counseling is not only ethically imperative but also beneficial to Black students' well-being. Black students need spaces in schools where they can talk openly and feel valued. By creating an environment where race can be discussed openly and honestly, counselors foster stronger relationships with their Black students and promote their healing.

CASE STUDY: *LIVING OUR BEST LIVES*—A CULTURALLY RESPONSIVE GIRLS' GROUP

At a midwestern urban high school where Black girls had the highest dropout and chronic absenteeism rates among tenth graders, a school counselor noticed a pattern of unaddressed mental health concerns. Black girls reported persistent symptoms of anxiety, depression, and stress linked to experiences of racism, gendered microaggressions, family pressures, and social isolation. Compounding the issue, few Black counseling resources existed in the surrounding community.

In response, the counselor launched a school-based group counseling initiative titled *Living Our Best Lives*, designed specifically for Black girls. A psychologist who was a Black woman was invited to co-facilitate the group, ensuring that both facilitation and content were grounded in cultural congruence and psychological safety. The program drew from a Black feminist theoretical framework and principles of Black psychology, both of which affirm the intersecting identities of Black girls and resist deficit-based narratives. Black girls navigate a society that often fails to see their full humanity. This group provided them a space where their whole selves were honored, the counselor later reflected.

The group, held weekly during elective periods, was advertised as a safe, affirming space for students who identify as Black and female (she/her/hers) to prioritize mental wellness, build community, and explore their identities. The format was strength based and interactive, incorporating storytelling, journaling, sister circles, music, culturally affirming media, and African diasporic practices such as *liberatory breathing*, praise poetry, and collective affirmations.

Group Sessions: *Living Our Best Lives*

1. Session 1: Getting to Know Each Other and Our Strengths

Students were invited to share affirmations, family traditions, and sources of pride. Group agreements were co-created using Swahili principles, such as *umoja* (unity) and *kujichagulia* (self-determination).

2. Session 2: Being Black—What Does That Mean?

Girls explored racial identity through visual journaling and discussed moments when they felt both celebrated and marginalized in their Blackness. Conversations highlighted colorism, hair politics, and cultural pride.

3. Session 3: Intersectionality—Being Black and a Girl

Drawing from the pioneering work of Kimberlé Crenshaw, who first coined the term *intersectionality* to explain how overlapping systems of oppression—such as racism, sexism, and classism—interact to shape the lived experiences of marginalized groups, we recognize the importance of attending to the multiple, intersecting identities of students.[67] Students identified how their gender and race intersect to shape their experiences in school and society. They role-played scenarios involving microaggressions and practiced responding assertively and safely.

4. Session 4: Focusing on Nia (Purpose)

Students reflected on their goals and strengths through the lens of *Nia* (Swahili for "purpose"), one of the Nguzo Saba (Seven Principles of Kwanzaa).

They created vision boards, set intentions, and discussed ways to protect their joy and purpose amid external pressures.

5. Session 5: Bringing It All Together—Next Steps

Girls shared reflections, celebrated their growth, and identified strategies to maintain their mental wellness. Each participant received a personalized "toolkit for thriving" that included affirmations, local resources, and words of encouragement from each group member.

The *Living Our Best Lives* group yielded meaningful outcomes:

- *Improved self-efficacy:* Participants reported increased confidence in advocating for themselves in school and personal settings.
- *Increased belonging:* Girls described the group as one of the few places in school where they felt "fully seen and understood."
- *Reduced absenteeism:* Half the group members showed improved attendance over the semester, citing the group as a motivating factor.
- *Emerging leadership:* Several students asked to co-lead a future cohort or start a schoolwide "Black Girls Wellness Week."
- *Trust in counseling:* Participants expressed a greater willingness to seek support from school counselors, naming the presence of culturally affirming facilitators as a key reason.

The group created a space of radical care and empowerment. Rather than focusing on pathology, it affirmed identity, purpose, and healing as collective endeavors. As one student wrote in her journal, *"This group reminded me that being a Black girl is powerful—even when the world tries to make it hard."*

CASE STUDY: "I JUST DON'T FEEL LIKE I MATTER"

Jade is a thirteen-year-old Black girl in eighth grade at a racially diverse suburban middle school. She lives with her grandmother, who has been her guardian since her mother's death. Although her grandmother is loving and supportive, she is managing multiple health issues and has a fixed income. Jade rarely talks about her mother, avoids drawing attention to herself in class, and has not sought counseling before.

Recently, Jade's English teacher noticed that she'd become increasingly withdrawn and turned in a poem that included phrases like, *"No one would miss me"* and *"I'm tired of pretending I'm okay."* The teacher, concerned about possible suicidal ideation, submitted a report to the school counselor. The school counselor, a Black woman trained in trauma-informed care and racial equity practices, arranges a private meeting with Jade the next day.

Initial Counseling Session (Excerpted Script)

COUNSELOR: Hi Jade. I'm really glad you came. I wanted to check in because your teacher shared a poem you wrote, and some of the words really stood out to me. Before we talk more, I want you to know that this is a safe and private space. I'm here to support you, no matter what.

JADE *(shoulders tense, avoids eye contact):* It's just something I wrote. I didn't mean anything by it.

COUNSELOR: Sometimes writing says what we don't feel like we can say out loud. That poem seemed to hold some big feelings. Can I ask—have you been feeling like you don't want to be here anymore?

JADE *(quietly)*: Maybe. I don't know. I feel invisible. At school, at home. Everyone thinks I'm fine, but I don't feel fine.

COUNSELOR: That sounds really painful. Feeling invisible is heavy. I want you to know that your feelings matter. *You* matter. What's been going on for you lately—at home, at school?

JADE: It's just hard. My grandma's tired. I don't want to be another thing for her to worry about. And sometimes . . . I just feel like I don't fit in anywhere.

COUNSELOR: I hear that. And I want you to know, you fit at this school. I'm here for you, and I'd love to work with you on ways to make things feel more manageable. Would that be okay?

(The counselor follows school protocol to complete a suicide risk assessment, coordinates with the grandmother for a family meeting, and refers Jade to a Black, culturally responsive community therapist. The counselor also checks in with Jade twice weekly for continued support.)

Outcomes (One-Month Follow-Up)

- Jade begins weekly therapy with a local Black female psychologist.
- She participates in a small healing circle at school with other girls of color, focusing on affirming identity, storytelling, and art.
- Her attendance and classroom engagement improve.
- Jade shares with her counselor that she's been journaling again and feels "less alone."

Guiding Questions for Jade's Case

- How did the counselor acknowledge both Jade's emotions and her cultural context? What would have been your response as a counselor, teacher, educator?
- In what ways did the counselor work to build trust during the first session?
- What assumptions might a school professional make about Jade's family situation?
- How can educators support students with empathy and without judgment who are being raised by extended family members?
- How might stigma around mental health, particularly in Black families, influence how students express distress?
- What culturally grounded strategies can you use to reduce that stigma in school spaces?
- Does your school have a clear and trauma-informed suicide prevention protocol?
- How might that protocol be adapted to reflect cultural humility and racial equity?
- What school-based supports (e.g., affinity groups, healing circles, peer mentoring) could affirm Jade's identity and reduce feelings of isolation?
- How do you make space in your classroom or office for Black girls to be heard, validated, and seen?

Jade's narrative is typical and underscores the significance of culturally responsive, healing-centered counseling that embraces the complete identities of Black girls. It serves as a reminder to educators that often the most impactful intervention is to listen with compassion, validate without judgment, and foster genuine relationships grounded in care and cultural understanding.

CONCLUSION

Black youth exemplify intelligence, resilience, and promise. However, they often encounter educators who misinterpret or simply don't take the time to understand their emotions and actions. It's essential for educators to prioritize the mental health and well-being of Black students. Teachers, counselors, and school administrators play a crucial role in breaking damaging patterns and collaboratively fostering environments of safety, belonging, and growth. This can be achieved through culturally relevant counseling, trauma-informed classroom practices, or by simply demonstrating compassion and cultural understanding. We need to rethink our perspective, viewing schools as hubs for healing and support. Prioritizing the mental health of Black youth is vital. When Black students are mentally well, they are more likely to attend school, engage more effectively with their peers, and view themselves as responsible and productive members of society.

Chapter Reflection Questions

1. Think about your own experiences with mental health. How do your beliefs, experiences, or cultural values shape the way you interpret student behavior?
2. What systems, programs, or resources currently exist to support Black students' mental health in your school? Where are the gaps?
3. Create a "community care map" identifying local Black therapists, elders, faith leaders, artists, or cultural practitioners who could support students.
4. Design a physical or virtual "healing space" in your school. What elements would make it feel culturally safe and affirming for Black youth?
5. Reread Jade's case study. What would you do differently as a teacher, counselor, or administrator? Draft a care plan grounded in culturally responsive strategies.

6. Look at the mental health staff in your school or district. How racially diverse are they? What are the implications of representation or lack of it?
7. Ask a group of Black students what they need to feel emotionally safe and supported in your school. Listen without defensiveness. Build with them, not for them.
8. Choose one concrete change you will commit to making in your school or practice to support Black students' mental well-being. Share it with a colleague for accountability.

CHAPTER 9

Resistance and Advocacy: The Promise of Healing

To understand the resilience of Black communities is to understand the history of Black resistance as a vital force for liberation. Resistance is a response to oppression; however, more important, it is a practice of self-definition, psychological reclamation, and community care. For Black youth navigating layered injustices such as criminalization, cultural erasure, and intergenerational trauma, resistance becomes both a survival mechanism and a pathway to self-efficacy.[1]

Throughout history, community advocacy and resistance have served as both a healing act and a demand for systemic change. During the civil rights movement, resistance manifested in protests and mass mobilizations, legal battles, and demands for racial integration and voting rights. In the 1960s and 1970s, the Black Panther Party expanded this resistance through grassroots programs, including community clinics, free breakfast for children, and liberation schools that taught Black history and political literacy. More recently, the Black Lives Matter (BLM) movement has continued this tradition by protesting the murders of Black men, such as George Floyd, Trayvon Martin, and Michael Brown. As psychologist Thema Bryant-Davis explains, advocacy is a form of trauma recovery: "Liberation is the antidote to racial trauma. When you feel like the world is against you, organizing reminds you that you are not alone—and that you have power."[2]

Yet every advancement in Black advocacy is historically followed by backlash. The end of slavery brought Black Codes and racial terror. *Brown v. Board of Education* was met with massive resistance and white flight. The election of the first Black president was followed by a surge in white nationalist organizing. Today's

DEI rollbacks, book bans, and anti-CRT legislation continue that legacy of retrenchment. Backlash is the predictable response of a system designed to preserve racial hierarchy.

This chapter examines the profound history of activism and resistance within Black communities. Educators committed to affirming Black students can partner with communities to stand in solidarity with Black families as they advocate for equality and justice. This chapter is an invitation to transform schools into places of hope, healing, and liberation. To resist is to affirm that Black life is worthy of joy, dignity, and freedom. The arts have long been central to that affirmation. From protest music and poetry to theater, visual storytelling, and hip-hop culture, artistic expression has served as a vital form of resistance, healing, and truth-telling within Black communities. This chapter is a call to action for educators to create space for activism and resistance in their curricula, enabling students to utilize their voices, stories, and creativity as tools of transformation.

DEFINING RESISTANCE

Resistance in Black communities is an enduring, multifaceted practice of asserting dignity and humanity in the face of systems designed to erase them. It is deeply embedded in cultural expression and community organizing. The author bell hooks reminded us of the power of resistance in this quote from *Teaching to Transgress*: *"Dominator culture has tried to keep us all afraid, to make us choose safety instead of risk, sameness instead of diversity. Moving through that fear, finding out what connects us, reveling in our differences—this is the process that brings us closer, that gives us a world of peace and possibility."*[3]

Resistance encompasses not only the fight for justice but also the fight for joy, healing, and wholeness. Resistance envisions new possibilities in a world that often denies Black people agency, affirmation, and safety. Psychologically, resistance can be understood as a protective factor, a refusal to internalize inferiority or victimhood. According to Anderson and Stevenson, acts of resistance serve as cultural buffers against racial stress and trauma, contributing to greater self-efficacy, especially among youth.[4] Black resistance is also collective and rooted in kinship and community memory. It draws from an African-centered worldview that connects the individual to the collective and struggles for ancestral survival. Black resistance in the United States began during enslavement. Enslaved Africans resisted through revolts (e.g., Nat Turner), flight (e.g., Harriet Tubman's

Underground Railroad), sabotage, spiritual retention, and intergenerational storytelling. These were psychological survival strategies. As historian Robin Kelley notes, "Even the quietest forms of refusal—refusing to forget, refusing to be broken—are radical."[5]

During Reconstruction, newly freed Black people built schools, churches, and mutual aid societies in the face of racial terror. When white backlash dismantled Reconstruction through Jim Crow laws and lynching, Black educators, journalists, and women's organizations carried the torch by resisting and mobilizing. Black teachers, especially in the South, were among the most consistent and courageous advocates for Black youth.[6]

The civil rights and Black Power movements significantly heightened national awareness of resistance. Although the civil rights movement emphasized nonviolence and legal recourse, the Black Power movement focused on reclaiming cultural pride, political sovereignty, and the right to self-defense. The Black Panther Party, for instance, developed more than sixty community survival programs, including free breakfast initiatives, health clinics, and liberation schools—each serving as a defiant response to state neglect and violence.[7]

In the 1980s and 1990s, Black resistance responded to the criminalization of Black youth through the war on drugs and zero-tolerance policies in schools. Advocacy groups like the Malcolm X Grassroots Movement and the African American Policy Forum fought against "school pushout" and the criminalization of Black girls and boys. Black feminist scholars, such as Kimberlé Crenshaw and Monique Morris, have exposed how Black girls' resistance is often misread as defiance, leading to exclusion rather than support.[8]

In the 2010s, the BLM movement, founded by Alicia Garza, Patrisse Cullors, and Opal Tometi revived global resistance ignited by state violence and the murders of Trayvon Martin, Michael Brown, Breonna Taylor, and others. Their advocacy extended beyond protest signs. BLM activists have stressed and recommended policy demands, reshaped public education discourse, and fought for police-free schools, mental health supports, and affirming curricula.[9]

Yet, as previously stated, resistance always invites backlash. Just as Black advancements during Reconstruction led to Jim Crow, the victories of the civil rights era were followed by mass incarceration. Now, in the wake of the impact of the BLM movement, we witness intensified attacks through anti-critical race theory (CRT) and anti-diversity, equity, and inclusion (DEI) laws, book bans, rollbacks of

DEI university programs, and the political scapegoating of Black educators and students. In the early part of the second Trump administration, for example, the administration targeted DEI training, labeled it "divisive," and amplified a moral panic around racial justice that continues to influence policy and public opinion.[10]

WHAT DOES RESISTANCE LOOK LIKE TODAY IN COMMUNITIES AND SCHOOLS?

Resistance is a central theme throughout this book and in all the interventions described within it. Resistance manifests in the way a Black grandmother gathers neighbors to prevent a school closure. It exists in a high school student who demands protection against hair discrimination. It lives in a culturally affirming classroom that teaches students about their ancestors' brilliance rather than focusing solely on their suffering. Resistance in schools encompasses organizing youth healing spaces, offering culturally responsive mental health support, and implementing policies that affirm identity rather than penalize behavior. As stated in earlier chapters, educators must shift their practices to healing-centered approaches that build upon principles of Black psychology, self-efficacy, and strength, prioritizing youth agency, dignity, and connection.

For Black youth, resistance acts as a psychological safeguard. It fosters racial pride, a sense of belonging to the community, and purpose, all essential for buffering against the adverse effects of racial stress. When students and families organize, they reclaim the power to articulate their needs and worth. Black children resist every day in school by emphasizing their lived experiences, cultural foundations, and self-preservation. These actions are often misinterpreted as defiance, disrespect, or disengagement, but they are powerful assertions of identity and autonomy. Viewing these moments through the lens of cultural responsiveness and racial justice can transform how educators interact with students.

Here are several common examples of resistance in schools—and how they are often misunderstood:

1. *Talking back or refusing to comply immediately*

   Often misinterpreted as insubordination, defiance

   What it may actually be is a challenge to unfairness, a demand for dignity, or an effort to be heard in systems where Black children's voices are often silenced.

Reflection: Are we listening to what students are saying or only reacting to how they say it?

2. *Refusing to stand for the pledge or national anthem*

   Often misinterpreted as being unpatriotic or disruptive

   What it may actually be is a protest rooted in political awareness and historical consciousness, especially in response to racial injustice.

   Reflection: Do we encourage critical thinking, or only conformity?

3. *Wearing culturally expressive hairstyles or clothing*

   Often misinterpreted as violating dress code, being unprofessional

   What it may actually be is cultural pride, self-expression, and resistance to assimilationist norms.

   Reflection: Do our dress code policies honor or police identity?

4. *Disengaging in class discussions (e.g., keeping camera off in Zoom sessions)*

   Often misinterpreted as laziness or lack of interest

   What it may actually be is self-protection in classrooms that feel unsafe, invalidating, or culturally irrelevant.

   Reflection: Have we created learning environments where Black students feel affirmed and psychologically safe?

5. *Using African American Vernacular English (AAVE)*

   Often misinterpreted as "improper" speech or poor grammar

   What it may actually be is culturally grounded communication that carries rhythm, meaning, and history.

   Reflection: Are we teaching code-switching as a skill or forcing linguistic erasure?

6. *Challenging curriculum content*

   Often misinterpreted as being argumentative or disruptive

   What it may actually be is a legitimate critique of Eurocentric materials and a call for inclusive, truthful education.

   Reflection: Do we see critical questions as threats or as signs of engagement?

7. *Forming peer groups or affinity spaces*

   Often misinterpreted as cliques or exclusion of white people (e.g., anti-white)

   What it may actually be is a search for safety, solidarity, and cultural affirmation in predominantly white or racially hostile environments.

Reflection: Are we providing spaces where Black students don't just survive, but thrive?

THE RISKS OF RESISTANCE

Resistance is powerful, but it comes at a cost. Those who resist often face surveillance, punishment, and retaliation. Take, for example, professional football player Colin Kaepernick's decision to kneel during the national anthem before a game; he was labeled unpatriotic and subsequently released from his team.[11] Or consider Barbara Johns, a sixteen-year-old Black student who led a school walkout in 1951 to protest the unequal and substandard conditions at her all-Black high school in Farmville, Virginia. On April 23, 1951, Johns led more than 450 students in a walkout, shutting down the school and making national headlines. Her actions caught the attention of civil rights lawyers from the NAACP, including Oliver Hill and Spottswood Robinson. However, Barbara Johns and her family faced harassment and death threats. Crosses were burned near her home, and her family feared for her safety. To protect her, Johns' parents sent her to live with relatives in Montgomery, Alabama, away from the backlash.[12]

The history of Black resistance and its consequences for those who stand up are marked by horrific outcomes. Enslaved individuals who resisted faced whippings and death. Civil rights organizers were jailed, beaten, and assassinated. Today, educators advocating for equity risk job loss, public harassment, and doxing. Youth organizers are policed and often excluded from decision-making spaces. However, history teaches us that the cost of silence is greater. Black communities continue to resist because the alternative is erasure.

DEFINING ADVOCACY THROUGH THE LENS OF BLACK RESISTANCE

Advocacy is often defined as the act of speaking up or taking action to support a cause, policy, or group. In the context of education and Black communities, the term "advocacy" should not be understood as neutral. Instead, it should be rooted in struggle. Advocacy is a form of resistance that confronts inequities, dismantles oppressive practices, and builds pathways for self-determination and healing. For Black educators, students, families, and allies, advocacy is about reclaiming Black narratives and reclaiming the dignity that systemic racism has tried to strip away. It is the legacy of generations who fought for books when literacy was punishable, for Black teachers when schools were segregated, and for justice when silence was safer. In essence, advocacy is a moral and cultural imperative to disrupting anti-Blackness in policy, pedagogy, and practice. Nobles frames resistance and advocacy as tools to reclaim cultural integrity and repair psychic harm caused by racism.[13] Advocacy helps restore what is often denied to Black youth in schools: *voice, visibility,* and *value*. Black feminist scholars, including Patricia Hill Collins and bell hooks, emphasize that advocacy also requires educators to challenge domination in all its forms and to stand in solidarity with Black youth who resist through voice, expression, and critique.[14] To advocate, then, is to engage in a liberatory practice that is both structural and morally imperative.

Advocacy comprises organized actions aimed at highlighting critical issues that have been overlooked, influencing public attitudes, and enacting and implementing laws and public policies to turn visions of "what should be" in a just society into reality. These efforts may involve challenging school policies (e.g., banning books) or raising critical issues (e.g., college-going disparities) that might otherwise be avoided.

There are three primary types of advocacy: self-advocacy, individual advocacy, and systems advocacy. *Self-advocacy* refers to the act of advocating for one's own interests. It involves skills such as knowing one's rights, understanding one's needs, and effectively communicating those needs to others. Black students must learn to advocate for themselves within schools, for example, by seeking more assistance with classwork or by helping educators understand their unique experiences. Self-advocacy is a crucial skill for Black students in the educational process, as it is essential for achieving a sense of well-being.

Individual advocacy occurs when a person (or group) focuses on the interests of one or a few individuals. This kind of advocacy can be informal or formal. For instance, Black parents might advocate at their child's school for the teaching of Black history year-round rather than only during Black History Month (e.g., February). Alternatively, a counselor might advocate for a Black student who was rejected from participating in a college tour at a local university. Formal individual advocacy often takes place through organizations such as government agencies, universities, or nonprofit organizations.

Systems advocacy addresses the needs of many people and seeks change through laws and policies at local, state, or national levels. This form of advocacy can be intricate because the goal is to enact long-term changes in larger systems. Multiple organizations often collaborate to research, raise awareness, and apply pressure on lawmakers. For example, an educator might partner with the local chapter of the NAACP to lift the ban on Black history books in the school district. The NAACP is a long-standing civil rights organization that advocates for justice for Black Americans.

Advocating for Black students and families requires more than good intentions. It demands transforming an educator's daily practice. It's not business as usual. True advocacy resides in a set of competencies that enable educators to move with courage, cultural humility, and critical clarity. These competencies are profoundly ethical, relational, and political. They influence how educators view Black children, how they respond to injustice, and how they co-create liberatory learning environments.

At the heart of advocacy is *critical consciousness*, a framework first articulated by Paulo Freire in *Pedagogy of the Oppressed*.[15] Educators must understand how structural racism, anti-Blackness, and intersecting oppressions manifest in schools and classrooms. Developing critical consciousness involves questioning whose knowledge is centered in the curriculum, who is most often disciplined, and whose voices are excluded from decision-making. Research indicates that when educators reflect on their own power and commit to antiracist practices, school climate and student outcomes improve.[16]

Equally important is cultivating *cultural competence and cultural humility* or the ability to engage with students and families across lines of race, culture, and history with deep respect and self-awareness. This requires educators to learn about African-centered worldviews, Black psychology principles, Black identity development, and the communal values that many Black families hold. Cultural humility moves beyond knowledge toward relational accountability. It challenges educators to unlearn white superiority and to co-create affirming spaces where all students' identities are not only acknowledged but celebrated.

Another essential advocacy competency is *racial literacy*, or the capacity to recognize, name, and navigate racialized dynamics in schools. According to Stevenson (2014), racially literate educators can spot microaggressions, respond to racial stress, and help students process racialized experiences. Racial literacy supports students' mental well-being and builds their capacity to respond with agency rather than internalized harm.[17]

Educators also need to master restorative communication, shifting from punitive reactions to conflict toward dialogue, empathy, and repair. When students act out, they are often communicating unspoken trauma, cultural disconnection, or unmet needs. Restorative approaches center on relationship and healing, allowing students to remain in the community while being held accountable in ways that affirm their dignity. These practices have been shown to reduce suspensions and improve school belonging, particularly for students of color.[18]

In the face of institutional barriers, effective advocates must also develop skills in navigating systems and disrupting them. This entails understanding how to utilize policy, legal protections, and organizational frameworks to prevent harm and foster justice. Holcomb-McCoy emphasizes the crucial role of school counselors and educators in advocating for and conducting equity audits, inclusive hiring practices, and eliminating exclusionary disciplinary policies.[19] Without systemic change, even the most culturally responsive classrooms remain susceptible to larger injustices.

Genuine advocacy also demands ongoing and meaningful partnerships with the community. It is disappointing that educators often perceive families as liabilities instead of leaders. Transitioning from "parent involvement" to collaborative leadership involves appreciating the knowledge of elders, caregivers, cultural advocates, and grassroots organizers. These alliances revive communal healing and decision-making methods that are essential to Black psychological traditions.

Ultimately, none of this work would be possible without courage and accountability. Advocacy means speaking up even when it is uncomfortable. It means being willing to disrupt silence, to take a stand when students are harmed, and to face backlash with integrity. However, it also means being willing to listen, accept feedback, reflect on one's own biases, and commit to continuous learning. The impact of advocacy is profound. When educators move from intention to action, they don't just create better classrooms, they contribute to a better world. They honor Black students' full humanity and build the conditions where joy, resistance, and thriving are possible.

EMPOWERMENT AS RESISTANCE: RECLAIMING AGENCY IN SCHOOLS AND COMMUNITIES

Empowerment plays a vital role in advocacy and resistance efforts, particularly in the pursuit of racial and educational justice. Being empowered means having the ability, confidence, and community backing to act, express oneself, and make choices that confront oppression and affirm personal worth. For Black students and families facing systems that are often exclusionary and anti-Black, empowerment transcends mere motivation; it is a transformational and liberating force. Fundamentally, empowerment is a process that enables individuals and groups to take charge of their lives and the circumstances that affect them. Julian Rappaport, a pioneering figure in empowerment theory, describes it as "a process by which people, organizations, and communities gain mastery over their affairs."[20] In the realm of education, this entails guiding students and families from being passive recipients to becoming active contributors in the development of learning environments and policies.

Empowerment is both individual and collective. Over three decades ago, psychologist Barbara Solomon emphasized that empowerment within Black communities involves resisting imposed powerlessness and building structures that affirm cultural identity and community strength.[21] Empowerment in this context must therefore confront both personal internalization of inferiority and systemic oppression. Empowerment is also contextual, meaning that it cannot be "given" by those in power but must be facilitated through reciprocal relationships, capacity-building, and solidarity. As Paulo Freire wrote in *Pedagogy of the Oppressed*, "No one liberates anyone else, and no one is liberated alone. People liberate themselves in fellowship with each other."[22] Freire's statement challenges simplistic ideas of empowerment as charity or saviorism. True empowerment is co-created through relational, political, and pedagogical work. Empowerment becomes a form of resistance when it disrupts systems of control and creates space for Black agency. In schools, this can take many forms:

- a Black student organizing a Black Student Union to affirm identity and challenge racial harassment
- a group of Black parents advocating for a curriculum that reflects Black history and literature
- a parent supporting a student-led protest against biased dress codes
- teachers co-creating classroom agreements with students to promote mutual respect and shared voice

Every one of these instances entails reclaiming voice, space, and power, which are fundamental to resistance work. When people who have historically been silenced begin to speak, organize, and build, they disrupt dominant narratives and make new futures possible. This disruption is not necessarily well received by others. Educators should be prepared to engage in continuous advocacy and empowerment.

CAN EDUCATORS EMPOWER OTHERS?

As alluded to in the previous section, empowerment is not something educators *do to* others; it is something they help facilitate, support, and co-construct. Educators cannot "empower" Black families or students in the hierarchical sense of bestowing power. Instead, they can help create environments that affirm power that already exists, although it is often marginalized or suppressed by institutional systems. This distinction matters. Empowerment work must resist the trap of benevolent paternalism. Education is most liberating when it is rooted in "mutual recognition" or when teachers see students not as empty vessels but as "bearers of critical knowledge." In practice, educators can support empowerment by:

- *sharing power:* inviting students and families into decision-making processes around curriculum, discipline, and school climate
- *building capacity*: offering training, leadership opportunities, and resources to support family and student advocacy
- *affirming culture*: validating and celebrating the cultural practices, languages, and leadership styles of Black families and youth
- *being allies in public*: using institutional privilege to amplify marginalized voices and challenge injustice at school board meetings, faculty gatherings, or policy forum.

As discussed in an earlier chapter, Black families have been mischaracterized as disengaged or "hard to reach," despite long-standing traditions of advocacy, education, and community organizing. For Black families to feel empowered, educators need to dismantle deficit narratives and recognize Black families existing wisdom and activism. Educators can begin by:

- hosting forums where Black caregivers define their own needs and priorities, rather than just responding to district agendas
- creating culturally responsive workshops on student rights, restorative justice, and navigating school systems

- partnering with Black-led organizations and churches that already support family well-being
- offering interpretation, transportation, and childcare to remove structural barriers to participation

When educators transition from gatekeepers to co-conspirators, schools become spaces where families don't just participate; they lead. In these environments, empowerment transcends mere concept. It evolves into a collective act of resistance, rooted in love, knowledge, and the urgent belief that Black children deserve to thrive.

THE ARTS AND RESISTANCE

An important factor in the lives of Black students' and communities' resistance is the arts. Throughout Black history, the arts have played a vital role in resisting oppression. From the rich body of music that served both cultural and functional purposes (e.g., work songs) during enslavement to the music of the contemporary Black Lives Matter movement, Black artistic expression, through music, poetry, drama, and literature, has consistently served as both a reflection of harsh realities and a platform for urgent calls for freedom and liberation. During slavery, spirituals conveyed hidden messages of escape and hope. Subsequently, artists associated with the Harlem Renaissance and the Black arts movement used cultural outputs to challenge racism, celebrate Black identity, and envision a better future. Neal famously asserted that Black music is the aesthetic of the Black Power concept.[23] Music has always been foundational to Black resistance. From spirituals and blues to jazz and gospel, and then to soul, funk, and hip-hop, music has chronicled the Black experience and provided emotional resilience in the face of challenges ahead.

Civil rights anthems such as "We Shall Overcome" and "A Change Is Gonna Come" communicated beliefs in faith and defiance, while the emergence of hip-hop in the 1970s and its transformation into political rap in the 1980s and 1990s voiced the struggles of generations confronting systemic injustice (Rose 2). Artists such as Public Enemy, Tupac Shakur, and Lauryn Hill highlighted issues such as police brutality, poverty, and racial inequality in their lyrics, setting the stage for the 2020s' protest music. Contemporary hip-hop continues this legacy with heightened urgency, as seen in Kendrick Lamar's "To Pimp a Butterfly" and "DAMN," J. Cole's "4 Your Eyez Only," and Noname's politically driven verses that challenge institutional racism, mass incarceration, and Black erasure, while embracing cultural pride. Lamar's Pulitzer Prize–winning track "Alright" evolved into a hallmark of the Black Lives Matter movement, often heard during protests as an expression of survival and hope. Similar contributions from artists such as Rapsody, Little Simz, and Janelle Monáe shape resistance culture through their lyrics, embodiment of futurism, and intersectional narratives that uplift Black queer voices and gender justice.[24] Therefore, modern rap transcends mere music. It serves as a protest and a prophecy.

The influence of hip-hop and the arts has increasingly permeated schools and the educational process through innovative methods, such as hip-hop counseling and arts-integration programs. Levy, a counselor educator, is a proponent of hip-hop counseling, which utilizes lyric writing, beat crafting, and storytelling as therapeutic and educational mechanisms to help youth navigate trauma, express their identities, and cultivate self-worth.[25] However, schools can achieve even more. Schools can foster resistance-based learning by incorporating poetry slams, spoken word initiatives, youth theater productions, community murals, and music composition projects into their curricula, enabling students to address injustice, celebrate their cultural identities, and envision new possibilities. These methodologies redefine education as a place of liberation. When students are given the chance to articulate their truths, perform their histories, and reshape their realities, they reclaim their agency within systems that typically marginalize them.

Schools that embrace the arts as a form of resistance foster healing-centered teaching, culturally relevant education, and social-emotional growth grounded in justice. These initiatives also connect students to the historical legacies of Black resilience, affirming that their voices are both valid and essential. Through beats, literature, or performance, Black art continues to invigorate the movement for Black liberation. In any classroom that emphasizes culture, creativity, and resistance, students are empowered to question, heal, and lead. James Baldwin remarked, *"The role of the artist is exactly the same as the role of the lover: if I love you, I have to make you conscious of the things you don't see."*[26] Today, educators need to partner with Black artists to support Black students and honor Black culture.

HONORING THE LEGACY: BLACK EDUCATION ACTIVISTS

To understand the landscape of resistance and to uplift Black education, honoring Black elders, advocates, scholars, teachers, and freedom fighters who laid its foundation is essential. These Black education activists were institution builders, community organizers, theorists, and truth tellers. Their work endures in classrooms, school policies, teacher preparation programs, and grassroots movements that continue to advocate for justice for Black students and families.

Marva Collins (1936–2015)

A visionary educator who refused to accept the failures of the public school system, Marva Collins founded Westside Preparatory School in Chicago in 1975 using her own savings. There, she taught low-income Black children classical literature, instilling high expectations and, demonstrating what culturally affirming, rigorous education could look like when educators believed in Black children. Her model has inspired countless equity-driven teachers and leaders.

Carter G. Woodson (1875–1950)

Known as the "Father of Black History," Woodson understood that education was political. He launched Negro History Week in 1926, which would evolve into Black History Month. Woodson believed that the erasure of Black contributions to history was a key tool of oppression. His work reminds educators today that culturally affirming curricula serve as acts of resistance and healing.

Mary McLeod Bethune (1875–1955)

Bethune, the daughter of formerly enslaved people, believed deeply in the power of education to transform lives. She founded the Daytona Educational and Industrial Training School for Negro Girls (now Bethune-Cookman University) and was a tireless advocate for Black women's education and civic participation. Her legacy endures in the ongoing fight for gender equity and access to higher education.

Mary Hatwood Futrell (1940–)

As one of the few Black women to lead a national education organization, Futrell served as president of the National Education Association (NEA) during the

1980s, adeptly navigating the complexities of desegregation, teacher equity, and funding disparities. Her leadership paved the way for unions and professional organizations to engage more actively in equity and social justice work.

Edmund Gordon (1921–)

A luminary in the fields of psychology and education, Gordon co-founded the Head Start program and developed the concept of "supplementary education," which focuses on community-based learning and cultural enrichment. His research continues to shape educators' understanding of achievement, opportunity gaps, and culturally relevant pedagogy.

Lois Jean White (1938–)

As the first Black president of the National Parent-Teacher Association (PTA), White advocated for increased family engagement and racial equity within an organization that had long marginalized Black voices. She championed the importance of Black parental involvement in education, recognizing that family leadership is crucial to school transformation.

Selena Sloan Butler (1872–1964)

Butler, a lesser-known yet crucial figure, founded the National Congress of Colored Parents and Teachers Association, an organization that advocated for Black students and families when they were excluded from the white-led PTA. Her advocacy laid the groundwork for inclusive family-school partnerships and community organizing models that are still used today.

Charlotte Forten Grimké (1837–1914)

Grimké was the first Black woman to teach at the Penn School in South Carolina during the Civil War. The Penn School was a school for formerly enslaved people. Her reflections, poetry, and teaching provided early insights into what it meant to educate for both freedom and dignity. She serves as a reminder that the Black teaching tradition is also a literary and moral one.

Nannie Helen Burroughs (1879–1961)

A fierce advocate for Black women and girls, Burroughs established the National Training School for Women and Girls in Washington, D.C., with support from the National Baptist Convention. Her school emphasized academic achievement, vocational training, and spiritual development, defying the limitations placed on Black education and Black womanhood.

These trailblazers were architects of resistance. They understood that schooling could be either a site of oppression or a tool for liberation. Their work reminds us that advocacy is not a new concept, and neither is excellence in Black educational leadership. In a time when equity work is under attack and public education is increasingly politicized, their legacies call us to act. Today's educators, policymakers, and advocates stand on the shoulders of these giants. Let us honor them not only by saying their names but by living their values of truth, justice, joy, and unwavering belief in the futures of Black students.

RACIAL JUSTICE ADVOCACY CHECKLIST FOR EDUCATORS: ADVOCACY IN ACTION

Below is a self-assessment checklist of essential advocacy behaviors for being an effective racial justice advocate for Black students:

Advocacy Behavior	*Completed (✓/✗)*
I listen to and amplify Black family/community stories to challenge harmful systems.	
I attend and speak at community meetings (e.g., school board, city council).	
I stand in solidarity with Black community members advocating for change.	
I volunteer with local, Black-led organizations or places of worship.	
I read and research issues affecting Black students (e.g., police brutality).	
I explore Black student issues through diverse sources and mediums.	
I reflect on personal privilege and systemic oppression.	
I boycott discriminatory or noninclusive companies/products.	
I write/call policymakers on issues impacting Black communities.	
I organize others to advocate for Black students and families.	

This checklist is not exhaustive, but it offers a foundation for intentional and sustained advocacy. Through deliberate action, educators can become powerful allies and co-conspirators in advancing racial justice and protecting the mental wellness of Black students.

TEACHING STUDENTS TO BE ADVOCATES AND COMMUNITY ORGANIZERS

Black student activism has long been a cornerstone of racial justice. From the early twentieth century to the present, young Black people have catalyzed transformative change, not because they were handed power, but because they demanded it and organized for it. The legacy of Black student organizing dates back to the 1920s, when youth began to publicly challenge injustice. One example is the mobilization around the Scottsboro Boys case, in which Black students, including student-led collectives at historically Black colleges and universities (HBCUs), took to the streets, raising national awareness about racial injustice in the legal system.[27] These early efforts foreshadowed decades of youth-led advocacy grounded in racial consciousness, solidarity, and liberation.

Simultaneously, in the early 1900s, the founding of Black Greek-letter organizations emerged as another critical form of student-led organizing. These organizations included:

Alpha Phi Alpha Fraternity, Inc. (ΑΦΑ): founded in 1906 at Cornell University
Alpha Kappa Alpha Sorority, Inc. (AKA): founded in 1908 at Howard University
Kappa Alpha Psi Fraternity, Inc. (ΚΑΨ): founded in 1911 at Indiana University
Omega Psi Phi Fraternity, Inc. (ΩΨΦ): founded in 1911 at Howard University
Delta Sigma Theta Sorority, Inc. (DST): founded in 1913 at Howard University
Phi Beta Sigma Fraternity, Inc. (ΦΒΣ): founded in 1914 at Howard University
Zeta Phi Beta Sorority, Inc. (ZPB): founded in 1920 at Howard University
Sigma Gamma Rho Sorority, Inc. (SGR): founded in 1922 at Butler University
Iota Phi Theta Fraternity, Inc. (ΙΦΘ): founded in 1963 at Morgan State University

Collectively known as *the Divine Nine*, the organizations were formed on campuses in response to the exclusionary climate of Jim Crow America. They championed racial uplift, service, civic engagement, and kinship values, shaping generations of student leaders who advanced justice from college campuses to Capitol Hill.[28]

During the 1960s and 1970s, the Black Panther Party for Self-Defense established over sixty-five survival programs, including breakfast and lunch services for children, free health clinics, and sickle cell anemia testing.[29] The Panther Party's actions transcended charity and represented a political stance based on the conviction that institutions had neglected Black communities, prompting the belief that Black people should be self-reliant and create new frameworks for care and education. Composed mainly of young Black men and women in their teens and early twenties, the Black Panther Party for Self-Defense emphasized community empowerment, self-determination, and mutual aid. Members were not only political activists but also educators, health workers, cooks, and organizers. This rich history underscores that student organizing is education in action. Research has shown that civic engagement contributes to academic motivation, self-efficacy, and well-being, especially for Black students.[30]

CONTEMPORARY COMMUNITY ORGANIZING: LESSONS FROM THE FIELD

Today, youth-led organizing remains essential. Black communities need young organizers who prioritize humility, listening, year-round engagement, and love. Below are core principles of grassroots advocacy[31]:

- rejecting transactional relationships that reduce people to votes or talking points
- building campaigns around what communities say they need, not what outsiders assume
- listening and following through with action
- organizing beyond election cycles, especially in the face of voter suppression
- centering those most impacted as leaders and truth-tellers

CADRE (*Community Asset Development Re-defining Education*) in Los Angeles is a powerful example of these principles in action. Founded as a parent- and student-led effort to transform punitive school environments, CADRE worked to shift schools from a "culture of discipline" to a "culture of dignity." They convened nearly forty stakeholders—parents, youth, educators, advocates, and administrators—in a collective process of self-reflection and systems redesign. Their work changed district policy and redefined school climate in South L.A.[32]

Educators have a vital role to play in sustaining this tradition. Although students must be the drivers of their own advocacy, schools can be the launchpads. Educators and school leaders can empower youth organizers by:

- assisting students in recognizing and leveraging their strengths—be it artistic, athletic, or academic—as catalysts for activism
- offering accessible venues—like classrooms, auditoriums, and after-school hours—for organizing meetings, teach-ins, or community gatherings
- encouraging connections between students and community leaders, local organizers, and alumni activists from different generations
- safeguarding students' rights to organize and voice their truths, even when their messages confront the institution

Activist and educator Dena Simmons (2019) reminds us, *"Students can't be civically engaged if they are not emotionally safe."*[33] Advocacy is about building school cultures that encompass belongingness and modeling justice. Educators who view their students as whole human beings foster generational transformation. When schools invest in youth organizing, they invest in democracy. When teachers support Black students in advocating for their communities, they carry on a legacy of resistance and liberation that has always begun in the classroom.

CASE STUDY: "WE DESERVE BETTER"—BLACK PARENT ADVOCACY AND SCHOOL TRANSFORMATION

Carter Elementary School, a historically Black K–5 school located in a disinvested urban neighborhood, has long been labeled "failing" by district and state officials. Despite a strong legacy of community presence, the school has faced declining resources, high teacher turnover, and persistent academic achievement gaps. Recent state test scores placed Carter in the bottom 10 percent of all schools in the district. For many parents, the data only confirmed what they already knew—their children weren't getting what they needed.

The catalyst for change emerged during a fall PTA meeting. Five mothers—Ms. Holloway, Ms. Bell, Ms. Ramsey, Ms. Taylor, and Ms. Nkosi—expressed their growing frustration with broken Chromebooks, missing reading materials, substitute teachers rotating through core classes, and concerns about school safety. *"We feel disposable," Ms. Holloway said. "You are throwing our kids away. But not mine. Not anymore."* The tone was sharp. Emotions were high. But beneath the anger was deep love for the children and the profound clarity that the mothers wanted more from the school.

Rather than dismissing the group's frustration, a small cohort of teachers, including Mr. Jones (fifth grade), Ms. Cash (special education), and Ms. Melendez (reading intervention specialist), invited the parents to stay after the meeting to discuss further. They listened without defensiveness, took notes, and asked, "What would justice look like to you?"

The next week, the group, now calling themselves the *Carter Collective for Justice*, met in the school library. The principal and teachers provided data showing disparities in reading access and chronic absenteeism. Parents shared stories of missed IEP meetings, outdated materials, and their feelings about their children being labeled as "behavior problems."

Together, they created a three-part advocacy plan:

1. *Organize listening sessions* with more families to gather data and build solidarity.
2. *Develop a "We Deserve Better" manifesto* outlining specific demands: full-time mental health staff, stable grade-level teachers, afterschool programs, and culturally responsive curriculum.
3. *Present to the local school board* in coordinated public testimony with visual displays of student art and family testimonials.

The district didn't anticipate what came next. In January, the Carter Collective filled the school boardroom with students displaying hand-drawn posters, administrators and teachers wearing solidarity shirts, and parents speaking boldly. Ms. Nkosi closed her statement with: "You may not value our ZIP code, but we will not let you ignore our children."

When a board member dismissed the group's concerns as "emotion-driven," Ms. Cash responded with district attendance and attrition data. Their organizing was emotional, but it was also factual, strategic, and fierce. Within the next year, the district:

- funded a full-time school counselor and a bilingual family liaison for the Carter Collective
- piloted a restorative justice program co-designed with the Carter Collective
- included Carter Collective parents on a district-wide family engagement task force
- developed a framework for *school-based equity teams* based on the Carter model

More important, the culture shifted. "We used to feel like outsiders," said Ms. Ramsey. "Now we know our power."

Reflection Questions

1. How did the parents in this case turn their anger into action?
2. What role did teachers play in either resisting or reinforcing institutional inequity? Do you think this was a risk for the small group of teachers?
3. What barriers might have stopped a group like the Carter Collective, and how were they overcome?
4. How can schools institutionalize, rather than tokenize, this kind of family advocacy?
5. What does it mean to empower without controlling? How was that reflected here?

This case illustrates that resistance doesn't always look like protest signs or walkouts. Sometimes, it starts with five mothers and a simple question: *"Why aren't our kids getting what they need?"* Advocacy, when rooted in truth and collective care, can be a site of healing, transformation, and enduring power.

CASE STUDY: "WE ARE THE HISTORY"—STUDENT ADVOCACY FOR BLACK HISTORY EDUCATION

Lincoln High School is located in a rural town in a state where new laws have prohibited teaching practices considered to promote "divisive concepts" related to race, gender, and sexual orientation. This legislation prohibits educational content that might evoke feelings of "discomfort, guilt, or anguish" in white students due to their race, a law that many interpret as excluding significant aspects of Black history. Although 75 percent of the student body identifies as white, Lincoln High serves a population of Black and multiracial students who have long felt marginalized within the school.

In early February, during what had traditionally been Black History Month, students noticed the absence of any schoolwide acknowledgments: no morning announcements, classroom lessons, or bulletin boards. A previously planned student-led assembly featuring poetry and historical presentations was abruptly canceled. The official reason given was "pending legal review."

Jasmine, a junior and president of the school's Diversity Club, met with friends after school. "This is not right," she said. "And we can't just sit here." That week, Jasmine and eight other students drafted a statement titled *"We Are the History."* In it, they demanded the reinstatement of Black History Month programming, the right to maintain the Diversity Club, and the inclusion of Black authors and historical figures in the curriculum.

When their request was denied, they organized a silent protest. On a Monday morning, twenty-five students (including white students) walked into school wearing black shirts with the phrase "We Are the History" hand-painted across the front. At 10:00 a.m., during the daily announcements, they stood in silence, holding signs bearing the names of Black historical figures omitted from their textbooks. Several teachers seemed visibly nervous. A few teachers pulled students aside and told them to "be careful." One administrator instructed the group to disperse or face "disciplinary consequences for disrupting learning." Local parents quickly got word. Some white parents flooded the school district office with complaints, accusing the students of being "un-American and shaming white kids." One white parent shouted, "You are the racist!" at the students as they stood in silence.

Now, under pressure from student activists and parent opposition, the school's leadership must decide how to respond. The district's legal counsel has warned against any curricular changes that might violate state law. The superintendent is facing a divided school board and a flurry of media coverage.

Within the school, teachers are divided. Some quietly express solidarity with the students. Others worry about job security. The counseling department is concerned about rising racial tensions and the emotional toll on all students, but particularly Black students and families who report experiencing overt racist events (e.g., racist emails). Meanwhile, the students continue to organize. They've started a petition, gained support from a statewide youth justice network, and have planned a public teach-in at a local church. Jasmine writes on Instagram: *"They say Black history makes people feel bad. But ignoring it makes us feel invisible. We're not going anywhere."*

Case Study Questions for Reflection and Discussion

1. How does this student-led protest exemplify resistance, advocacy, and empowerment?
2. What ethical responsibilities do school leaders have when student needs conflict with state law?
3. What role should teachers and school counselors play in moments of racial tension and student protest? What should the school tell parents and families about that role?
4. How should schools navigate the tension between compliance with policy and the pursuit of equity and inclusion?
5. Stakeholders are experiencing this dilemma differently. What role would you take? One of resistance? How would you address the needs of all students and families?
6. In what ways does censorship of Black history harm all students, not just Black students?
7. What are the risks and consequences of responding to or ignoring the students' demands?

CONCLUSION

This culminating chapter examines the enduring legacy of resistance within the Black community, with a particular focus on the pivotal role of youth-led activism in the struggle for educational justice. From the student sit-ins and organizing of the civil rights movement to today's school-based movements for racial justice, young Black people have been at the heart of transformative change. Changemakers such as Dr. Martin Luther King Jr., who began his activism as a young preacher, and current young Black activists exemplify the power of early engagement in resistance as a form of leadership and liberation.

The chapter underscores that the path to affirmation and freedom for Black students requires courageous pushback against racism and racist beliefs in curriculum, discipline, representation, and policy. This resistance is not easy. Yet, it is through resistance that Black students reclaim their voices, assert their humanity, and demand schools that see, value, and reflect their full selves.

Chapter Reflection Questions

1. Sadly, anti-Black racism is the norm in many schools. Advocating for Black students can be tough, particularly when your colleagues believe you are "causing trouble." Which advocacy strategies are you most *uncomfortable* with? Most comfortable with? Why?
2. You overhear a teacher in your school stating, "Black students don't need assistance. They need to have more stable home lives." What would you say to this teacher?
3. What does it mean to help others feel empowered in a school setting? Discuss how you and other educators can create spaces for Black parents to embrace their power. What are the consequences for you?
4. Reflect on your assumptions about power, control, and leadership in relationships with Black students and families.
5. What historical and systemic barriers have shaped Black parents' relationships with schools, and how do these legacies show up in your current school context? How can schools repair trust and reframe engagement as a partnership rather than compliance?
6. How are expressions of advocacy by Black parents often misread as aggression, defiance, or disruption? Reflect on how implicit bias, racism, and

institutional culture may affect how parent advocacy is received and responded to.

7. How can educators distinguish between defiance and activism? What biases must be unlearned to make this distinction?
8. Reflect on your personal and professional capacity for risk-taking. What support systems do you need to stay committed to advocacy?

Epilogue

In 1972, as a third grader in Hampton, Virginia, I walked into my first racially integrated school. It marked a transition (eighteen years after *Brown v. Board of Education* in 1954) and was also profoundly personal. For the first time, I was taught by a white teacher. Until then, I had been nurtured by exceptional Black educators who believed in me. That year, my new teacher—a white woman—looked me in the eye and told me that I would be an excellent teacher one day.

That simple affirmation, grounded in care and possibility, stayed with me. It reminds me that although racism is systemic, the capacity to love, nurture, and uplift Black children is not limited by race. What is required is humanity, empathy, and a deep commitment to the well-being of every child. What my teacher gave me that day was not just encouragement, it was a mirror of worth and a glimpse into a future I could claim as my own.

For years, I've asked myself why so many educators, regardless of race, continue to see Black children through a deficit lens rather than through a lens of potential, brilliance, and resilience. We are still wrestling with the findings of Mamie and Kenneth Clark's famous doll studies, which revealed how anti-Black racism shapes the self-concept of children. The tragedy is not only that the findings were true then but that they remain disturbingly relevant now. We have not yet undone the psychological harm that the Clarks so clearly exposed.

Today, we find ourselves again in a struggle to preserve the civil rights of Black students and all students who are deemed "other." In this moment, as inclusive education is under attack and diversity efforts are being dismantled, we are called to defend not just pedagogy, but people. As Johnnetta Cole reminds us, *"The content of the curriculum should never exclude the realities of the very students who must intellectually wrestle with it."*[1] When Black students study every world but their own, they are not only miseducated—they are erased.

Decades after desegregation, anti-Black racism still shapes how Black students are treated, seen, and taught. Educators must confront this head on. If we don't, we are complicit in the continued denial of Black students' right to learn and thrive. The stakes are moral and democratic. Schools in all settings—urban, suburban, and rural—need educators who understand the weight of historical trauma and are willing to disrupt systems that perpetuate it. When we affirm and support Black youth, we uplift all students and move closer to the ideals of equity and justice.

Ironically, I completed this book during a moment of profound contradiction. As the first Black woman was nominated for the US presidency by a major political party, the country elected a federal administration steeped in anti-education, anti-Black rhetoric. It was staggering. "Law and order" once again became code for criminalizing Black youth. At the same time, the intellect and integrity of a sitting Black woman vice president were openly diminished. History doesn't just repeat, it resists. And so do we.

Affirming Black students is not a feel-good initiative or a political talking point. It is a sacred charge. Black students walk into our schools every day carrying the dreams, brilliance, and burdens of their ancestors. They don't need our pity. They need our radical love, transformative policies, and a commitment to dismantling the systems that harm them. They need teachers who will not simply teach content but will speak to their full humanity, their culture, their gifts, and their futures.

My deep hope is that every educator reading this remains steadfast—because your courage matters, especially now. The erasure of Black history, the retreat from equity, and the assault on truth all demand bold, principled action. Those who hold anti-Black sentiments will continue to hate. But we can't roll over and let them. Keep listening. Keep learning. Keep affirming. We've weathered storms before, and we will again.

Because when we choose to see Black children clearly, love them deeply, and teach them powerfully, we don't just change their lives, we change the world.

APPENDIX A

African Slave Trade Map

The African Slave Trade was global in scale and brutal in execution. According to historical records and estimates displayed on the map, more than ten million Africans were enslaved and transported across the Atlantic Ocean to the Americas, with the largest numbers arriving in Brazil and the Caribbean. This trade formed one leg of the infamous Triangular Trade, in which European goods were exchanged for African slaves, who were then transported to the Americas, where their labor produced goods that were subsequently exported back to Europe. However, the Atlantic routes were only part of the story. Millions more were

FIGURE A.1 Overview of the slave trade out of Africa, 1500–1900

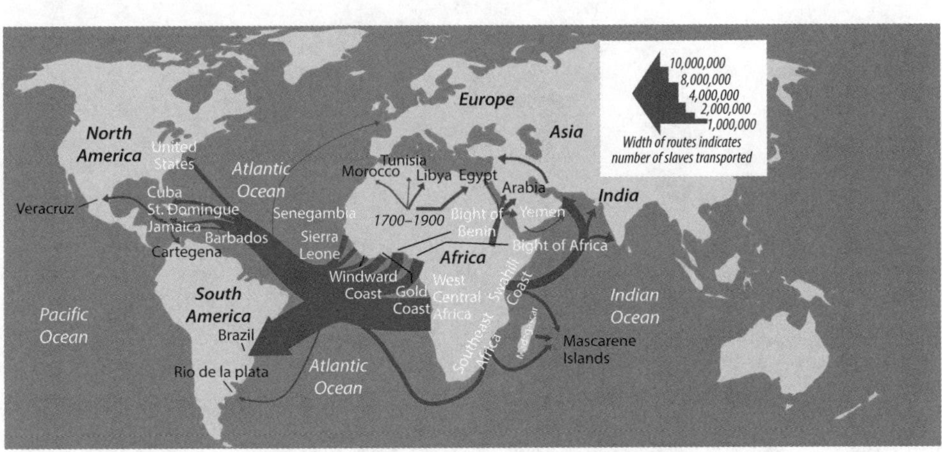

Source: KuroNekoNiyah, via Wikimedia Commons. https://commons.wikimedia.org/wiki/File:African_Slave_Trade.png

trafficked along Arabian and Indian Ocean routes, involving East African captives being sent to North Africa, the Middle East, India, and the Mascarenes (islands in the Indian Ocean). These lesser known but equally brutal trades show how slavery was embedded in both Western and Eastern imperial economies.

Meanwhile, the descendants of enslaved Africans shaped the cultural, political, and economic life of the Americas and beyond, even as they resisted dehumanization through rebellion, culture, and resilience.

APPENDIX B

Family Letter

Understanding Restorative Justice in Our School Community

Dear Families,

We know you care deeply about your child's learning, well-being, and sense of safety at school. At [School Name], we are committed to fostering a respectful, inclusive environment where every student feels seen, heard, and valued. As part of this commitment, we are implementing *restorative justice* (RJ) practices in our school.

WHAT IS RESTORATIVE JUSTICE?

Restorative justice is an approach to discipline that focuses on repairing harm and strengthening relationships—not just punishing behavior. Rather than asking, "What rule was broken and what punishment is deserved?," restorative justice asks:

- What happened?
- Who was affected and how?
- What needs to be done to repair the harm?
- How can we work together to make things right?

WHY ARE WE USING RESTORATIVE JUSTICE?

Research shows that traditional punishment often pushes students out of the learning environment and does not address the root of the issue. Restorative practices help us:

- keep students in school and learning
- teach responsibility, accountability, and empathy
- create a stronger, more caring school community
- reduce repeated conflict and harm

WHAT DOES THIS LOOK LIKE IN PRACTICE?

Your child may participate in:

- *restorative circles*: group conversations used to build community or resolve conflicts
- *mediation*: a structured dialogue to address specific issues between students or between students and staff
- *community service*: actions that help repair harm and restore relationships
- *reintegration support*: helping students feel welcome and supported after a conflict or disciplinary issue

FREQUENTLY ASKED QUESTIONS

Is RJ too lenient? Not at all. RJ holds students accountable by encouraging them to take responsibility and repair harm, while also recognizing their capacity to grow and learn.

Will students still face consequences? Yes. RJ is not about avoiding consequences, it's about making sure consequences are meaningful, fair, and focused on healing rather than punishment.

How can families be involved? We encourage family participation in restorative processes, especially when your child is directly involved. Families are essential to healing and supporting student growth.

LET'S WORK TOGETHER

Restorative justice is a philosophy. It's a commitment to seeing each child as a whole person and building a school culture where every student thrives.

Thank you for your continued partnership in supporting your child's success.

For more information, or to speak with our RJ coordinator, please contact: [insert contact information].

In partnership,

[Principal/Counselor Name]

[School Name]

[Date]

APPENDIX C

Banned or Challenged Books Featuring Black Characters or by Black Authors

These books have faced challenges or bans for various reasons, including discussions of race, sexuality, and social justice. For more detailed information on book bans and challenges, refer to resources such as PEN America's Index of School Book Bans and the American Library Association's Office for Intellectual Freedom.

1. *The Bluest Eye* by Toni Morrison
2. *Beloved* by Toni Morrison
3. *The Hate U Give* by Angie Thomas
4. *All Boys Aren't Blue* by George M. Johnson
5. *The Color Purple* by Alice Walker
6. *I Know Why the Caged Bird Sings* by Maya Angelou
7. *Stamped: Racism, Antiracism, and You* by Ibram X. Kendi and Jason Reynolds
8. *Between the World and Me* by Ta-Nehisi Coates
9. *The 1619 Project: A New Origin Story* by Nikole Hannah-Jones
10. *Roll of Thunder, Hear My Cry* by Mildred D. Taylor
11. *Ghost Boys* by Jewell Parker Rhodes
12. *New Kid* by Jerry Craft
13. *Monday's Not Coming* by Tiffany D. Jackson
14. *Go Tell It on the Mountain* by James Baldwin
15. *Native Son* by Richard Wright

16. *Black Boy* by Richard Wright
17. *Kindred* by Octavia Butler
18. *Homegoing* by Yaa Gyasi
19. *The New Jim Crow* by Michelle Alexander
20. *Caste: The Origins of Our Discontents* by Isabel Wilkerson
21. *Half of a Yellow Sun* by Chimamanda Ngozi Adichie
22. *The Fire Next Time* by James Baldwin
23. *The Hill We Climb* by Amanda Gorman
24. *The Story of Little Black Sambo* by Helen Bannerman
25. *Kaffir Boy* by Mark Mathabane
26. *A Lesson Before Dying* by Ernest J. Gaines
27. *Things Fall Apart* by Chinua Achebe
28. *The Autobiography of Malcolm X* by Malcolm X and Alex Haley
29. *Pet* by Akwaeke Emezi
30. *The Poet X* by Elizabeth Acevedo

Notes

Chapter 1

1. Kimberlé Crenshaw et al., *Black Girls Matter: Pushed Out, Overpoliced, and Underprotected* (African American Policy Forum, 2015), https://www.aapf.org/reports.
2. Bettina L. Love, *We Want to Do More Than Survive: Abolitionist Teaching and the Pursuit of Educational Freedom* (Beacon Press, 2019).
3. Kenneth B. Clark and Mamie P. Clark, "Racial Identification and Preference in Negro Children," *Journal of Negro Education* 19, no. 3 (1950): 169–71.
4. Richard Kluger, *Simple Justice: The History of Brown v. Board of Education and Black America's Struggle for Equality* (Vintage Books, 2004), 313.
5. Daina Ramey Berry, *The Price for Their Pound of Flesh: The Value of the Enslaved, from Womb to Grave, in the Building of a Nation* (Beacon Press, 2017).
6. David Theo Goldberg, *Dread: Facing Futureless Futures* (Polity Press, 2021), 101–3.
7. Isabel Wilkerson, *Caste: The Origins of Our Discontents* (Random House, 2020).
8. Heather Andrea Williams, *Self-Taught: African American Education in Slavery and Freedom* (University of North Carolina Press, 2005), 28–30.
9. Frederick Douglass, *Narrative of the Life of Frederick Douglass, an American Slave* (Anti-Slavery Office, 1845), 47.
10. James D. Anderson, *The Education of Blacks in the South, 1860–1935* (University of North Carolina Press, 1988), 245.
11. *Plessy v. Ferguson*, 163 U.S. 537 (1896).
12. *Brown v. Board of Education of Topeka*, 347 U.S. 483 (1954).
13. Gloria Ladson-Billings, "From the Achievement Gap to the Education Debt: Understanding Achievement in U.S. Schools," *Educational Researcher* 35, no. 7 (2006): 3–12; Monique W. Morris, *Pushout: The Criminalization of Black Girls in Schools* (The New Press, 2016).
14. US Department of Education, Office for Civil Rights, "Annual Report to Congress" (US Department of Education, 2020); The Education Trust, "Equity and Justice in Education Policy," https://edtrust.org/wp-content/uploads/2014/09/Getting-Things-Done_Advancing-Racial-Justice-and-Equity-in-Education_June-2021.pdf.
15. Love, *We Want to Do More.*
16. Love, *We Want to Do More*; Anderson, *Education of Blacks.*
17. Derrick Bell, *Faces at the Bottom of the Well: The Permanence of Racism* (Basic Books, 1992).
18. Dorinda J. Carter Andrews, "Black Students' Perceptions of School-Based Racial Microaggressions: Implications for School Psychologists," *School Psychology International* 33, no. 5 (2012): 535–50.
19. Peggy McIntosh, "White Privilege: Unpacking the Invisible Knapsack," *Independent School* 49, no. 2 (1988): 31.
20. Derrick Bell, *Faces at the Bottom of the Well: The Permanence of Racism* (Basic Books, 1992), 12.
21. Anderson, *Education of Blacks.*

22. Christopher Bonastia, *Southern Stalemate: Five Years Without Public Education in Prince Edward County, Virginia* (University of Chicago Press, 2012), 3–4.
23. Gary Orfield and Erica Frankenberg, *Brown at 60: Great Progress, a Long Retreat and an Uncertain Future* (Civil Rights Project/Proyecto Derechos Civiles, UCLA, 2014).
24. James H. Fultz, "The Displacement of Black Educators Post-Brown: An Overview and Analysis," *History of Education Quarterly* 44, no. 1 (2004): 11–45; Linda C. Tillman, "(Un)Intended Consequences?: The Impact of the Brown v. Board of Education Decision on the Employment Status of Black Educators," *Education and Urban Society* 36, no. 3 (2004): 280–303.
25. Seth Gershenson, Cassandra M. D. Hart, Constance A. Lindsay, and Nicholas W. Papageorge, "The Long-Run Impacts of Same-Race Teachers," *American Economic Journal: Economic Policy* 10, no. 4 (2018): 165–92.
26. Brookings Institution, "Black Teachers Are Still Left Behind," Brown Center Chalkboard, March 1, 2023, https://www.brookings.edu/articles/black-teachers-are-still-left-behind/.
27. National Center for Education Statistics, "Characteristics of Public School Teachers. Condition of Education" (US Department of Education, Institute of Education Sciences, 2023), https://nces.ed.gov/programs/coe/indicator/clr; National Center for Education Statistics, "Characteristics of Traditional Public, Public Charter, and Private School Teachers" and "Characteristics of Public School Teachers. The Condition of Education" (US Department of Education, Institute of Education Sciences, 2023), https://nces.ed.gov/programs/coe/indicator/sld and https://nces.ed.gov/programs/coe/indicator/clr.
28. Desiree Carver-Thomas, Diversifying the *Teaching Profession: How to Recruit and Retain Teachers of Color* (Learning Policy Institute, 2018), https://learningpolicyinstitute.org/product/diversifying-teaching-profession-report.
29. US Department of Education, Office for Civil Rights, *Civil Rights Data Collection: The 2017–18 Civil Rights Data Collection: An Overview of Exclusionary Discipline Practices in Public Schools* (US Department of Education, 2021), https://ocrdata.ed.gov.
30. Natasha Warikoo, Stacey Sinclair, Jessica Fei, and Drew Jacoby-Senghor, "Examining Racial Bias in Education: A New Approach," *Educational Researcher* 45, no. 9 (2016).
31. Walter S. Gilliam, Angela N. Maupin, Chin R. Reyes, Maria Accavitti, and Frederick Shic, *Do Early Educators' Implicit Biases Regarding Sex and Race Relate to Behavior Expectations and Recommendations of Preschool Expulsions and Suspensions?* (Yale University Child Study Center, 2016), https://medicine.yale.edu/childstudy/services/community/zigler/publications/Preschool%20Implicit%20Bias%20Policy%20Brief_final_9_26_276766_5379_v1.pdf; Jason A. Okonofua and Jennifer L. Eberhardt, "Two Strikes: Race and the Disciplining of Young Students," *Psychological Science* 26, no. 5 (2015): 617–24.
32. Rebecca Epstein, Jamilia J. Blake, and Thalia González, *Girlhood Interrupted: The Erasure of Black Girls' Childhood* (Georgetown Law Center on Poverty and Inequality, 2017), https://genderjusticeandopportunity.georgetown.edu/wp-content/uploads/2020/06/girlhood-interrupted.pdf.
33. Crenshaw et al., *Black Girls Matter*; Morris, *Pushout.*
34. Geneva Gay, *Culturally Responsive Teaching: Theory, Research, and Practice*, 3rd ed. (Teachers College Press, 2018); Maisha T. Winn, *Justice on Both Sides: Transforming Education Through Restorative Justice* (Harvard Education Press, 2018); Anne Gregory, Kathleen Clawson, Alycia Davis, and Jennifer Gerewitz, "The Promise of Restorative Practices to Transform Teacher-Student Relationships and Achieve Equity in School Discipline," *Journal of Educational and Psychological Consultation* 26, no. 4 (2016): 325–53.

35. Albert Bandura, "Moral Disengagement in the Perpetration of Inhumanities," *Personality and Social Psychology Review* 3, no. 3 (1999): 193–209; Henry V. Perkins and Matthew J. Corrigan, "Moral Disengagement in School: A Mechanism for the Perpetuation of Bullying," *Journal of School Violence* 14, no. 1 (2015): 47–66.
36. Thomas F. Pettigrew and Linda R. Tropp, *When Groups Meet: The Dynamics of Intergroup Contact* (Psychology Press, 2011).
37. Robin DiAngelo, *White Fragility: Why It's So Hard for White People to Talk About Racism* (Beacon Press, 2018).
38. Cheryl E. Matias and Michalinos Zembylas, "When Saying You Care Is Not Really Caring: Emotions, Whiteness, and Education," *Critical Studies in Education* 55, no. 1 (2014): 1–18.
39. Paulo Freire, *Pedagogy of the Oppressed*, trans. Myra Bergman Ramos (Herder and Herder, 1970); Scott Seider, Daren Graves, Shelby Clark, and Samantha Soutter, "Investigating the Effects of Critical Consciousness on Academic Achievement and Civic Engagement Among Adolescents," *Child Development* 91, no. 4 (2020): 1239–56.
40. Carolyn C. Speight, "Internalized Racism: One More Piece of the Puzzle," *Counseling Psychologist* 35, no. 1 (2007): 126–34; Thema Bryant-Davis and Carlota Ocampo, "The Trauma of Racism: Implications for Counseling, Research, and Education," *Counseling Psychologist* 33, no. 4 (2005): 574–78.
41. Love, *We Want to Do More*; Gloria Ladson-Billings, "Just What Is Critical Race Theory and What's It Doing in a Nice Field Like Education?" *International Journal of Qualitative Studies in Education* 11, no. 1 (1998): 7–24.
42. Equal Justice Initiative, *Reconstruction in America: Racial Violence after the Civil War, 1865–1876* (Equal Justice Initiative, 2020), https://eji.org/report/reconstruction-in-america/.
43. Scott Ellsworth, *Death in a Promised Land: The Tulsa Race Riot of 1921* (Louisiana State University Press, 1992).
44. Joy DeGruy, *Post Traumatic Slave Syndrome: America's Legacy of Enduring Injury and Healing*, rev. ed. (Joy DeGruy Publications, 2017).
45. Equal Justice Initiative, *Lynching in America: Confronting the Legacy of Racial Terror*, 3rd ed. (Equal Justice Initiative, 2017), https://eji.org/reports/lynching-in-america/.
46. Stephen J. Whitfield, *A Death in the Delta: The Story of Emmett Till* (Johns Hopkins University Press, 1991); Amy Louise Wood, *Lynching and Spectacle: Witnessing Racial Violence in America, 1890–1940* (University of North Carolina Press, 2009).
47. Danielle D. Loyd, Courtney D. Cogburn, and Riana Elyse Anderson, "Black Children's Racial Trauma: Historical and Contemporary Influences on Mental Health," *Annual Review of Clinical Psychology* 20 (2024): 1–24, https://doi.org/10.1146/annurev-clinpsy-081021-124208.
48. Richard Rothstein, *The Color of Law: A Forgotten History of How Our Government Segregated America* (Liveright Publishing Corporation, 2017).
49. H. Richard Milner IV, *Start Where You Are but Don't Stay There: Understanding Diversity, Opportunity Gaps, and Teaching in Today's Classrooms* (Harvard Education Press, 2012).
50. Django Paris and H. Samy Alim, eds., *Culturally Sustaining Pedagogies: Teaching and Learning for Justice in a Changing World* (Teachers College Press, 2017).
51. William E. Cross Jr., *Shades of Black: Diversity in African-American Identity* (Temple University Press, 1991).
52. Beverly Daniel Tatum, *"Why Are All the Black Kids Sitting Together in the Cafeteria?": And Other Conversations About Race* (Basic Books, 1997).

53. Tyrone C. Howard, *Black Male(d): Peril and Promise in the Education of African American Males* (Teachers College Press, 2014).
54. Tatum, *"Why Are All the Black Kids?"*
55. Margaret L. Hunter, *Race, Gender, and the Politics of Skin Tone* (Routledge, 2005); Kathy Russell, Midge Wilson, and Ronald Hall, *The Color Complex: The Politics of Skin Color among African Americans*, rev. ed. (Anchor Books, 2013).
56. Diane M. Hughes, James Rodriguez, Emilie P. Smith, Deborah J. Johnson, and Howard C. Stevenson, "Parents' Ethnic–Racial Socialization Practices: A Review of Research and Directions for Future Study," *Developmental Psychology* 42, no. 5 (2006): 747–70; JeffriAnne Wilder, *Color Stories: Black Women and Colorism in the 21st Century* (Routledge, 2010).
57. Michael J. Dumas and Kihana Miraya Ross, "Be Real Black for Me: Imagining BlackCrit in Education," *Urban Education* 51, no. 4 (2016): 415–42.
58. Jamilia J. Blake, Bettie Ray Butler, and Chance W. Lewis, "Unmasking the Inequitable Discipline Experiences of Urban Black Girls: Implications for Urban Educational Stakeholders," *Urban Review* 43, no. 1 (2011): 90–106.
59. Ingrid Banks, *Hair Matters: Beauty, Power, and Black Women's Consciousness* (New York University Press, 2000); Maxine Leeds Craig, *Ain't I a Beauty Queen? Black Women, Beauty, and the Politics of Race* (Oxford University Press, 2006).
60. Derald Wing Sue, Christina M. Capodilupo, Gina C. Torino, et al., "Racial Microaggressions in Everyday Life: Implications for Clinical Practice," *American Psychologist* 62, no. 4 (2007): 271–86.
61. Gilliam et al., *Do Early Educators' Implicit Biases?*
62. James P. Comer, *School Power: Implications of an Intervention Project* (Free Press, 1980).
63. Signithia Fordham and John Ogbu, "Black Students' School Success: Coping with the 'Burden of 'Acting White,'" *Urban Review* 18, no. 3 (1986): 176–206.
64. Tatum, *"Why Are All the Black Kids?"*
65. Cheryl Holcomb-McCoy, *School Counseling to Close Opportunity Gaps: A Social Justice and Antiracist Framework for Success* (Corwin Press, 2021).
66. DeGruy, *Post Traumatic Slave Syndrome*; Bryant-Davis and Ocampo, "Trauma of Racism."
67. Cynthia García Coll, Gontran Lamberty, Renee Jenkins et al., "An Integrative Model for the Study of Developmental Competencies in Minority Children," *Child Development* 67, no. 5 (1996): 1891–914; Michael Ungar, "The Social Ecology of Resilience: Addressing Contextual and Cultural Ambiguity of a Nascent Construct," *American Journal of Orthopsychiatry* 81, no. 1 (2011): 1–17.
68. Christina M. J. Byrd and Tabbye M. Chavous, "Racial Identity, School-Based Racial Socialization, and Academic Engagement among African American Youth: A Mediation Model," *Journal of Youth and Adolescence* 40, no. 5 (2011): 568–76.
69. Enrique W. Neblett Jr., Robert Sellers, and Michelle R. Ford, "Social Support and Racial Identity as Protective Factors Against the Influence of Racial Discrimination on the Psychological Adjustment of African American Adolescents," *Journal of Youth and Adolescence* 37, no. 5 (2008): 621–32; Loyd et al., "Black Children's Racial Trauma"; Hope et al., "Racial Identity and Academic Attitudes."

Chapter 2

1. Faye Z. Belgrave and Kevin W. Allison, *African American Psychology: From Africa to America*, 4th ed. (Sage, 2018).

2. Na'im Akbar, *Breaking the Psychological Chains of Slavery* (Mind Productions & Associates, 1996).
3. Joseph L. White, "Toward a Black Psychology," *Psychologist* 28, no. 9 (1970): 1–9.
4. Maulana Karenga, *Introduction to Black Studies*, 3rd ed. (University of Sankore Press, 2002), 360–61.
5. Kevin O. Cokley and Jessica Garber, "An Historical Perspective of the Association of Black Psychologists' Contributions to Psychology," *Journal of Black Psychology* 44, no. 8 (2018): 695–721.
6. Janice E. Hale, *Black Children: Their Roots, Culture, and Learning Styles* (Johns Hopkins University Press, 1986).
7. Bettina L. Love, *Punished for Dreaming: How School Reform Harms Black Children and How We Heal* (St. Martin's Press, 2023).
8. Carter G. Woodson, *The Mis-Education of the Negro* (Associated Publishers, 1933), 84.
9. bell hooks, *Teaching to Transgress: Education as the Practice of Freedom* (Routledge, 1994).
10. Prisca M. Chioneso, Jioni A. Lewis, Della V. Mosley, and Bryana H. French, "C-HeARTS: A Culturally Responsive Framework for Community Healing and Resistance Through Storytelling," *American Psychologist* 78, no. 3 (2023): 297–311.
11. Betty Achinstein, Rodney T. Ogawa, Daniel Sexton, and Cynthia Freitas, "Retaining Teachers of Color: A Pressing Problem and a Potential Strategy for 'Hard-to-Staff' Schools," *Review of Educational Research* 80, no. 1 (2010): 71–107; Lauren Proctor, *Black Educators Matter: A Call to Action for Racial Equity in the Teaching Profession* (Teachers College Press, 2022).
12. Asa G. Hilliard III, quoted in Lisa Delpit, *Multiplication Is for White People: Raising Expectations for Other People's Children* (The New Press, 2012), 76.
13. Asa G. Hilliard III, Lucretia Payton-Stewart, and Larry Obadele Williams, *Infusion of African and African American Content in the School Curriculum: Proceedings of the First National Conference* (Aaron Press, 1996).
14. Asa G. Hilliard III, "No Mystery: Closing the Achievement Gap Between Africans and Excellence," in *The Black Academic's Guide to Winning Tenure—Without Losing Your Soul*, ed. Kerry Ann Rockquemore and Tracey Laszloffy (Lynne Rienner Publishers, 2008), 139–52.
15. Anderson J. Franklin, Nancy Boyd-Franklin, and Saundra Kelly, "Racism and Invisibility: Race-Related Stress, Emotional Abuse, and Psychological Trauma for People of Color," *Journal of Emotional Abuse* 6, no. 2–3 (2006): 9–30.
16. White, "Toward a Black Psychology."
17. Wade W. Nobles, "The Infusion of African and African American Content: A Question of Content and Intent," in *Infusion of African and African American Content in the School Curriculum*, ed. Asa G. Hilliard III, L. P. Payton-Stewart, and L. O. Williams (Black Child Development Institute, 1990), 5.

Chapter 3

1. Margot Lee Shetterly, *Hidden Figures: The American Dream and the Untold Story of the Black Women Mathematicians Who Helped Win the Space Race* (William Morrow, 2016).
2. Martin E. P. Seligman and Mihaly Csikszentmihalyi, "Positive Psychology: An Introduction," *American Psychologist* 55, no. 1 (2000): 5–14.
3. Zaretta Hammond, *Culturally Responsive Teaching and the Brain: Promoting Authentic Engagement and Rigor Among Culturally and Linguistically Diverse Students* (Corwin, 2015);

Chezare A. Warren, Arlene Bogan, and Uche Anyanwu, "Centering Strengths and Identity to Promote Academic Persistence: A Framework for Black Student Success," *Journal of Urban Learning, Teaching, and Research* 18 (2022): 24–38.

4. Kimberly A. Griffin, "Striving for Success: A Qualitative Exploration of Competing Theories of High-Achieving Black College Students' Academic Motivation," *Journal of College Student Development* 51, no. 6 (2010): 676–700; Terrell L. Strayhorn, *College Students' Sense of Belonging: A Key to Educational Success for All Students*, 2nd ed. (Routledge, 2015).
5. Beth Harry and Janette K. Klingner, *Why Are So Many Minority Students in Special Education? Understanding Race and Disability in Schools* (Teachers College Press, 2006); Gloria Ladson-Billings, "Toward a Theory of Culturally Relevant Pedagogy," *American Educational Research Journal* 32, no. 3 (1995): 465–91.
6. Sherrie L. Proctor, "From Beckham Until Now: Recruiting, Retaining, and Including Black People and Black Thought in School Psychology," *School Psychology International* 43 (2022): 545–59; Gloria Ladson-Billings, *The Dreamkeepers: Successful Teachers of African American Children*, 2nd ed. (Jossey-Bass, 2009), 42.
7. Geneva Gay, *Culturally Responsive Teaching: Theory, Research, and Practice*, 3rd ed. (Teachers College Press, 2018).
8. Matthew A. Kraft, David Blazar, and Dylan Hogan, "The Effect of Teacher Coaching on Instruction and Achievement: A Meta-Analysis of the Causal Evidence," *Review of Educational Research* 88, no. 4 (2018): 547–88; Robert C. Pianta, Andrew J. Mashburn, Jason T. Downer, Bridget K. Hamre, and Laura Justice, "Effects of Web-Mediated Professional Development Resources on Teacher–Child Interactions in Pre-Kindergarten Classrooms," *Early Childhood Research Quarterly* 23, no. 4 (2008): 431–51; Anne Gregory, Mikki Hebl, and Rebecca A. M. Green, "Making Classrooms More Equitable: Teaching Practices That Support Student Voice," *Theory Into Practice* 55, no. 2 (2016): 122–29; Elena Aguilar, *Coaching for Equity: Conversations That Change Practice* (Jossey-Bass, 2020).
9. Tara J. Yosso, "Whose Culture Has Capital? A Critical Race Theory Discussion of Community Cultural Wealth," *Race Ethnicity and Education* 8, no. 1 (2005): 69–91, https://doi.org/10.1080/1361332052000341006.
10. Django Paris and H. Samy Alim, *Culturally Sustaining Pedagogies: Teaching and Learning for Justice in a Changing World* (Teachers College Press, 2017).
11. Mark VanDenBerg and Mary Ellen Grealish, *Individualized Services and Supports Through the Wraparound Process* (National Wraparound Initiative, 1996).
12. John P. Galassi and Patrick Akos, *Strengths-Based School Counseling: Promoting Student Development and Achievement* (Lawrence Erlbaum Associates, 2007); Dennis Saleebey, *The Strengths Perspective in Social Work Practice*, 4th ed. (Allyn & Bacon, 2006).
13. Steve de Shazer, Yvonne Dolan, Harry Korman, Terry Trepper, Wallace Gingerich, and Eric McCollum, *More Than Miracles: The State of the Art of Solution-Focused Brief Therapy* (Routledge, 2007).
14. Cynthia Franklin, Johnny S. Kim, Sue C. Salloum, and Laura J. S. Spector, "Evidence-Based Practice in School Mental Health: Addressing Disparities and Advancing Equity in Practice," *Children and Schools* 30, no. 1 (2008): 15–26.
15. Michael White, and David Epston, *Narrative Means to Therapeutic Ends* (Norton, 1990).
16. William R. Miller, and Stephen Rollnick, *Motivational Interviewing: Helping People Change*. 3rd ed. (Guilford Press, 2013).

17. Gill Strait, Linda Glosoff, James P. Myers, and Brian R. Miller, "Motivational Interviewing: Improving the Delivery of Psychological Services to Minority Youth," *Journal of Counseling & Development* 90, no. 4 (2012): 466–74, https://doi.org/10.1002/j.1556-6676.2012.00058.x.
18. Yosso, "Whose Culture Has Capital?"
19. Joseph E. Zins, Roger P. Weissberg, Margaret C. Wang, and Herbert J. Walberg, eds., *Building Academic Success on Social and Emotional Learning: What Does the Research Say?* (Teachers College Press, 2004).

Chapter 4

1. Albert Bandura, *Self-Efficacy: The Exercise of Control* (W. H. Freeman, 1997).
2. Frank Pajares, "Self-Efficacy Beliefs in Academic Settings," *Review of Educational Research* 66, no. 4 (1996): 543–78; Dale H. Schunk and Maria K. DiBenedetto, "Motivation and Social-Emotional Learning: Theory, Research, and Practice," *Contemporary Educational Psychology* 60 (2020): 101830.
3. Ellen L. Usher and Frank Pajares, "Sources of Self-Efficacy in School: Critical Review of the Literature and Future Directions," *Review of Educational Research* 78, no. 4 (2008): 751–96.
4. Ronald F. Ferguson, 'Teachers' Perceptions and Expectations and the Black-White Test Score Gap," *Urban Education* 38, no. 4 (2003): 460–507.
5. Deborah Witherspoon, Faye Z. Belgrave, and Thomas L. Mays, "Self-Efficacy and Academic Achievement in Black Adolescents," *Journal of Black Psychology* 23, no. 4 (1997): 331–43; Barry J. Zimmerman, "Self-Efficacy: An Essential Motive to Learn," *Contemporary Educational Psychology* 25, no. 1 (2000): 82–91.
6. Yu S. Cherng, Peter F. Halpin, and Luis A. Rodriguez, "Teaching Bias? Relations between Teaching Quality and Classroom Demographic Composition," *American Journal of Education* (2022), https://doi.org/10.1086/717676.
7. David S. Yeager, Valerie Purdie-Vaughns, Julio Garcia, et al., "Breaking the Cycle of Mistrust: Wise Interventions to Provide Critical Feedback Across the Racial Divide," *Journal of Experimental Psychology: General* 143, no. 2 (2014): 804–24, https://doi.org/10.1037/a0033906.
8. Shawn O. Utsey, Cheryl A. Giesbrecht, Cheryl E. Hook, and Richard S. Stanard, "Cultural, Sociofamilial, and Psychological Resources That Inhibit Psychological Distress in African Americans Exposed to Stressful Life Events and Race-Related Stress," *Counseling Psychologist* 30, no. 3 (2002): 439–53, https://doi.org/10.1177/0011000002303004.
9. Bettina L. Love, *We Want to Do More Than Survive: Abolitionist Teaching and the Pursuit of Educational Freedom* (Beacon Press, 2020).
10. William Surr, Jenny Scala, Julie Kochanek, and Kori Hamilton Biagas, *Measuring School Climate and Social and Emotional Learning and Their Relationship to Academic Achievement: Evidence from Chicago Public Schools* (American Institutes for Research, 2018).
11. Lev S. Vygotsky, *Mind in Society: The Development of Higher Psychological Processes*, ed. Michael Cole, Vera John-Steiner, Sylvia Scribner, and Ellen Soubermanet (Harvard University Press, 1978).
12. Gabriel Trujillo, Amanda J. Gravelle, and Marvin W. Berkowitz, "The Impact of Peer Mentorship on Academic and Social-Emotional Outcomes in Urban Schools," *Urban Education* 50, no. 2 (2015): 146–73; Kisha Taylor, Andrea L. Dennis, and Ronald D. Whitaker, "Culturally Relevant Mentoring: Affirming Black Students' Identity and Potential," *Journal of Negro Education* 92, no. 1 (2023): 77–95.

13. Lumina Foundation, *Transformational Relationships: The Power of Mentoring in Advancing Equity* (Lumina Foundation, 2025).
14. Gloriana Trujillo, Pauline Aguinaldo, Chelsie Anderson et al., "Near-peer STEM Mentoring Offers Unexpected Benefits for Mentors from Traditionally Underrepresented Backgrounds," *Perspectives on Undergraduate Research and Mentoring: PURM* 4, no. 1 (2015); Audrey J. Murrell, Doris Rubio, Maya Thakar, Natalia Morone, and Gretchen White, "Mentoring as a Buffer for the Impact of Social Unrest due to Systemic Racism and Ambient Discrimination," *Chronicle of Mentoring & Coaching* 8, no. 1 (2024): 116–25.
15. Lumina Foundation, *College Advising Corps: Near-Peer Advising Helps More Students Enroll and Succeed in College* (Lumina Foundation, 2014), https://www.luminafoundation.org/files/resources/college-advising-corps.pdf.
16. Michelle Scott and Lindsay Page, *The Impact of Near-Peer College Mentoring on FAFSA Completion and College Access* (College Advising Corps, 2017), https://collegeadvisingcorps.org/wp-content/uploads/2017/11/CAC_Research_Brief_Near_Peer_Mentoring.pdf.

Chapter 5

1. Jing Chen, Linda M. Reddy, and Charles R. Beitzel, "Examination of Disciplinary Disproportionality in Schools: A Meta-Analysis," *Review of Educational Research* 91, no. 4 (August 2021): 551–98, https://doi.org/10.3102/0034654321997317; Paul Fenning and Jennifer Rose, "Overrepresentation of African American Students in Exclusionary Discipline: The Role of School Policy," *Urban Education* 42, no. 6 (November 2007): 536–59, https://doi.org/10.1177/0042085907305039.
2. Meghan E. Cuellar and Sara Markowitz, "School Suspension and the School-to-Prison Pipeline," *International Review of Law and Economics* 45 (June 2016): 98–106, https://doi.org/10.1016/j.irle.2016.06.001.
3. Andrew Bacher-Hicks, Stephen B. Billings, and David J. Deming, "The School to Prison Pipeline: Long-Run Impacts of School Suspensions on Adult Crime," *American Economic Review: Insights* 1, no. 1 (June 2019): 29–42, https://doi.org/10.1257/aeri.20180173.
4. Tony Fabelo, Michael D. Thompson, Martha Plotkin, Dottie Carmichael, Miner P. Marchbanks III, and Eric A. Booth, *Breaking Schools' Rules: A Statewide Study of How School Discipline Relates to Students' Success and Juvenile Justice Involvement* (Council of State Governments Justice Center, 2011); Tracey Shollenberger, *Racial Disparities in School Suspension and Subsequent Outcomes: Evidence from the National Longitudinal Survey of Youth* (Columbia University, Center for Civil Rights Remedies, 2015), https://www.civilrightsproject.ucla.edu/resources/projects/center-for-civil-rights-remedies/school-to-prison-folder/state-reports/racial-disparities-in-school-suspension-and-subsequent-outcomes-evidence-from-the-national-longitudinal-survey-of-youth.
5. Carter G. Woodson, *The Mis-Education of the Negro* (Associated Publishers, 1933); Na'im Akbar, *Breaking the Chains of Psychological Slavery* (Mind Productions, 1996); Shawn C. T. Jones, Riana Elyse Anderson, and Howard C. Stevenson, "Toward a Mental Health Equity Framework for Racial Trauma," *American Psychologist* 76, no. 7 (2021): 1197–210.
6. Ian Haney Lopez, *Dog Whistle Politics: How Coded Racial Appeals Have Reinvented Racism and Wrecked the Middle Class* (Oxford University Press, 2015).
7. Elizabeth Hinton, *America on Fire: The Untold History of Police Violence and Black Rebellion Since the 1960s* (Liveright Publishing, 2021); Vesla M. Weaver, "Frontlash: Race and the Development of Punitive Crime Policy," *Studies in American Political Development* 21, no. 2 (Fall 2007): 230–65; 2020 Presidential Debate, September 29, 2020, Cleveland, OH,

Commission on Presidential Debates, https://www.debates.org/voter-education/debate-transcripts/september-29-2020-debate-transcript/.

8. US Department of Education, Office for Civil Rights, *Civil Rights Data Collection: School Climate and Safety* (US Department of Education, 2021), https://ocrdata.ed.gov/.
9. Kimberlé Crenshaw, Priscilla Ocen, and Jyoti Nanda, *Black Girls Matter: Pushed Out, Overpoliced, and Underprotected* (African American Policy Forum and Center for Intersectionality and Social Policy Studies, 2015); US Department of Education, Office for Civil Rights, *2013–2014 Civil Rights Data Collection: Key Data Highlights on Equity and Opportunity Gaps in Our Nation's Public Schools* (US Department of Education, 2016), https://ocrdata.ed.gov/.
10. Kelly Welch and Allison Ann Payne, "Racial Threat and Punitive School Discipline," *Social Problems* 57, no. 1 (2010): 25–48.
11. Russell J. Skiba, Robert H. Horner, Choong-Geun Chung, M. Karega Rausch, Seth L. May, and Tary Tobin, "Race Is Not Neutral: A National Investigation of African American and Latino Disproportionality in School Discipline," *School Psychology Review* 40, no. 1 (2011): 85–107.
12. Jonathan Zimmerman, *Whose America? Culture Wars in the Public Schools*, rev. ed. (Harvard University Press, 2024).
13. Fabelo et al., *Breaking Schools' Rules.*
14. Jason P. Nance, "Students, Police, and the School-to-Prison Pipeline," *Washington University Law Review* 93, no. 4 (2016): 919–87.
15. Michael Rocque and Raymond Paternoster, "Understanding the Antecedents of the 'School-to-Jail' Link: The Relationship Between Race and School Discipline," *Journal of Criminal Law and Criminology* 101, no. 2 (2011): 633–65.
16. Aaron Kupchik and Geoff K. Ward, "Race, Poverty, and Exclusionary School Security: An Empirical Analysis of U.S. Elementary, Middle, and High Schools," *Youth Violence and Juvenile Justice* 12, no. 4 (2014): 332–54; National Center for Education Statistics, *Indicators of School Crime and Safety: 2022*, US Department of Education, https://nces.ed.gov/programs/crimeindicators/.
17. Howard Zehr, *The Little Book of Restorative Justice* (Good Books, 2002).
18. Anne Gregory, Kathleen Clawson, Alycia Davis, and Jennifer Gerewitz, "The Promise of Restorative Practices to Transform Teacher-Student Relationships and Achieve Equity in School Discipline," *Journal of Educational and Psychological Consultation* 26, no. 4 (2016): 325–53.
19. Priscilla Ocen, Monique W. Morris, and Janelle R. White, "Suspending Progress: Examining the Impact of Discipline Policies on Black Girls in Oakland Schools," *African American Policy Forum* and *National Women's Law Center*, 2014; Thalia González, "Social Justice, Health, and Legal Education: A Collaborative Framework for Inquiry and Action," *Journal of Legal Education* 65, no. 2 (2015): 282–302.
20. Frank Pajares, "Self-Efficacy Beliefs in Academic Settings," *Review of Educational Research* 66, no. 4 (1996): 543–78; Linda James Myers, *Understanding an Afrocentric Worldview: Introduction to an Optimal Psychology* (Kendall/Hunt Publishing, 1993); Wade W. Nobles, *African Psychology: Toward Its Reclamation, Reascension, and Revitalization* (Institute for the Advanced Study of Black Family Life and Culture, 1986).
21. Karen M. Witherspoon, Velma McRoy, and Linda M. Lichtenstein, "Racial Identity, Academic Achievement, and Psychological Adjustment: An Examination of African American Adolescents," *Journal of Black Psychology* 23, no. 4 (1997): 363–77; Tynisha D.

Butler-Barnes, Sheretta T. Butler, Tabbye M. Chavous, and Robert M. Zimmerman, "Promoting Resilience Among African American Girls: Racial Identity as a Protective Factor," *Youth & Society* 45, no. 2 (2013): 158–81.

22. Julia Anyon et al., "Restorative Interventions and School Discipline Sanctions in a Large Urban School District," *American Educational Research Journal* 53, no. 6 (2016): 1663–97; Catherine H. Augustine, John Engberg, Geoffrey E. Grimm, Emma Lee, Elaine Lin Wang, Karen Christianson, and Andrea Joseph, *Can Restorative Practices Improve School Climate and Curb Suspensions?* (RAND Corporation, 2018), https://www.rand.org/pubs/research_reports/RR2840.html.
23. Kathy Evans and Dorothy Vaandering, *The Little Book of Restorative Justice in Education: Fostering Responsibility, Healing, and Hope in Schools* (Good Books, 2016).
24. US Department of Education, Office for Civil Rights, *Civil Rights Data Collection: The Status and Trends of Racial Equity in School Discipline* (US Department of Education, 2021), https://ocrdata.ed.gov/.
25. Catherine H. Augustine, Jonathan Schweig, Kyle C. Siler-Evans, and Geoffrey Grimm, "Can Restorative Practices Improve School Climate and Curb Suspensions? Evidence from a Randomized Controlled Trial," *American Economic Review* 110, no. 5 (2020): 124–29.
26. Gregory et al., "Promise of Restorative Practices."
27. Ted Wachtel, *Restorative Circles in Schools: Building Community and Enhancing Learning* (International Institute for Restorative Practices, 2016).
28. David R. Karp and Beau Breslin, "Restorative Justice in School Communities," *Youth & Society* 33, no. 2 (2001): 249–72.
29. Heather Strang, Lawrence W. Sherman, Evan Mayo-Wilson, Daniel Woods, and Barak Ariel, *Restorative Justice Conferencing (RJC) Using Face-to-Face Meetings of Offenders and Victims: A Review of the Empirical Evidence* (US Department of Justice, Office of Justice Programs, National Institute of Justice, 2013), https://www.ojp.gov/pdffiles1/nij/grants/244756.pdf.
30. Brenda Morrison and Dorothy Vaandering, "Restorative Justice: Pedagogy, Praxis, and Discipline," *Journal of School Violence* 11, no. 2 (2012): 138–55.
31. Thalia González, "Keeping Kids in Schools: Restorative Justice, Punitive Discipline, and the School to Prison Pipeline," *Journal of Law & Education* 41, no. 2 (2012): 281–335.
32. Sharada Jain, Trevor Fronius, Sarah Persson, and Nancy Guckenburg, *Restorative Justice in Oakland Schools: Implementation and Impacts* (WestEd, 2014).
33. Gwynedd McCluskey, Sheila Lloyd, Vicky Kane, and Ruth Riddell, "Can Restorative Practices in Schools Make a Difference?" *Educational Review* 60, no. 4 (2008): 405–17.
34. Dorothy Vaandering, "The Significance of Critical Theory for Restorative Justice in Education," *Review of Education, Pedagogy, and Cultural Studies* 32, no. 2 (2010): 145–76.
35. International Institute for Restorative Practices (IIRP), *Restorative Practices: Fostering Healthy Relationships & Promoting Positive Discipline in Schools* (IIRP, 2015), https://www.iirp.edu/images/pdf/IIRP-WhitePaper-2015.pdf.
36. Nadine A. Burrell, *Peer Mediation and School Climate: A Study of Conflict Resolution in Urban Schools* (PhD diss., University of Southern California, 2013), 89.
37. National Center for Restorative Justice, *Restorative Practices in Schools: A National Scan* (National Center for Restorative Justice, 2021), 12.
38. Brenda Morrison, Peta Blood, and Margaret Thorsborne, "Practicing Restorative Justice in School Communities: Addressing the Challenge of Culture Change," *Public Organization Review* 5, no. 4 (2005): 335–57.

39. Shelley Zion, Maureen Connolly, and Ramona Cutri, "Urban High School Students' Engagement in Restorative Justice: A Case Study," *Journal of Urban Education* 50, no. 4 (2015): 446–62.
40. Marc A. Brackett, Susan E. Rivers, Maria R. Reyes, and Peter Salovey, "Enhancing Academic Performance and Social and Emotional Competence with the RULER Feeling Words Curriculum," *Learning and Individual Differences* 22, no. 2 (2012): 218–24.
41. Morrison and Vaandering, "Restorative Justice."
42. Jain et al., *Restorative Justice in Oakland Schools*, 21.
43. Gregory et al., "Promise of Restorative Practices"; Russell J. Skiba, Mariella I. Arredondo, and M. Karega Rausch, *New and Developing Research on Disparities in Discipline* (The Equity Project at Indiana University, 2011), 5.
44. Augustine et al., *Can Restorative Practices Improve*, 45.
45. Evans and Vaandering, *Little Book of Restorative*, 23; Shawn Ginwright, *The Future of Healing: Shifting from Trauma-Informed Care to Healing-Centered Engagement* (Flourish Agenda, 2018), 4.
46. Myers, *Understanding an Afrocentric Worldview*, 15; Shawn Ginwright, *Future of Healing*, 6.
47. Catherine H. Augustine, John Engberg, Geoffrey E. Grimm, Emma Lee, Elaine Lin Wang, Karen Christianson, and Andrea A. Joseph, "Can Restorative Practices Improve School Climate and Curb Suspensions? An Evaluation of the Impact of Restorative Practices in a Mid-Sized Urban School District" (RAND Corporation, 2018).

Chapter 6

1. Meredith Anderson, *Hear Us, Believe Us: Centering African American Parent Voices in K–12 Education* (United Negro College Fund, 2024).
2. Kobi K. Kambon, *African/Black Psychology in the American Context: An African-Centered Approach* (Nubian Nation Publications, 2012).
3. Nancy E. Hill and Ming-Te Wang, "From Middle School to College: Developing Aspirations, Promoting Engagement, and Indirect Pathways from Parenting to Post High School Enrollment," *Developmental Psychology* 51, no. 2 (2015): 224–35.
4. John B. Diamond and Kimberly Gomez, "African American Parents' Educational Orientations: The Importance of Social Class and Parents' Perceptions of Schools," *Education and Urban Society* 36, no. 4 (2004): 383–427; L'Heureux Lewis-McCoy, *Inequality in the Promised Land: Race, Resources, and Suburban Schooling* (Stanford University Press, 2014).
5. Herbert G. Gutman, *The Black Family in Slavery and Freedom, 1750–1925* (Pantheon Books, 1976).
6. Diana Slaughter-Defoe, *Racing to the Top: Reclaiming Black Education* (University of Chicago Press, 2012), 141; Sarah Rall, "Community-Responsive Education: Building Power with Families of Color," *Phi Delta Kappan* 103, no. 6 (2022): 40–45; Gloria Ladson-Billings, *The Dreamkeepers: Successful Teachers of African American Children*, 2nd ed. (Jossey-Bass, 2009), 39.
7. American Psychological Association, *Empowerment: Definition and Discussion*, APA Dictionary of Psychology, 2022, https://dictionary.apa.org/empowerment.
8. Jay A. Conger and Rabindra N. Kanungo, "The Empowerment Process: Integrating Theory and Practice," *Academy of Management Review* 13, no. 3 (1988): 471–82.
9. Camille Wilson Cooper, "School Reform and Black Parental Engagement: The Intersections of Race, Poverty, and Parental Involvement," *Urban Education* 44, no. 5 (2009): 545–70; Diamond and Gomez, "African American Parents' Educational Orientations."

10. Richard Rothstein, *The Color of Law: A Forgotten History of How Our Government Segregated America* (Liveright Publishing, 2017).
11. Annette Lareau, *Unequal Childhoods: Class, Race, and Family Life*, 2nd ed. (University of California Press, 2011); Erin McNamara Horvat, Elliot B. Weininger, and Annette Lareau, "From Social Ties to Social Capital: Class Differences in the Relations Between Schools and Parent Networks," *American Educational Research Journal* 40, no. 2 (2003): 319–51.
12. Tara J. Yosso, "Whose Culture Has Capital? A Critical Race Theory Discussion of Community Cultural Wealth," *Race Ethnicity and Education* 8, no. 1 (2005): 69–91.
13. Pierre Bourdieu, "The Forms of Capital," in *Handbook of Theory and Research for the Sociology of Education*, ed. John G. Richardson (Greenwood Press, 1986), 241–58.
14. James S. Coleman, "Social Capital in the Creation of Human Capital," *American Journal of Sociology* 94 (Supplement: Organizations and Institutions) (1988): S95–S120.
15. McNamara Horvat et al., "From Social Ties to Social Capital."
16. Julia Bryan and Lynette Henry, "Strengths-Based Partnerships: A School-Community Partnership Approach to Empowering Latino Students' and Parents' Engagement in School," *Professional School Counseling* 15, no. 3 (2012): 215–22; Ann M. Ishimaru, *Just Schools: Building Equitable Collaborations with Families and Communities* (Teachers College Press, 2019).
17. Conger and Kanungo, "Empowerment Process."
18. James D. Anderson, *The Education of Blacks in the South, 1860–1935* (University of North Carolina Press, 1988); Charles M. Payne, *Getting What We Need Ourselves: How Food and Resistance Led to the Black Panther Party's Most Successful Program* (University of Illinois Press, 2023).
19. Rothstein, *Color of Law*; Lareau, *Unequal Childhoods*.
20. Ishimaru, *Just Schools*.
21. Black and Brown Coalition for Educational Equity and Excellence, *About Us*, accessed May 31, 2025, https://www.bandbcoalition.org/about-us.
22. Oakland Unified School District, Office of Equity, "Equity," accessed May 31, 2025, https://www.ousd.org/equity.
23. Ann M. Ishimaru and Mollie K. Galloway, "Beyond Individual Effectiveness: Conceptualizing Organizational Leadership for Equity," *Leadership and Policy in Schools* 13, no. 1 (2014): 93–146.
24. Ann M. Ishimaru and Satoshi Takahashi, "Disrupting Parental Roles in Reproducing Inequalities: Toward Equity-Oriented School Leadership," *Peabody Journal of Education* 92, no. 3 (2017): 409–25.
25. Concha Delgado-Gaitán, *The Power of Community: Mobilizing for Family and Schooling* (Rowman & Littlefield, 2001); Connie Wun, "Against Captivity: Black Girls and School Discipline Policies in the Afterlife of Slavery," *Educational Policy* 30, no. 1 (2016): 171–96.
26. Charles M. Payne, *I've Got the Light of Freedom: The Organizing Tradition and the Mississippi Freedom Struggle* (University of California Press, 1995).
27. Beth Harry, *Cultural Diversity, Families, and the Special Education System: Communication and Empowerment* (Teachers College Press, 1992); Jewelle Taylor Gibbs, *Young, Black, and Male in America: An Endangered Species* (Auburn House, 1985).
28. Diane Hughes, James Rodriguez, Emilie P. Smith, Deborah J. Johnson, Howard C. Stevenson, and Paul Spicer, "Raising Culturally Conscious and Competent Children: A Comprehensive Review of Racial Socialization Practices in Black Families," *Counseling Psychologist* 34, no. 6 (2006): 867–909; Marie Ferguson Peters, "Racial Socialization of

Young Black Children," in *Black Children: Social, Educational, and Parental Environments*, ed. Harriette Pipes McAdoo (Sage, 1985), 159–73.

29. Bettina L. Love, *We Want to Do More Than Survive: Abolitionist Teaching and the Pursuit of Educational Freedom* (Beacon Press, 2019), 19; Wade W. Nobles, *African Psychology: Toward Its Reclamation, Reascension, and Revitalization* (Institute for the Advanced Study of Black Family Life and Culture, 1986), 6.
30. Dorothy Roberts, *Shattered Bonds: The Color of Child Welfare* (Basic Books, 2002).
31. Roberts, *Shattered Bonds.*

Chapter 7

1. M. Suggs, I. U. Iruka, and N. A. Telfer, *Black Child National Agenda Statewide Analysis Report* (Equity Research Action Coalition, Frank Porter Graham Child Development Institute, The University of North Carolina at Chapel Hill, December 2023).
2. US Department of Education Office for Civil Rights, *2021 Civil Rights Data Collection (CRDC): School Climate and Safety Data Highlights* (US Department of Education, 2021).
3. Rebecca Epstein, Jamilia J. Blake, and Thalia González, *Girlhood Interrupted: The Erasure of Black Girls' Childhood* (Georgetown Law Center on Poverty and Inequality, 2017).
4. National Center for Education Statistics, "Safety and Security Practices at Public Schools," *Condition of Education* (US Department of Education, July 2024).
5. Urban Institute, *Police in Schools: Disparities in School-Based Law Enforcement* (Urban Institute, 2023).
6. Scott Kupchik, *The Real School Safety Problem: The Long-Term Consequences of Harsh School Punishment* (University of California Press, 2016).
7. National Women's Law Center and Southern Poverty Law Center, *Held Back: Black Girls and School Pushout in the South* (NWLC, 2024).
8. Sarah Jain, Pedro Noguera, and Rei Blakely, "Restorative Justice in Oakland Schools: Implementation and Impacts," Oakland Unified School District, 2014; Iheoma U. Iruka, Stephanie M. Curenton, Tonia R. Durden, and Kerry-Ann Escayg, *Don't Look Away: Embracing Anti-Bias Classrooms* (NAEYC, 2021).
9. Trina Payne-Patterson, "Policing Black Hair in Schools: A Legal and Ethical Perspective," *Journal of Law and Education Policy* 38, no. 2 (2023): 142–65; Tamika L. Johnson, *Crowned in Their Glory: The Politics of Black Hair in Schools and Society* (Beacon Press, 2020).
10. Eleanor K. Seaton, Enrique W. Neblett, Jr., Gene H. Brody, and Rand D. Conger, "Racial Discrimination and Psychological Well-Being: The Moderating Role of Racial Socialization for African American Adolescents," *Cultural Diversity and Ethnic Minority Psychology* 14, no. 2 (2008): 125–33; Melissa L. Greene, Angela D. Wallace, and Dana T. Johnson, "The Impact of Hair-Based Discrimination on the Mental Health of Black Adolescents," *Journal of Black Psychology* 49, no. 1 (2023): 3–21.
11. Whitney Gaskins, Kyla Allen, and Renée M. Jones, "Hair Politics: How Hair-Based Discrimination Affects Black Girls in Schools," *Journal of African American Women and Girls in Education* 1, no. 2 (2021): 45–60.
12. US House of Representatives, *Creating a Respectful and Open World for Natural Hair (CROWN) Act of 2021*, H.R. 2116, 117th Cong. Passed House March 18, 2022, https://www.congress.gov/bill/117th-congress/house-bill/2116; The CROWN Coalition, "The Official Campaign of the CROWN Act." accessed May 2024, https://www.thecrownact.com.
13. Patricia O'Brien-Richardson, "Hair It Is: Examining the Experiences of Black Women With Natural Hair," *International Journal of Qualitative Studies in Education* 32, no. 2 (2019):

153–64; LaTasha Henning, Shantel E. Crosby, Mariam D. Doumbia, and J'Quita A. Sampson, "School-Based Hair Discrimination: Understanding Black Girls' Experiences," *Journal of School Psychology* 90 (2022): 50–61; Janelle Yang and Logan McKnight, "Bullying, Bias, and Black Hair: The Role of Appearance-Based Harassment in Educational Settings," *Youth & Society*, published online April 2023.

14. US Department of Education Office for Civil Rights, "Civil Rights Data Collection, 2017–18: Gifted and Talented Enrollment" (US Department of Education, 2021), https://ocrdata.ed.gov.
15. Davis Pitre, "The Historical Foundations of Gifted Education: Eugenics and Exclusion," in *Gifted Education and Equity: A Critical Examination*, edited by Joy Lawson Davis and Deb Douglas, 15–34 (Routledge, 2020).
16. National Association for Gifted Children, *Equity and Excellence: Access to Gifted Education for All Students* (NAGC, 2024); Donna Y. Ford and James L. Moore III, "Gifted Education and the Promise of Equity: New Directions for Identification and Access," *Journal for the Education of the Gifted* 46, no. 1 (2023): 7–30.
17. Donna Y. Ford, *Reversing Underachievement Among Gifted Black Students: Promising Practices and Programs*, 2nd ed. (Prufrock Press, 2011).
18. Donna Y. Ford, *Multicultural Gifted Education*, 2nd ed. (Prufrock Press, 2013).
19. Donald J. Trump, "Executive Order on Combating Race and Sex Stereotyping," *Federal Register* 85, no. 188 (September 22, 2020): 60683–87.
20. White House, *Executive Order 13950 on Combating Race and Sex Stereotyping* (Office of the Federal Register, September 22, 2020).
21. Henry A. Giroux, *Race, Politics, and Pandemic Pedagogy: Education in a Time of Crisis* (Bloomsbury Academic, 2021); Kimberlé Crenshaw, *#SayHerName: Black Women's Stories of Police Violence and Public Silence* (The New Press, 2023).
22. US Executive Order 14151: Ending Radical and Wasteful Government DEI Programs and Preferencing, January 29, 2025.
23. Donald J. Trump for President 2024, "Agenda47: Ending the Left's Marxist Diversity, Equity, and Inclusion Regime," Donald J. Trump Campaign Website, 2023, https://www.donaldjtrump.com/news/307-agenda47-ending-the-left-s-marxist-diversity-equity-and-inclusion-regime.
24. W. E. B. Du Bois, *The Souls of Black Folk* (A.C. McClurg & Co., 1903), 78.
25. PEN America, "Index of School Book Bans" (PEN America, 2024), https://pen.org/index-of-school-book-bans/.
26. Daniel J. Losen and Gary Orfield, eds., *Racial Inequity in Special Education* (Harvard Education Press, 2002).
27. Education for All Handicapped Children Act of 1975, Public Law 94-142, 94th Congress, November 29, 1975; Individuals with Disabilities Education Act (IDEA), 20 US Code, Chapter 33, 1990.
28. M. Suzanne Donovan and Christopher T. Cross, eds., *Minority Students in Special and Gifted Education* (National Academies Press, 2002).
29. Ann Arnett Ferguson, *Bad Boys: Public Schools in the Making of Black Masculinity* (University of Michigan Press, 2000).
30. Mitchell L. Yell, *The Law and Special Education*, 4th ed. (Pearson, 2015).
31. Rehabilitation Act of 1973, Section 504, Public Law 93-112, 93rd Congress, September 26, 1973.

32. US Department of Education, Office for Civil Rights, *Protecting Students with Disabilities: Frequently Asked Questions About Section 504 and the Education of Children with Disabilities*, 2016, www2.ed.gov/about/offices/list/ocr/504faq.html.
33. Margo A. Mastropieri and Thomas E. Scruggs, *The Inclusive Classroom: Strategies for Effective Differentiated Instruction*, 6th ed. (Pearson, 2017).
34. Stephen Jay Gould, *The Mismeasure of Man* (W. W. Norton & Company, 1996); Richard R. Valencia, ed., *Dismantling Contemporary Deficit Thinking: Educational Thought and Practice* (Routledge, 2010).
35. Jack A. Naglieri and Donna Ford, "Addressing Underrepresentation of Gifted Minority Children Using the Naglieri Nonverbal Ability Test (NNAT)," *Gifted Child Quarterly* 47, no. 2 (2003): 155–60.

Chapter 8

Epigraph: Taraji P. Henson, quoted in "Taraji P. Henson Launches Foundation to Tackle Mental Health in Black Community," *The Root*, April 8, 2019.

1. American School Counselor Association, "Student-to-School-Counselor Ratio 2020–2021" (ASCA, 2021), https://www.schoolcounselor.org/About-School-Counseling/State-Student-to-Counselor-Ratio-Report.
2. US Department of Education Office for Civil Rights, "Civil Rights Data Collection: School Climate and Safety" (US Department of Education, 2021), https://ocrdata.ed.gov.
3. US Department of Health and Human Services, "Protecting Youth Mental Health: The U.S. Surgeon General's Advisory" (Office of the Surgeon General, 2021), https://www.hhs.gov/surgeongeneral/reports-and-publications/youth-mental-health/index.html.
4. World Health Organization, "Mental Health: Strengthening Our Response" (WHO, 2022), https://www.who.int/news-room/fact-sheets/detail/mental-health-strengthening-our-response.
5. Justine M. Gatt, Emma M. Melvin, Julie R. Williams, et al., "Facets of Mental Health: Development of the Positive Mental Health Scale (PMHS)," *Frontiers in Psychology* 5 (2014): 634, https://doi.org/10.3389/fpsyg.2014.00634.
6. National Institute of Mental Health, "Mental Illness" (National Institute of Mental Health, 2023), https://www.nimh.nih.gov/health/statistics/mental-illness.
7. National Center for Health Statistics, "Mental Health Treatment Among Adults: United States, 2020" (Centers for Disease Control and Prevention, 2021), https://www.cdc.gov/nchs/products/databriefs/db419.htm.
8. Centers for Disease Control and Prevention, *Youth Risk Behavior Survey Data Summary & Trends Report: 2011–2021* (US Department of Health and Human Services, 2022), https://www.cdc.gov/healthyyouth/data/yrbs/pdf/YRBS_Data-Summary-Trends_Report2023_508.pdf.
9. William A. Smith, Walter R. Allen, and Lynette L. Danley, "'Assume the Position . . . You Fit the Description': Psychosocial Experiences and Racial Battle Fatigue Among African American Male College Students," *American Behavioral Scientist* 51, no. 4 (2007): 551–78.
10. McLean Hospital, "Mental Health in the Black Community" (McLean Hospital, 2024), https://www.mcleanhospital.org/essential/mental-health-black-community.
11. Rheeda Walker and Nayeli Y. Chavez-Dueñas, *Latinx and Black Mental Health: Practices and Social Justice Approaches* (Springer, 2019); Centers for Disease Control and Prevention (CDC), *Mental Health—Household Pulse Survey* (US Department of Health and Human Services, 2021).

12. CDC, *Youth Risk.*
13. Joseph L. White, "Toward a Black Psychology," *Ebony Magazine,* November 1970, 44–52.
14. American Psychological Association, "APA Resolution on Racism and Racial Disparities in Mental Health" (American Psychological Association, 2021), https://www.apa.org/about/policy/resolution-racism-health-equity.
15. Lillian Comas-Díaz, Gordon C. Hall, and Helen A. Neville, "Racial Trauma: Theory, Research, and Healing: Introduction to the Special Issue," *American Psychologist* 74, no. 1 (2019): 1–5, https://doi.org/10.1037/amp0000442.
16. Joy DeGruy, *Post Traumatic Slave Syndrome: America's Legacy of Enduring Injury and Healing,* 2nd ed. (Joy DeGruy Publications, Inc., 2017).
17. Na'im Akbar, *Visions for Black Men* (Mind Productions & Associates, 1991).
18. Wade W. Nobles, *Seeking the Sakhu: Foundational Writings for an African Psychology* (Third World Press, 2006).
19. Linda James Myers, *Understanding an Afrocentric Worldview: Introduction to an Optimal Psychology* (Kendall Hunt, 1993).
20. Kevin Cokley, Leann Smith, Bernard Donte et al., "Impostor Feelings as a Moderator and Mediator of the Relationship between Perceived Discrimination and Mental Health among Racial/Ethnic Minority College Students," *Journal of Counseling Psychology* 64, no. 2 (2017): 141–54, doi:10.1037/cou0000198.
21. Thomas A. Parham, *Counseling Persons of African Descent: Raising the Bar of Practitioner Competence* (SAGE Publications, 2002).
22. Courtland C. Lee, *Multicultural Issues in Counseling: New Approaches to Diversity* (American Counseling Association, 2007).
23. Cirecie West-Olatunji, Lauren Shure, Rose Pringle et al., "Exploring How School Counselors Position Low-Income African American Girls as Mathematics and Science Learners," *Professional School Counseling* 13, no. 3 (2010): 184–95, SAGE Journals, https://doi.org/10.1177/2156759X1001300306.
24. US Department of Health and Human Services, Office of the Surgeon General, *Protecting Youth Mental Health: The U.S. Surgeon General's Advisory* (HHS, 2021).
25. A. Oshri, A. J. Reck, S. E. Carter et al., "Racial Discrimination and Risk for Internalizing and Externalizing Symptoms Among Black Youths," *JAMA Network Open* 7, no. 6 (2024): e2416491, doi:10.1001/jamanetworkopen.2024.
26. Howard C. Stevenson, Deborah L. Reed, and Patrick J. Bodison, "Racial Socialization Beliefs and the Use of Cultural Resources in African American Families," *Journal of Black Psychology* 28, no. 2 (2002): 155–78; Sydney Adams, Tennisha Riley, Patrick D. Quinn et al., "Racial-Ethnic Differences in ADHD Diagnosis and Treatment During Adolescence and Early Adulthood," *Psychiatric Services* 75 (2024): 513–612.
27. Paula Allen-Meares, Wendy Montgomery Kolka, and Ramona J. Washington, "Urban Adolescents and Depression: The Role of School Social Workers in School-Based Mental Health Services," *Children & Schools* 25, no. 1 (2003): 39–57; Ijeoma Opara, Guy M. Weissinger, David T. Lardier et al., "Mental Health Burden among Black Adolescents: The Need for Better Assessment, Diagnosis and Treatment Engagement," *Social Work in Mental Health* 19, no. 2 (2021): 88–104, doi:10.1080/15332985.2021.1879345.
28. Wenhua Lu, "Adolescent Depression: National Trends, Risk Factors, and Healthcare Disparities," *American Journal of Health Behavior* 43, no. 1 (2019): 181–94, doi:10.5993/AJHB.43.1.15.

29. American Psychological Association, *Ethnic and Racial Disparities in Youth Mental Health and Juvenile Justice: Current Research and Future Directions* (APA, 2023).
30. Jacob A. Gale and Lenna Nepomnyaschy, "School Belonging and Depressive Symptoms among Black Adolescents: The Moderating Role of School Racial Composition," *Journal of Youth and Adolescence* 53, no. 1 (2024): 45–61.
31. Centers for Disease Control and Prevention (CDC), "U.S. Public Health Service Syphilis Study at Tuskegee," accessed March 2, 2020, https://www.cdc.gov/tuskegee/index.html.
32. "Black Americans and Mistrust of the U.S. Health Care System and Medical Research," Pew Research Center, June 15, 2024, https://www.pewresearch.org/race-and-ethnicity/2024/06/15/black-americans-and-mistrust-of-the-u-s-health-care-system-and-medical-research/; Sirry M. Alang, "Mental Health Care among Blacks in America: Confronting Racism and Recognizing Resilience" (PMC / National Institutes of Health, 2019), https://pmc.ncbi.nlm.nih.gov/articles/PMC6407345/.
33. Derald Wing Sue, Annie I. Lin, Gina C. Torino, Christina M. Capodilupo, and David P. Rivera, "Racial Microaggressions and Difficult Dialogues on Race in the Classroom," *Cultural Diversity and Ethnic Minority Psychology* 15, no. 2 (2009): 183–90.
34. Alfiee M. Breland-Noble, Michele J. Wong, Trenita Childers, Sidney Hankerson, and Jason Sotomayor, "Spirituality and Religious Coping in African-American Youth with Depressive Illness," *Mental Health, Religion & Culture* 18, no. 5 (2015): 330–41, doi:10.1080/13674676.2015.1056120.
35. A. Glasofer, C. Dingley, and A. T. Reyes, "Medication Decision Making Among African American Caregivers of Children With ADHD: A Review of the Literature," *Journal of Attention Disorders* 25, no. 12 (2020): 1687–98, https://doi.org/10.1177/1087054720930783.
36. Thema Bryant-Davis, *Surviving Sexual Violence: A Guide to Recovery and Empowerment* (Rowman & Littlefield Publishers, 2011), 108.
37. Theodore J Corbin, Loni. P. Tabb, Daria B. Waite, Yang Waite, Yang Xu, Shanna-Kay Townsend et al., "Association Between Healing Hurt People Hospital-Based Violence Intervention Program Participation and Trauma-Related Psychological Symptoms for Violent Injury Survivors," *Journal of the American College of Emergency Physicians Open* (July 24, 2025), doi:10.1016/j.acepjo.2025.100199; Stoneleigh Foundation, "Healing Hurt People: Hospital- and Community-based Violence Intervention" (November 14, 2023), https://stoneleighfoundation.org/healing-hurt-people-hospital-and-community-based-violence-intervention/.
38. American School Counselor Association, *ASCA National Model: A Framework for School Counseling Programs*, 4th ed. (American School Counselor Association, 2019).
39. Nobles, *Seeking the Sakhu.*
40. Kevin Cokley, "A Meta-Analysis of the Relationship Between the Impostor Phenomenon and Race and Gender," *Journal of Counseling Psychology* 62, no. 3 (2015): 363–79.
41. Stephanie Moore, Anna Long, Samantha Coyle et al., "A Roadmap to Equitable School Mental Health Screening," *Journal of School Psychology* 96 (2023): 57–74, doi:10.1016/j.jsp.2022.11.001; Shinwoo Choi, Hyejoon Park, Kim, Yeongbin Kim, and Ching-Hsuan Lin, "School-Based Mental Health Services for Racial Minority Children in the United States," *International Journal of School Social Work* 7, no. 1 (2022), https://doi.org/10.4148/2161-4148.1058.
42. Shawn Ginwright, *The Future of Healing: Shifting from Trauma-Informed Care to Healing-Centered Engagement* (Flourish Agenda, 2018).

43. Caryn R. R. Rodgers, Michael W. Flores, Obioesio Bassey et al., "Racial/Ethnic Disparity Trends in Children's Mental Health Care Access and Expenditures From 2010-2017: Disparities Remain Despite Sweeping Policy Reform," *Journal of the American Academy of Child and Adolescent Psychiatry* 61, no. 7 (2022): 915–25, doi:10.1016/j.jaac.2021.09.420.
44. Christine M. Walrath, Eric J. Bruns, Karen L. Anderson, M. Glass-Siegal, and Mark D. Weist, "Understanding Expanded School Mental Health Services in Baltimore City," *Behavior Modification* 28, no. 4 (2004): 472–90, doi:10.1177/0145445503259501.
45. Qiyang Zhang, J. Wang, and A. Neitzel, "School-based Mental Health Interventions Targeting Depression or Anxiety: A Meta-analysis of Rigorous Randomized Controlled Trials for School-aged Children and Adolescents," *Journal of Youth and Adolescence* 52, no. 1 (2023): 195–217. doi:10.1007/s10964-022-01684-4.
46. Angela L. Duckworth, Christopher Peterson, Michael D. Matthews, and Dennis R. Kelly, "Grit: Perseverance and Passion for Long-Term Goals," *Journal of Personality and Social Psychology* 92, no. 6 (2007): 1087–1101, https://doi.org/10.1037/0022-3514.92.6.1087; Kiara M. Robinson, "Rethinking Grit: Examining the Structural Conditions That Impact Student Success," *Urban Education* (2021): 1–28.
47. Jasmine A. Abrams, Morgan Maxwell, Mitchell Pope, and Faye Belgrave, "Carrying the World with the Grace of a Lady and the Grit of a Warrior," *Psychology of Women Quarterly* (2014), https://doi.org/10.1177/0361684314541418.
48. Faye Z. Belgrave and Julia Brevard, *African American Boys: Identity, Culture, and Developmental Pathways* (Springer, 2015).
49. Ginwright, *Future of Healing.*
50. Camille Johnson and Linda Lee, "Centering the Family: A Systems Approach to Counseling Black Youth." *Journal of Black Psychology* 49, no. 1 (2023): 45–62.
51. Christine McWayne, Maria Cheung, Marisha Wright, and Brenda Hahs-Vaughn, "Strength-Based Parent–Teacher Relationships in Early Childhood: A Cultural Context Lens," *Early Childhood Research Quarterly* 28, no. 1 (2013): 135–46.
52. M. Fortes and E. E. Evans-Pritchard, *African Political Systems*, first ed. (Routledge, 1987), https://doi.org/10.4324/9781315683461.
53. Enrique W. Neblett, Eleanor K. Chavous, Dyonne M. Caldwell, Ciara L. Zimmerman, and Robert M. Sellers, "Racial Identity and Academic Attainment Among African American Adolescents," *Child Development* 81, no. 1 (2010): 186–202.
54. Edward C. Fletcher, Jr., Tanya J. Middleton, Erik M. Hines, and Donna Ford, "Lift Every Voice and Succeed: The Need for More Black School Counselors," *Diverse: Issues In Higher Education*, October 6, 2022.
55. ACLU, "Cops And No Counselors," 2019, https://www.aclu.org/news/juvenile-justice/cops-and-no-counselors.
56. American School Counselor Association, "Updated Student-to-School-Counselor Ratio Data," 2025, https://www.schoolcounselor.org/getmedia/1282baef-9128-44cf-8b4b-63fa5cfda2b6/pr_ratios-23-24.pdf?utm_source=chatgpt.com.
57. The Education Trust, *School Counselors Matter: The Role of School Counselors in Increasing Access to College and Career Readiness for Students of Color and Students from Low-Income Backgrounds* (The Education Trust, 2021), 5.
58. Collaborative for Academic, Social, and Emotional Learning (CASEL), "What Is SEL?" (CASEL, n.d.), https://casel.org/fundamentals-of-sel/what-is-the-sel-framework/.

59. Robert J. Jagers, Erin Skoog-Hoffman, and Dena Simons, "Toward a Culturally Affirming Social and Emotional Learning: Addressing Race, Culture, and Equity," *Educational Leadership* 78, no. 6 (2021): 28–35.
60. Shawn O. Utsey, Vanessa Adams, Cheryl Bolden, and James A. Belvet, "Development and Initial Validation of the Africultural Coping Systems Inventory," *Journal of Black Psychology* 26, no. 2 (2000): 194–215.
61. J. M. Jones, "Surviving While Black: Systemic Racism and Psychological Resilience," *Annual Review of Psychology* 74 (2023): 1–25.
62. Brooke Nodeland, Susan E. Rivers, and Marc A. Brackett, "Creating Emotionally Intelligent Schools with RULER," *Emotion Review* 10, no. 4 (2018): 290–300.
63. Cheryl Holcomb-McCoy, *School Counseling to Close Opportunity Gaps: A Social Justice and Antiracist Framework for Success* (Corwin, 2022), 3.
64. Norma L. Day-Vines, Julia Bryan, Jennifer R. Brodar, and Dana Griffin, "Grappling with Race: A National Study of the Broaching Attitudes and Behavior of School Counselors, Clinical Mental Health Counselors, and Counselor Trainees," *Journal of Multicultural Counseling and Development* 50, no. 1 (2022): 25–34, https://doi.org/10.1002/jmcd.12231.
65. Chanelle N. King, "Exploring the Role of Racial Dialogue in Counseling: A Qualitative Study of Black Clients' Experiences," *Journal of Counseling Psychology* 68, no. 4 (2021): 405–17. Lillian Comas-Díaz, "Multicultural Psychotherapy," *Psychotherapy* 49, no. 1 (2012): 87–91.
66. Joshua N. Hook, Jesse Owen, Don E. Davis, Everett L. Worthington Jr., and Cirleen DeBlaere, "Cultural Humility and Racial Microaggressions in Counseling," *Journal of Counseling Psychology* 60, no. 3 (2013): 45.
67. Kimberlé Crenshaw, "Demarginalizing the Intersection of Race and Sex: A Black Feminist Critique of Antidiscrimination Doctrine, Feminist Theory and Antiracist Politics," *University of Chicago Legal Forum* 1989, no. 1 (1989): 139–67.

Chapter 9

1. Carl A. Anderson and Howard C. Stevenson, *Radical Healing: Pathways to Self-Efficacy for Black Youth* (Teachers College Press, 2019).
2. Thema Bryant-Davis, *Thriving in the Wake of Trauma: A Multicultural Guide* (Rowman & Littlefield, 2011), 142.
3. bell hooks, *Teaching to Transgress: Education as the Practice of Freedom* (Routledge, 1994), 183.
4. Stevenson and Anderson, *Radical Healing.*
5. Robin D. G. Kelley, *Freedom Dreams: The Black Radical Imagination* (Beacon Press, 2002), 8.
6. Vanessa Siddle Walker, *The Lost Education of Horace Tate: Uncovering the Hidden Heroes Who Fought for Justice in Schools* (The New Press, 2018).
7. Joshua Bloom and Waldo E. Martin Jr., *Black Against Empire: The History and Politics of the Black Panther Party* (University of California Press, 2016).
8. Kimberlé Crenshaw, Andrea J. Ritchie, and Jyoti Nanda, *Black Girls Matter: Pushed Out, Overpoliced and Underprotected* (African American Policy Forum, 2015); Monique W. Morris, *Pushout: The Criminalization of Black Girls in Schools* (The New Press, 2016).
9. Adreana Clay, *The Hip-Hop Generation Fights Back: Youth, Activism and Post–Civil Rights Politics* (NYU Press, 2012).
10. US Department of Education, *Fact Sheet: Executive Order on Combating Race and Sex Stereotyping* (US Department of Education, 2025).

11. Jemele Hill, "The Destruction of Colin Kaepernick," *The Atlantic*, October 2020.
12. Martha B. Katz-Hyman, *Barbara Johns and the Farmville Student Strike* (Longwood University, 2001); J. Douglas Smith, *Managing White Supremacy: Race, Politics, and Citizenship in Jim Crow Virginia* (University of North Carolina Press, 2002).
13. Wade W. Nobles, *Seeking the Sakhu: Foundational Writings for an African Psychology* (Third World Press, 2006), 245.
14. Patricia Hill Collins, *Black Feminist Thought: Knowledge, Consciousness, and the Politics of Empowerment* (Routledge, 2000); bell hooks, *Teaching to Transgress.*
15. Paulo Freire, *Pedagogy of the Oppressed*, trans. Myra Bergman Ramos (Continuum, 1970).
16. Paul C. Gorski and Katy Swalwell, "Equity Literacy for All," *Educational Leadership* 72, no. 6 (2015): 34–40.
17. Howard C. Stevenson, *Promoting Racial Literacy in Schools: Differences That Make a Difference* (Teachers College Press, 2014).
18. Anne Gregory, Kathleen Clawson, Alycia Davis, and Jennifer Gerewitz, "The Promise of Restorative Practices to Transform Teacher-Student Relationships and Achieve Equity in School Discipline," *Journal of Educational and Psychological Consultation* 26, no. 4 (2016): 325–53, https://doi.org/10.1080/10474412.2014.929950.
19. Cheryl Holcomb-McCoy, *School Counseling to Close Opportunity Gaps: A Social Justice and Antiracist Framework for Success* (Corwin, 2022).
20. Julian Rappaport, *Studies in Empowerment: Steps Toward Understanding and Action* (Haworth Press, 1984), 122.
21. Barbara P. Solomon, *Black Empowerment: Social Work in Oppressed Communities* (Columbia University Press, 1976).
22. Freire, *Pedagogy of the Oppressed*, 66.
23. Mark Anthony Neal, *What the Music Said: Black Popular Music and Black Public Culture* (Routledge, 1999), 29.
24. Gwendolyn Pough, "Check It While I Wreck It: Black Womanhood, Hip Hop Culture, and the Public Sphere," Choice Reviews Online, Association of College and Research Libraries, 2004.
25. B. Michael Levy, Ian Levy, and Regine Jean-Charles, "Hip-Hop and Spoken Word Therapy with Urban Youth," in *Expressive Arts Interventions for School Counselors*, ed. Suzanne Degges-White and Bonnie R. Colon (Springer, 2022), 119.
26. James Baldwin, *The Cross of Redemption: Uncollected Writings*, ed. Randall Kenan (Vintage, 2011), 131.
27. Thomas L. Bynum, *NAACP Youth and the Fight for Black Freedom, 1936–1965* (University of Tennessee Press, 2010).
28. Tamara L. Brown, Gregory S. Parks, and Clarenda M. Phillips, *African American Fraternities and Sororities: The Legacy and the Vision* (University Press of Kentucky, 2005).
29. Bloom and Martin Jr., *Black Against Empire.*
30. Elan C. Hope and Margaret Beale Spencer, "Civic Engagement as an Adaptive Coping Response to Conditions of Inequality: An Application of Phenomenological Variant of Ecological Systems Theory (PVEST)," in *Handbook on Positive Development of Minority Children and Youth*, ed. Natasha J. Cabrera and Brian E. Livingston (Springer, 2017), 421–35.
31. Tamara Lang, *How We Get Free: Black Organizing for Education and Justice* (Communities for Just Schools Fund, 2022), 6.

32. Myesha Chin, *Parent Power and School Discipline: The Story of CADRE and the Transformation of South Los Angeles Schools* (CADRE, 2015).
33. Dena Simmons, "Why We Can't Afford Whitewashed Social-Emotional Learning," *ASCD Educational Leadership* 77, no. 5 (2019): 54.

Epilogue

1. Johnnetta B. Cole, *Conversations: Straight Talk with America's Sister President* (Doubleday, 1993).

About the Author

Cheryl Holcomb-McCoy, PhD, is president and CEO of the American Association of Colleges for Teacher Education (AACTE), where she leads national efforts to strengthen and advocate for high-quality educator preparation. She assumed this role in January 2025 after more than eight transformative years as Dean of the School of Education at American University (AU), where she elevated the school to a stand-alone academic unit and increased enrollments.

Holcomb-McCoy has led major initiatives to diversify and expand the educator pipeline, including the Summer Institute on Education Equity and Justice (SIEEJ), AU/District of Columbia Public Schools Teacher Pipeline Project, and Advancing Early Education Collaborative, which was funded by JPMorgan-Chase, and provided credentialing for early childhood educators in the Washington, DC, region. Prior to her tenure at American University, she held senior leadership roles at Johns Hopkins University, where she launched the Faculty Diversity Initiative and School Counseling Fellows Program.

A former kindergarten teacher and school counselor, she has served on the faculties of the University of Maryland and Brooklyn College. She is the author of *School Counseling to Close Opportunity Gaps* (Corwin Press), a national bestseller, and *Antiracist Counseling in Schools and Communities* (ACA Press). A 2023 Aspen Institute ASCEND Fellow and Fellow of the American Counseling Association, she is a nationally recognized leader in equity, education, and educator development.

About the Author

Index